This book is an invaluable resource for understanding the developmental dynamics that create financial exclusion, particularly in emerging economies. It also serves as a rich toolkit for tackling a specific law-and-policy environment to shape it into a financially inclusive one. Finally, it readily commends itself as a handy reference book for a variety of actors in the financial services space, including researchers, lawyers, policymakers, corporate leads, fintech practitioners, students and other friends of financial inclusion.

— **Professor Ada Ordor**
Director, Centre for Comparative Law in Africa,
Faculty of Law, University of Cape Town

Using refreshing insights from Africa (her home region), Asia and Latin America, this study is truly lateral thinking in the service of financial inclusion. The case studies are a rich mixture of eleven jurisdictions and nine emerging technologies, mixing law, finance, technology, regulatory and social policy. Those of us struggling through the 21st century financial, economic and social crises from a perspective frequently dominated by the orthodoxies and controversies of the rich economies should take note of the sheer eclecticism of Ogo Monye's truly innovative thinking.

— **Robin Simpson**
An old consumer war horse and consultant to UNCTAD,
with decades of experience garnered at the Consumers International,
World Bank, OECD, ISO and UK National Consumer Council

The COVID-19 pandemic exposed our economic and digital inequalities thus creating impetus to centre inclusion in our digital and financial development goals. This work by Dr. Ogochukwu Monye outlines financial inclusion in a digital landscape as well as emphasizing the importance of mainstreaming inclusion in policy and regulatory frameworks for digital economies.

— **Onica N. Makwakwa**
Head of Africa Region
Alliance for Affordable Internet (A4AI)

Digital Financial Inclusion and Regulation

This book explores the various considerations for achieving an effective regulatory strategy to improve financial access and usage in Nigeria and beyond. Gaps in the legal and institutional framework for digital financial services (DFS) as well as the barriers that contribute to financial exclusion are identified as are the policy changes needed to provide more extensive, accessible and sustainable financial inclusion value. In addition, the book covers divergent themes around the use of and insights for regulating industry financial services providers and challenger entities that herald industry disruption.

The book adopts three research methods. The doctrinal research method is used to buttress the law and development analysis and the themes around regulation, adoption and usage of financial services. To elucidate the application of financial innovations, comparative case studies are drawn from selected jurisdictions including Kenya, South Africa, Ghana, the Philippines, Brazil, Mexico, Uganda, Pakistan, India and Bangladesh. Lastly, using the empirical research method, the author reports the burden experienced by the residents of a community without banks in accessing finance. Included in this discussion are the barriers to finance as well as the coping strategies adopted by community residents to access formal and informal finance.

Ogochukwu Monye is a technology law specialist with expertise in digital financial inclusion. She is a senior law lecturer at the University of Benin, Nigeria with a well-rounded experience in research, litigation, consulting, government and advocacy roles. She holds an LLB from the University of Nigeria, an LLM from the Queen Mary University of London, and a PhD from the University of Cape Town, South Africa. Her research published in journals, book chapters and technical reports traverses access to finance, Fintech, consumer protection, digital inclusion and gender bias, recourse mechanisms, data privacy, telecommunications law, regional trade in Africa, e-health and IP, clean energy transition and e-commerce. She also researches the opportunities and challenges around emerging technologies including peer-to-peer lending, cryptocurrency, CBDCs, API, blockchain, artificial intelligence, Internet of Things and digital identification.

Routledge Studies in Development Economics

Neoliberalism and Unequal Development
Alternatives and Transitions in Europe, Latin America and Sub-Saharan Africa
Edited by Fernando López Castellano, Carmen Lizárraga and Roser Manzanera Ruiz

Industrialization and Economic Diversification
Post-Crisis Development Agenda in Asia and Africa
Banji Oyelaran-Oyeyinka and Kaushalesh Lal

Digitalization and Economic Development
Edited by Mohamed Sami Ben Ali

The Political Economy of Universal Healthcare in Africa
Evidence from Ghana
Philip C. Aka, Hassan Wahab and Yvette M. Alex-Assensoh

State Building and Social Policies in Developing Countries
The Political Economy of Development
Rashed Al Mahmud Titumir

Taxation in the Digital Economy
New Models in Asia and the Pacific
Edited by Nella Hendriyetty, Chris Evans, Chul Ju Kim and Farhad Taghizadeh-Hesary

Human Capital and Gender Inequality in Middle-Income Countries
Schooling, Learning and Socioemotional Skills in the Labour Market
Elizabeth M. King and Dileni Gunewardena

Digital Financial Inclusion and Regulation
Ogochukwu Monye

For more information about this series, please visit: www.routledge.com/Routledge-Studies-in-Development-Economics/book-series/SE0266

Digital Financial Inclusion and Regulation

Ogochukwu Monye

Routledge
Taylor & Francis Group
LONDON AND NEW YORK

First published 2023
by Routledge
4 Park Square, Milton Park, Abingdon, Oxon OX14 4RN

and by Routledge
605 Third Avenue, New York, NY 10158

Routledge is an imprint of the Taylor & Francis Group, an informa business

British Library Cataloguing-in-Publication Data
A catalogue record for this book is available from the British Library

Library of Congress Cataloging-in-Publication Data
Names: Monye, Ogochukwu, author.
Title: Digital financial inclusion and regulation / Ogochukwu Monye.
Description: Abingdon, Oxon ; New York, NY : Routledge, 2023. |
Series: Routledge studies in development economics | Includes bibliographical references and index.
Identifiers: LCCN 2022018320 (print) | LCCN 2022018321 (ebook) |
ISBN 9781032109558 (hbk) | ISBN 9781032109572 (pbk) |
ISBN 9781003217886 (ebk)
Subjects: LCSH: Financial exclusion--Prevention--Technological innovations. | Financial services industry--State supervision--Nigeria. | Financial services industry--State supervision--Developing countries.
Classification: LCC HG176.55 .M66 2023 (print) | LCC HG176.55 (ebook) |
DDC 332.09669--dc23/eng/20220718
LC record available at https://lccn.loc.gov/2022018320
LC ebook record available at lccn.loc.gov/2022018321

ISBN: 978-1-032-10955-8 (hbk)
ISBN: 978-1-032-10957-2 (pbk)
ISBN: 978-1-003-21788-6 (ebk)

DOI: 10.4324/9781003217886

To all persons seeking and working to achieve access to affordable and convenient financial services offered with dignity.

Contents

Foreword xiii
Preface xv
Table of statutes and other legal instruments xvii
Abbreviations xix
Book summary xxii

1 Introduction **1**

1.1 Background 1
1.2 Definition of relevant financial inclusion concepts 2
1.2.1 Financial inclusion 2
1.2.2 Digital financial services 4
1.2.3 Bank/non-bank institutions 4
1.2.4 Mobile network operator 5
1.2.5 Inclusive finance 5
1.2.6 Financial health 5
1.2.7 Financial stress 6
1.2.8 Financial literacy and capability 6
1.3 Dimensions of financial inclusion 7
1.3.1 Banked 7
1.3.2 Formal other 7
1.3.3 Informal only 7
1.3.4 Financially excluded 8
1.4 Why is financial inclusion important for Nigeria? 8
1.5 Chronicling Nigeria's journey to achieving financial inclusion 9
1.5.1 Demographic profile of the excluded in the pre-2011 era 10
1.5.2 Financial inclusion access strands 10
1.5.3 Financial exclusion by gender 10
1.5.4 Age range of the financially excluded 10

1.5.5 Rural/urban exclusion 10
1.5.6 Financial exclusion by level of education 10
1.5.7 Geographical representation of financial inclusion by geo-political zones 11
1.5.8 Stakeholder and industry profile 11
1.6 Nigeria's commitment to the Maya Declaration 11
1.7 Regulatory initiatives since the Maya Declaration 12
1.8 The CBN 2018 National Financial Inclusion Strategy (NFIS) refresh 13
1.9 Legal landscape for financial inclusion in Nigeria 16
1.10 Institutional landscape for financial inclusion in Nigeria 18
1.10.1 Central Bank of Nigeria 19
1.10.2 National Insurance Commission (NAICOM) 20
1.10.3 Nigerian Communications Commission (NCC) 20
1.10.4 Nigeria Deposit Insurance Corporation 21
1.10.5 National Pension Commission (PENCOM) 21
1.10.6 Securities and Exchange Commission (SEC) 22
1.10.7 National Bureau of Statistics (NBS) 22
1.10.8 The National Identification Management Commission 22
1.10.9 The Nigerian Postal Service 23
1.11 How have we fared in the financial inclusion journey? 23
1.12 Conclusion 24

2 Financial Inclusion in the Context of Law and Development 31

2.1 Introduction 31
2.2 The law and development moments 31
2.3 Law and development intersections 33
2.4 Law and development theory in the context of financial inclusion 35
2.5 Legal transplants 36
2.5.1 Background to legal transplants 36
2.5.2 The motivating factors for legal transplants 37
2.6 Financial inclusion transplants in Nigeria 40
2.7 Conclusion 44

3 Regulation of Digital Financial Services 49

3.1 Introduction 49
3.2 The financial sector regulator 49

3.3 *Regulation and market competition* 53
3.4 *The place of competitive advantages for DFS providers* 54
3.5 *Determining dominance and anti-competition in DFS* 56
3.6 *Regulatory sandboxes and prospective use cases in Nigeria* 59
3.7 *Conclusion* 61

4 Dislodging the Barriers to Accessing Financial Services in Nigeria **66**

4.1 *Introduction* 66
4.2 *Barriers to financial inclusion in Nigeria* 67
4.2.1 *Irregular income and unemployment* 67
4.2.2 *Cost of financial services* 68
4.2.3 *Illiteracy* 70
4.2.4 *Distance* 72
4.2.5 *Cash preference* 77
4.2.6 *Identification documentation* 78
4.2.7 *Complexity of account opening* 80
4.3 *Conclusion* 82

5 Rural Digital Financial Exclusion – Community Case Study (Ubulu-Uku, Nigeria) **88**

5.1 *Introduction* 88
5.1.1 *Outline of study* 88
5.1.2 *Aims and objectives* 89
5.1.3 *Method of identifying and selecting participants* 89
5.1.4 *Key messages* 90
5.2 *Background* 91
5.3 *Financial inclusion themes* 91
5.3.1 *Knowledge about financial inclusion initiatives* 91
5.3.2 *Financial service adoption and usage patterns* 92
5.3.3 *Barriers to accessing finance* 94
5.3.4 *Coping strategies* 97
5.3.5 *Consumer perception of DFS* 99
5.3.6 *User recommendations* 101
5.4 *Lessons for financial inclusion* 102
5.4.1 *Conventional banks are trusted but not easily accessible* 102
5.4.2 *Cash is still king* 103
5.4.3 *Tailored regulatory policies are essential* 104

5.5 *Summary of findings* 105
5.6 *Conclusion* 106

6 Emerging Technology and Implications for Financial Inclusion 109

6.1 *Introduction* 109
6.2 *The financial technology sector in Nigeria: A brief overview* 109
6.3 *Emerging trends in technology and potential for improving financial inclusion* 111
6.3.1 *Distributed ledger technology* 111
6.3.2 *Cryptocurrencies* 113
6.3.3 *Central bank digital currencies* 116
6.3.4 *Data analytics and big data* 120
6.3.5 *Artificial intelligence* 122
6.3.6 *Robo-advisors* 123
6.3.7 *Application programming interface* 124
6.3.8 *Peer-to-peer lending* 126
6.3.9 *Digital identification* 128
6.4 *Summary of legal issues raised by foregoing financial service technologies* 131
Concluding remarks 132

Appendix 143
Bibliography 146
Index 164

Foreword

In its 2018 report on Digital Access and the Future of Financial Inclusion in Africa, the International Finance Corporation called financial inclusion one of Africa's great success stories of the second decade of this century. By 2018, just over 43 per cent of adults on the African continent had access to formal financial services, compared to about a quarter in 2011. This success is primarily due to the adoption of digital financial services. According to the GSMA's State of the Industry Report on Mobile Money 2021 Africa in 2020 had more than a half of the live mobile money services on offer globally, with 562 million accounts, transaction volumes of 27,5 billion and total transaction value of USD 496 billion.

I have been privileged to observe and study these developments and in some cases also help to remove global and national regulatory barriers that unnecessarily inhibited financial inclusion. African policymakers and regulators have played leading roles to develop responsive frameworks that support financial inclusion while mitigating a range of risks introduced by the new technologies and business models. Their solutions have informed regulatory and supervisory innovation in many countries around the world.

Financial inclusion is not an end in itself but rather a means to economic empowerment and financial resilience. Financial resilience – the ability of people and firms to recover from adverse economic shocks without suffering a decline in living standards – has long been viewed as an important aspect of financial inclusion. The importance of this element became very clear during the COVID-19 pandemic and is set to increase in relevance as the world works towards post-pandemic recovery. An inclusive recovery that supports the United Nations Sustainable Development Goals will require appropriate financial inclusion policy and regulatory frameworks that respond to the opportunities and risks posed by fast-developing digital technologies and models.

What has been attained deserves to be celebrated, but the celebration should not detract from the work that remains. Financial inclusion entails more than mere access to an account but also appropriate use of such accounts. Yet, of the 562 million accounts in Africa in 2020, GSMA advised that only 161 million were in active use. More needs to be done to facilitate active use of formal financial services by those who can access them while work continues to provide access to the millions of adult Africans that still lack such access.

Furthermore, the focus on the financial inclusion of women needs to sharpen. Financial inclusion successes in Africa to date reflect a gender bias. According to the GSMA's Mobile Gender Gap Report, 2020 women in Sub-Saharan Africa are 13 per cent less likely than men to own a mobile phone and are 37 per cent less likely to use the mobile Internet. This gap has not reduced in Sub-Saharan Africa while it has significantly reduced in South Asia over the same period. This gap entrenches the relatively lower access by African women to financial services.

The digital financial inclusion objective should also not distract from the attendant risks. Consumer risks, such as predatory lending, and privacy and data protection risk must be appropriately addressed to ensure the levels of trust required to sustain and advance financial inclusion.

This book focuses on digital financial inclusion in Nigeria and the regulatory and supervisory hurdles to be navigated to broaden digital financial inclusion in the country. These hurdles are also considered from the perspective of a community in a small regional town to identify lived experiences and perspectives of adults who should benefit from financial inclusion initiatives. The book is published at the key juncture when the world's economic focus is on the post-pandemic recovery phase where digital financial innovation is set to play a key role. The analysis and findings presented in this book are therefore of significant value not only to Nigerian policymakers but also to global policymakers and stakeholders who study financial inclusion developments in Nigeria to inform regulatory innovation.

Professor Louis de Koker
La Trobe Law School
Melbourne, Australia

Preface

Financial inclusion has remained the bane of 1.4 billion people globally according to the World Bank Findex. In Nigeria, the Enhancing Financial Innovation and Access (EFInA) 2020 reveals that 35.9 per cent of adults have no access to financial services. The efforts to dismantle the hurdles to financial inclusion are ongoing. With the increasing use of digital finance, growth in financial literacy, and tailored regulatory policies, the opportunity to lift more people out of poverty through improved access to available, affordable, convenient financial services shows promise.

Using a combination of doctrinal and empirical methods, this book analyses the suitability of the enabling laws and institutions for digital financial services in Nigeria for addressing the needs of the financially excluded. The reasons for exclusion, burden of financial access, and regulatory strategies to curb these are explored. Insights are drawn from ten jurisdictions to buttress strategies adopted to overcome different financial inclusion barriers. These are Kenya, South Africa, Ghana, Uganda, the Philippines, Brazil, Mexico, Pakistan, India and Bangladesh.

Broadening the market to an array of alternative providers to innovate niche services, adopting consumer-centred policies, and increasing financial literacy and transactional capacity of financially excluded populations are small steps to achieving significant results for financial inclusion. The efforts at adjusting policies to suit the needs of the financially excluded ensure that as users get comfortable with these systems, usage will grow steadily, particularly since improved trust will help knock down concerns and barriers regarding digital financial services (DFS).

I have, in the course of this research been aided by many. I therefore, extend my gratitude to everyone who in any way has made this book a reality. I wish to express my profound gratitude to Professor Ada Ordor for inspiring in me the possibility that I could write this and for continued encouragement. To Professor Louis de Koker for his unwavering support, mentorship and confidence in my abilities through the course of the research. My affiliation with the Centre for Comparative Law in Africa, Faculty of Law, the University of Cape Town during the substantial part of this work is acknowledged. I am also grateful to my colleagues at the University of Benin for providing the needed academic and collegial environment for this research.

My deepest gratitude goes to my family, the Monyes and the Eziashis, particularly my parents Mr Felix and Professor Felicia Monye and my sisters Ngo, Ify and Ebele who ensured I maintained a stable academic, mental, emotional, financial and spiritual state of mind and body throughout the course of this work.

Finally, I am most grateful to the Almighty God, the source of my inspiration who ensured that all my needs mentally, physically, financially and spiritually were catered for and never let me lose hope from inception to completion.

Table of Statutes and Other Legal Instruments

Banks and Other Financial Institutions Act (as amended) Cap C4 Laws of the Federation of Nigeria 2004 at 1991 amended 2020

Constitution of the Federal Republic of Nigeria 1999 (as amended)

Central Bank of Nigeria Act Cap C4 Laws of the Federation of Nigeria 2004 at 2007

Central Bank of Nigeria Anti Money Laundering and Counterfeiting of Terrorism Regulations Schedule 2 of 2013

Central Bank of Nigeria Anti-Money Laundering/Counter Terrorism Financing Regulations 2013

Central Bank of Nigeria Guidelines for Card Issuance and Usage in Nigeria 2014

Central Bank of Nigeria Guidelines for the Regulation of Agent Banking and Agent Banking Relationships in Nigeria 2003

Central Bank of Nigeria Guidelines on Electronic Banking in Nigeria 2003

Central Bank of Nigeria Guidelines on Operations of Electronic Payment Channels in Nigeria 2020

Central Bank of Nigeria Guidelines on Transactions Switching in Nigeria 2016

Central Bank of Nigeria Regulatory Framework for Mobile Payments Services in Nigeria 2015

Central Bank of Nigeria, Guidelines for the Regulation of Agent Banking and Agent Banking Relationships 2013

Central Bank of Nigeria Guidelines on Mobile Money Services in Nigeria 2015

Central Bank of Nigeria Know-Your-Customer Guidelines 2013

Central Bank of Nigeria National Financial Literacy Framework 2015

Central Bank of Nigeria Regulatory Framework for Licensing Super-Agents in Nigeria 2016

Central Bank of Nigeria Regulatory Framework for Mobile Money Services in Nigeria, Regulation 2015

Federal Competition and Consumer Protection Act 2019

National Deposit Insurance Corporation Framework for the Establishment of Passthrough Deposit Insurance for Subscribers of Mobile Money Operators in Nigeria 2016

National Electoral Act 2010

National Identification Management Commission Act 23 of 2007

National Identification Management Commission Mandatory Use of Identification Number Regulation 2015

Abbreviations

AEPS	Aadhaar-Enabled Payment System
AFI	Alliance for Financial Inclusion
AI	Artificial Intelligence
AML/CFT	Anti-Money Laundering and Combating the Financing of Terrorism
API	Application Programming Interface
BOG	Bank of Ghana
BSP	Bangko Sentral ng Pilipinas
BVN	Bank Verification Number
CDF	Comprehensive Development Framework
CGAP	Consultative Group to Assist the Poor
CICO	Cash-In-Cash-Out
CNIC	Computerised National Identity Card
CBA	Commercial Bank of Africa
CBN	Central Bank of Nigeria
CPS	Compulsory Pensions Scheme
CRA	Credit Reporting Act
CTC	Competition and Tariff Commission
DFS	Digital Financial Services
DI	Digital Identification
DL	Distributed Ledgers
EAC	East Africa Community
EFInA	Enhancing Financial Innovation and Access
FAFT	Financial Action Task Force on Money Launderings
FCCPA	Federal Competition and Consumer Protection Act
FCCPC	Federal Competition and Consumer Protection Commission
FGN	Federal Government of Nigeria
FRSC	Federal Road Safety Commission
FSI	Financial Service Innovators Association of Nigeria
FSP	Financial Service Provider
GPF	Global Policy Forum
GMPC	General Multipurpose Card

GNP	Gross National Product
HDI	Human Development Index
ID	Identification Documentation
IFC	International Financial Corporation
INEC	Independent National Electoral Commission
ITU	International Telecommunications Union
KYC	Know-Your-Customer
LGA	Local Government Area
MFB	Microfinance Banks
MNO	Mobile Network Operator
MPOS	Mobile Point of Sale
MVNO	Mobile Virtual Network Operator
NADRA	National Database and Registration Authority
NAICOM	National Insurance Commission
NBS	National Bureau of Statistics
NCC	Nigeria Communication Commission
NDIC	Nigeria Deposit Insurance Corporation
NHIC	Nigeria Health Insurance Scheme
NEFT	NIBSS Electronic Funds Transfer
NFIS	National Financial Inclusion Strategy
NFLF	National Financial Literacy Framework
NIBSS	Nigerian Interbank Settlement System
NIMC	National Identity Management Commission
NIN	National Identification Number
NIP	NIBSS Instant Payments
NIPOST	Nigerian Postal Service
NITEL	Nigeria Telecommunications Limited
NSIS	National Security Information System
NSSLA	Non-Stock Savings and Loan Associations
NUBAN	Nigeria Uniform Bank Account Number
OTC	Over-the-Counter
OTF	Open Technology Foundation
P2P	Peer-to-Peer
PENCOM	Pension Commission
POS	Point of Sale
PSB	Payment Service Banks
PVC	Permanent Voter Card
SANEF	Shared Agent Network Expansion Facility
SEC	Securities and Exchange Commission
SMEDAN	Small and Medium Enterprise Development Agency of Nigeria
SMP	Significant Market Power
SMS	Short Messaging Service
SSNIP	Significant and Non-Transitory Increase in Price
TWAIL	Third World Approaches to International Law

UFA	Universal Finance Access
UIDAI	Unique Identification Authority of India
UNDRD	United Nations Declaration on the Right to Development
USSD	Unstructured Supplementary Service Data
WBG	World Bank Group

Book Summary

The burden of financial exclusion is borne by about 1.4 billion people globally according to the World Bank Global Findex Database due to varied barriers. Financial inclusion aids poverty reduction, better financial health, economic empowerment, capacity to adequately respond to family emergencies and economic shocks, improved quality of life, better financial management and consumption smoothing. Nigeria, like many other countries, has committed to removing the barriers to accessing financial services and has launched the national financial inclusion strategy. Particularly in the era of the COVID-19 pandemic, it is crucial to pursue policies that ensure the affordability and accessibility of fitting products that foster consumer dignity and trust and meet users' varied financial expectations. The growing deployment of complex financial services, increasing difficulty in regulating new technology and the scourge and extent of financial exclusion are additional reasons to advance the financial inclusion discourse.

This book considers financial inclusion from the perspective of digital finance for underserved groups. The ubiquity and decreasing cost of smartphones, automated teller machines (ATMs) and point of sale (POS) devices, helps providers to expand finance to persons residing at a distance from banks or other financial access points. In addition, the use of emerging technology such as artificial intelligence, data analytics, and blockchain are augmenting incomplete identification systems and lack of collateral registries in some countries and prove useful in offering credit to persons without formal financial footprints and credit histories.

Specifically, this book explores various considerations for achieving an effective regulatory strategy to improve financial access and usage in Nigeria and beyond. Gaps in the legal and institutional framework for DFS that contribute to this exclusion are identified as are the policy changes that need to be made to provide more extensive, accessible and sustainable financial inclusion value for users. Specifically, the book covers divergent themes around the legal issues arising from the use of digital financial services (DFS) and insights for regulating industry financial services regulators and challenger entities that herald industry disruption. This ensures that major and minor voices in the digital financial inclusion discourse are represented.

The book applies a doctrinal research method in the main, as well as some components of comparative and empirical research to exhaustively consider appropriate strategies for regulating and driving financial inclusion. The doctrinal method is also used to buttress the law and development analysis and the themes around regulation, adoption and usage of financial services. To elucidate the application of financial innovations, comparative case studies are drawn from selected jurisdictions including Kenya, South Africa, Ghana, the Philippines, Brazil, Mexico, Uganda, Pakistan, India, and Bangladesh. Lastly, using the empirical research method, the author reports the burden experienced as well as the coping strategies adopted by the residents of a community without banks in accessing finance.

In summary, the book comprises six chapters. A background to financial inclusion from a global and national perspective is provided in the first chapter, tracing Nigeria's journey to achieving financial inclusion since 2010, as well as the definitions of key concepts. Furthermore, the legal and institutional framework for financial inclusion in Nigeria is outlined. Chapter 2 examines the financial inclusion concept from a law and development viewpoint, tracing the legal transplants by Nigeria to formulate its framework. In Chapter 3, the dynamics of regulating financial services providers are described including a section on regulating competition among traditional and alternative finance providers and the use of sandboxes to drive innovation.

Chapter 4 describes the barriers to financial inclusion from the demand- and supply-sides and examines regulatory barriers, while Chapter 5 presents the results of an empirical study on the barriers to financial inclusion, conducted in Ubulu-Uku, a rural community in Nigeria without a bank. In Chapter 6 the final chapter, the author outlines nine emerging technologies, namely, distributed ledger technology, data analytics, robo-advising, application programme interface, peer-to-peer lending, artificial intelligence, cryptocurrency, central bank digital currencies and digital identity. The description, relevance and detriments of each with regard to financial inclusion are detailed. The chapter equally illuminates the legal issues heralded by these financial services technologies.

1 Introduction

1.1 Background

Worldwide, about 1.4 billion people are excluded from formal finance services according to the World Bank Global Financial Index on Financial Inclusion.[1] According to the World Bank, the reasons for this include a lack of funds, the cost of financial services, distance, account ownership by a family member, the lack of documentation, distrust in the financial system and religious concerns.[2] In Nigeria, the financial exclusion rate stands at 35.9 per cent, with a banked population of only 44.8 per cent.[3] Factors such as distance to banks, inadequate financial literacy, irregular income, unemployment, the complexity of account opening, a lack of proof of identity documentation, distance and preference for cash are responsible indices for the low rate of inclusion in Nigeria.[4] These have been summed up by the Enhancing Financial Innovation and Access (EFInA) 2020 survey as institutional exclusion, affordability, access and low awareness.[5] Specifically, factors such as geographic location, gender, age, level of education, sources and level of income are also at play in this low level of financial inclusion.[6]

In recent years, financial inclusion has gained the interest of national governments, development organisations, research institutions, technology corporations, not-for-profit organisations and the academia. The attention does not come as a surprise because financial inclusion promotes 7 of the 17 Sustainable Development Goals (SDGs) of the United Nations.[7] Targeted financial inclusion initiatives by national governments, regulators and financial services providers ensure that financially excluded persons, represented mainly by low-income earners, rural dwellers, women and youth can access quality financial services and obtain inclusion benefits. Poverty reduction, better financial health, economic empowerment, capacity to adequately respond to family emergencies and economic shocks, improved quality of life, better financial management and consumption soothing are some of these benefits.

The World Bank and the International Financial Corporation (IFC) launched Universal Finance Access (UFA) with the goal of 'providing access to a transaction account or electronic instrument to store money, send and receive payments for adults who are not currently within the formal financial

DOI: 10.4324/9781003217886-1

sector by 2020'.[8] These two organisations have committed to 'enabling one billion people to gain access to transaction accounts through targeted interventions'.[9] Likewise, the International Telecommunications Union (ITU) hosts focus group meetings on digital financial inclusion to stimulate discussions on digital financial services by regulators; services providers, payment platform providers, international organisations and other industry stakeholders.[10] The organisation also publishes specialised reports on varied aspects of Digital Financial Services (DFS).[11]

Similar strides have been achieved by not-for-profit organisations. The Bill and Melinda Gates Foundation has initiated the Financial Services for the Poor programme to expand low-cost DFS to the poor by helping to improve digital payment systems and lending support to strengthen national and regional strategies to foster financial inclusion.[12] The foundation provides funding for DFS programmes including the publication of the World Bank Global Findex on Financial Inclusion and the DFS Observatory of the Columbia University.[13]

Academia is not left behind as universities around the world are involved in research addressing issues around barriers as well as the enablers for financial inclusion. Columbia University, for example, set up a DFS observatory to monitor financial inclusion progress globally as well as maintain a repository of financial inclusion policies and initiatives from countries around the world.[14] Financial institutions such as Credit Suisse are also invested in the topic, by serving as a founding partner for the Centre for Financial Inclusion since 2008 'to engage and challenge the financial services industry to better serve, protect and empower clients'.[15]

There are also some global collaborations on financial inclusion. For instance, the Alliance for Financial Inclusion brings together financial regulatory institutions, central banks and finance ministries from 90 countries.[16] It is this alliance that introduced the Maya Declaration, the first global initiative to remove barriers to accessing finance by encouraging nations to commit to a set of targets and dates to achieve financial inclusion. Similarly, the Consultative Group to Assist the Poor (CGAP) is an international alliance of about 30 development organisations that work to improve financial inclusion using action-oriented research to help build inclusive and responsible financial systems.[17]

1.2 Definition of relevant financial inclusion concepts

1.2.1 Financial inclusion

In defining financial inclusion the elements of quality, convenience, availability, affordability and dignity usually receive attention as designing models that are out of the financial reach of the intended users or one that offers a lower quality or a more arduous system of use defeats the purpose of inclusion.

Financial inclusion is described by the Central Bank of Nigeria (CBN) as

> enhancing access and usage of financial services at affordable costs to the vast majority of disadvantaged and vulnerable low income groups; it is the

> availability and accessibility of financial products and services to the entire population without discrimination.[18]

The definition advanced by the CBN stresses the need to design financial services to reach all consumers including the last mile of consumers usually disadvantaged by reason of low income and vulnerability (including social or economic disadvantage) without discrimination. This definition, therefore, envisages that services will be designed in ways that open opportunities for all excluded persons. As outlined in the CBN's National Financial Inclusion Strategy (NFIS), the definition of financial inclusion embodies elements such as ease of access to financial products and services, use of a broad range of financial products and services, financial product designs that meet the needs of clients and affordable financial services even for low-income groups.[19]

The Centre for Financial Inclusion additionally defines financial inclusion as:

> a state in which all who can use them have access to a full suite of quality financial services, provided with quality to everyone who can use financial services with financial capability through a diverse and competitive marketplace.[20]

This definition envisions a situation where consumers are afforded the opportunity to access varied and quality financial services in a competitive environment. Implicitly, the definition takes into consideration, the fact that a competitive market place provides the consumer with the element of choice to select from suitable services according to personal needs. Also, the element of financial capability emphasises the need for consumers to understand clearly the advantages and disadvantages of each service offered, leading to a state where consumers become financially capable of making wise financial decisions independently.

The International Telecommunications Union (ITU) describes financial inclusion as 'the sustainable provision of affordable digital financial services that bring the poor into the formal economy'.[21] Simply, this alludes to designing financial services with low-income earners in mind to ensure that this category of persons receive seamless admission into the formal financial system.

Furthermore, the Financial Action Task Force on Money Laundering (FATF) 2011 guidance note on Anti-Money Laundering and Terrorist Financing Measures and Financial Inclusion defines the term as,

> In general terms, financial inclusion involves providing access to an adequate range of safe, convenient and affordable financial services to disadvantaged and other vulnerable groups, including low income, rural and undocumented persons, who have been underserved or excluded from the formal financial sector. Financial inclusion also involves making a broader range of financial products and services available to individuals who currently only have access

> to basic financial products. Financial inclusion can also be defined as ensuring access to appropriate financial products and services at an affordable cost in a fair and transparent manner.[22]

This definition provides the broadest range of elements and makes specific reference to persons excluded as a result of being undocumented. Remarkably, it contemplates offering a broader range of services to financially included persons that only have access to basic financial services. Again, the definition introduces the element of the suitability of financial products offered to vulnerable consumers. Consumer protection is advocated here as the definition suggests affordability, fairness and transparency

1.2.2 Digital financial service

DFS is defined as

> a broad category that encompasses mobile financial services and all branchless banking services enabled via electronic channels including mobile phones, points-of-sale (POS) devices, electronic cards (credit, debit, smart cards, etc.), and computers.[23]

Digital financial services are also defined by the International Telecommunications Union as 'methods to electronically store and transfer funds; to make and receive payments; to borrow, save, insure and invest; and to manage a person's or enterprise's finances'.[24]

Digital financial services are mainly offered using one or a combination of three models bank-led, MNO-led (provided by a Mobile Network Operator) and the corporation-led models depending on the regulatory strategy adopted in a jurisdiction. Significantly, the 2015 Regulatory Framework for Mobile Money Services in Nigeria defines the bank-led as

> one where a bank or consortium of banks (as lead initiator(s) delivers banking services alone or in partnership with other central bank approved organizations leveraging on the mobile money system while the non-bank-led model, is one where a duly licensed corporate organisation as lead initiator delivers mobile payment services to subscribers.[25]

1.2.3 Bank/non-bank institutions

A bank is defined as 'a chartered financial system within a country that has the ability to accept deposits and make/receive payments into those accounts'.[26] A non-bank institution on the other hand is as 'an entity that is not a chartered bank, but which is providing financial services to end-users; the requirements of non-banks to do this, and the limitations of what they can do, are specified by national law'.[27]

1.2.4 Mobile network operator

A mobile network operator (MNO) is defined as 'a telecommunications service provider organisation that provides wireless voice and data communication for its subscribed mobile users'.[28] These are 'independent communication service providers that own the complete telecom infrastructure for hosting and managing mobile communications between the subscribed mobile users with users in the same and external wireless and wired telecom networks'.[29]

1.2.5 Inclusive finance

Inclusive finance 'is concerned with financial products and services destined to aid low-income populations'.[30] This should not be confused with microfinance which is a type of banking service provided to unemployed or low-income individuals or groups who otherwise would have no other access to financial services.[31] Inclusive finance ensures that people are not cut off from fair and transparently offered financial services such as savings, credit, and micro-insurance because of lack of funds. Inclusive finance initiatives should take account of the peculiarities of target population that may lack be historically debarred from accessing finance due to a lack of funds or credit history, limited understanding of financial offerings, inadequate digital sophistication, regressive cultural norms and challenges of mobility, particularly for women. Here, financial providers could offer low-value accounts, micro-loan and insurance offerings, using alternative data for loan assessments of persons without collateral, providing financial services on user-friendly digital channels and deploying agents at financial access points to tackle customers' queries and concerns.

Inclusive finance models could also consider persons living with disability by offering terms and conditions on braille to the blind and iris scan for identification of quadriplegic clients. Inclusive finance models should consider the needs of excluded populations such as women, rural, poor, youth, marginalised, homeless, nomads, migrants, asylum seekers, internally displaced persons and vulnerable populations such as aged persons. Some inclusive finance examples include the use of boats and animals in Bolivia, skis in Pakistan, and helicopters in Cote D'Ivoire to drive identification documentation and enrolment that enables financial access.[32] Similarly, the widespread use of civic engagement campaigns on posters, press releases, television and radio broadcasts in Chichewa, spoken by more than half the population in Malawi, are other examples.[33]

1.2.6 Financial health

Financial health 'identifies how people manage their finance with available tools, the resort to risky financial services for the reason of lacking financial health and the relationship between policies relating to employment, health-care, pensions and social welfare and whether access and usage patterns lead to better financial health'.[34] Financial health is signified by the ability to meet ongoing financial obligations and consumption needs, manage financial shocks, meet financial goals and advance wellbeing and confidence and is influenced by the resources available to a person, choices, and economic status, access to financial services and social safety nets.[35]

This concept encompasses financial security, financial freedom and financial control and creates financially engaged consumers that save, borrow, manage risk, are financially capable and use varied financial services and helps to pinpoint which products and services work for whom and in what settings.[36] It is outcome-focused and considers objective and subjective ways to define impact, using conventional data on the number of registered and active accounts as well as transaction volumes and value.[37] Studies show a direct correlation between financial health and financial inclusion.[38]

1.2.7 Financial stress

Financial stress has been defined as 'a condition that is the result of financial and/or economic events that create anxiety, worry, or a sense of scarcity, and is accompanied by a physiological stress response'.[39] A related term, chronic financial stress, 'is ongoing and frequently intermittent financial stress'.[40] Financial stress includes stress about how to manage loans including auto, housing and student loans, saving for retirement, managing debt, security of jobs, having debts that surpass earnings, paying for utilities and recurrent bills, not having an emergency fund, and guarantees for the future.

Research reveals that there is a strong correlation between financial stress, interpersonal stress, and psychological distress and wellbeing, and persons who experienced major financial stressors, demonstrate higher greater levels of psychological distress and lower levels of psychological wellbeing.[41] This could be improved by cultivating good financial habits such as budgeting and expense tracking, inventory keeping and financial journaling, intentional debt management including scheduled repayment plans. Unhealthy and unsustainable financial habits such as impulse buying, particularly of luxury items should be jettisoned to get back on track.

1.2.8 Financial literacy and capability

Financial literacy and capability are related concepts that improve financial inclusion. Financial literacy and capability help individuals understand the value of finance products. It has been described as the cognitive understanding of financial components and skills such as budgeting, investing, borrowing, taxation, and personal financial management.[42] A financially literate person is able to manage financial affairs by competently allocating available funds to financial needs, avoiding debt and reserving savings for future needs such as retirement.

Financial capability has been defined as 'the addition of behaviour to the knowledge, skills and attitudes that make up financial literacy and the step in which prior endowments and preparations lead to the strategies and actions people actually carry out – in short, financial behaviours'.[43] In essence, it is the application of learned financial knowledge and skillset to make financial decisions confidently and independently.

Financial capability comprises financial behaviours that enable one to make important and sound financial decisions such as spending responsibly, planning for the future (including saving for education, retirement and emergencies) and avoiding over-indebtedness. A financially capable person would apply sharpened financial skills and knowledge to appropriately express choice of suitable financial services to meet peculiar needs. This also includes the mastery of financial skills such as budgeting, expense tracking, investment and portfolio broadening and diversification, skilful funds apportionment and a grasp of the correlation between product risks and returns to maximise the latter.

1.3 Dimensions of financial inclusion

Financial inclusion is measurable by assessing whether an individual is banked, formally included, included through the informal sector or totally excluded from financial services.[44] There can also be some overlaps such as when financially included persons utilise financial products from banks and other formal institutions or where formally included persons additionally utilise informal finance channels including rotating savings clubs and moneylenders. The meanings of these strands, adopted from the EFInA survey 2016 are specified below.

1.3.1 Banked

The banked are 'persons who currently have access to or use a deposit money bank, in addition to having/using any one of automated teller machine (ATM) cards, credit card, savings account, current account, fixed deposit account, mortgage, overdraft, loan or Islamic banking product'.[45]

1.3.2 Formal other

This refers to 'all adults who have access to or use other formal institutions and financial products not supplied by deposit money banks, including insurance companies, microfinance banks, pension schemes or equity including remittances (via formal channels)'.[46]

1.3.3 Informal only

These are adults who do not have any banked or formal other products but have access to or use only informal services and products such as savings clubs/pools, *esusu, ajo,* or moneylenders; as well as remittances (through informal channels such as a bus transport services or recharge card transfers).[47]

1.3.4 Financially excluded

This term refers to adults not in the banked, formal other or informal only categories, even though the persons may be using or have access to any of the following: loan/gift from friends or family and loan from employers, as well as remittances via a friend/family member.[48]

1.4 Why is financial inclusion important for Nigeria?

Financial inclusion holds many benefits. First, the scale of global financial exclusion at 1.4 billion people as well the proof that financial inclusion can help people escape poverty, makes this concept crucial.[49] In Nigeria, about 35.9 per cent of adults are excluded from finance and only 44.8 per cent are banked.[50] According to the World Bank Global Findex Database on Financial Inclusion, Nigeria, along with six other countries, namely, China, India, Pakistan, Indonesia, Egypt and Bangladesh, account for nearly half of the global unbanked population.[51]

Secondly, as it is easier to regulate money within the formal finance sector, access to these services, enables regulatory oversight by the CBN. Insights from patterns of adoption of financial services could help the government to fulfil welfare responsibilities through government disbursements and help citizens to adequately respond to financial shocks or family emergencies. This could also provide policy recommendations for better fiscal planning as the government is in a better position to understand the spending/investment behaviour and financial needs of the people. Furthermore, these could serve as insights to formulate useful policy strategies for other nations that grapple with financial exclusion. Access to financial services could improve the financial health and wellbeing of citizens by instilling healthy financial habits such as saving for investments, household recurrent expenditure, unforeseen events and emergencies and retirement.

Furthermore, there is evidence of the capacity of financial inclusion to include more people with lower cost DFS channels which, according to McKinsey, reduce set-up cost by as much as 80–90 per cent compared to physical bank branches.[52] Advancing financial products to unserved populations such as SMEs, rural populations and the poor therefore needs research that identifies the specific needs and product expectations of these populations to ensure adoption, usage and sustainability. This additionally saves regulators and providers the economic and resource waste that can arise from a lack of patronage of financial inclusion initiatives.

Fourthly, a study of digital financial inclusion from a country-specific context provides tailored recommendations that are suitable for the excluded. The story of M-Pesa in Kenya reveals how similar initiatives deployed in different countries can wield completely different results. While M-Pesa originated in Kenya and succeeded tremendously there, contributing to the increase of financial inclusion figures to about 83 per cent, the deployment of the model in South Africa's financial market failed to make the same impact.[53] Notably, South Africa's financial market was quite advanced and many already had significant access to traditional providers of finance such as banks unlike in Kenya where the concentration of banking services in the urban centres opened up the opportunity to create a platform for remittances.[54] Using the slogan 'send money home', in commercials, the company encouraged urban-rural remittances to dependents.[55] Like Kenya, Nigeria also has a significant unbanked population and high rural exclusion rate which require tailored solutions such as the M-Pesa model.

A fifth point is that financial inclusion provides the opportunity for the adoption of varied financial services such as payment, credit, savings, and pension. It also improves social inclusion by providing the opportunity to access additional social services in terms of providing access to payment platforms for utilities (energy, water and television). In addition, achieving universal financial inclusion will usher in a departure from the present situation of a mainly included urban segment of the population and a predominantly excluded rural population. In Nigeria, the rural financial exclusion rate stands at about 81 per cent compared to 19 per cent of the urban population even though 70 per cent of the 106 million adult population reside in these areas.[56]

Lastly, the increasing availability and affordability of DFS channels such as mobile phones, ATMs and POS devices and the relative affordability of Internet data plans make the prospects for the success of digital financial inclusion more attainable. Particularly with regard to digital financial inclusion, Nigeria can benefit from the high mobile phone and penetration rates to foster Unstructured Supplementary Service Data (USSD) banking and peer-to-peer financial transactions. Presently, about 81 per cent of Nigerians own a mobile phone and mobile subscription rate in Nigeria stands at 204 214 647.[57] DFS has the potential to increase the coverage of remittances including low-value transfers and makes sending funds directly for savings, health and education possible.[58]

1.5 Chronicling Nigeria's journey to achieving financial inclusion

The specific journey to financial inclusion in Nigeria has spanned about a decade starting with the CBN's commitment to the Maya Declaration in 2011. Before this time, there were no dedicated regulatory policies on financial inclusion or as the CBN focused more on distribution channels such as ATM, POS and the regulatory intervention programmes adopted, addressed credit enhancement rather than savings mobilisation.[59] Regulations, such as the Guidelines on Electronic Banking 2003, which became the first legal instrument that introduced digital finance, as well as the Point of Sales Guidelines 2009 and the Guidelines on ATM Operations 2011, were the few existing guidelines in the finance sector.

1.5.1 Demographic profile of the excluded in the pre-2011 era

This section provides some information on the demographic representation of the excluded as of 2010 and shows components relating to age, gender, geographical distribution and access strands. In this section, figures from the Enhancing Financial Innovation and Access (EFInA) survey 2010 are used. The survey shows that 39.2 million Nigerians or 46.3 per cent of the adult population did not have access to finance of which 54.4 per cent were males, 73.8 per cent were younger than 45 years and 34 per cent had not obtained formal education.[60] Financial exclusion was also more prevalent in the rural areas and in some parts of the North.

1.5.2 Financial inclusion access strands

In 2010, only 30 per cent of Nigerians were banked, 6.3 per cent were served by other formal financial institutions, 17.4 per cent by informal financial services and 46.3 per cent were excluded.[61]

1.5.3 Financial exclusion by gender

There was a gender bias towards men in relation to financial inclusion. About 54.4 per cent of females were financially excluded, while about 45.6 per cent of men were included.[62]

1.5.4 Age range of the financially excluded

Young adults were most likely to be excluded. The figures for financial exclusion reduced as the population aged. According to the CBN, while as much as 32.6 per cent of the population aged 18–24 was excluded, only 5.7 of the population aged 65 and above was excluded.[63] Similarly, only 7.8 per cent of the population aged 55–64 compared to 25.1 per cent of the 25–34 age grade was excluded.[64]

1.5.5 Rural/urban exclusion

There was a financial exclusion bias towards the rural population. Rural exclusion stood at a staggering 80.4 per cent of the population while, in contrast, only 19.6 per cent of the urban population lacked access to finance with factors such as distance, level of formal and financial literacy and lower levels of economic activities in rural areas contributing to this wide gap.[65]

1.5.6 Financial exclusion by level of education

There was no clear correlation between financial exclusion and the level of education attained by the individual. Remarkably, the population with a tertiary education had an exclusion rate of 3.1 while the group classified as 'other' are represented by a 1.8 per cent exclusion rate.[66] According to the survey, the percentage of excluded persons with no formal education at 34 per cent was lower than the population that had completed a secondary school education, i.e. 37.6 per cent and another 23.4 per cent had a primary school education.

1.5.7 Geographical representation of financial inclusion by geo-political zones

There was an uneven distribution of the included population by region. Urban dwellers were more financially included particularly in the South than in the North-East and North-West where as much as 68 per cent of adults in each region was shown to be excluded.[67] The North-Central followed at 44 per cent with the South-South at 36 per cent while the South-East and South-West had the best figures at 32 per cent and 33 per cent, respectively.[68]

1.5.8 Stakeholder and industry profile

Stakeholders in the industry ranged from development financial institutions, financial services providers, technology companies, public institutions and donors including the Small and Medium Enterprise Development Agency of Nigeria (SMEDAN), the National Identity Management Commission (NIMC) and the Nigeria Postal Service (NIPOST).[69] There were four payment processing companies, namely, Interswitch, Valuecard, Cams, and eTranzact and nine mobile network operators (MNOs) with 3 operators-MTN, Globacom and Airtel collectively dominating 85 per cent of the market share.[70] There were also 21 deposit money banks and 866 microfinance banks (MFBs) operating through branches across Nigeria.[71] At the time, the insurance industry only served 1 per cent of the population.[72]

1.6 Nigeria's commitment to the Maya Declaration

In 2011, Nigeria, along with other nations, committed to certain country targets on financial inclusion at the Maya summit hosted by the Global Policy Forum (GPF) in Riviera, Maya in Mexico. Here, members committed themselves to deliberately pursuing national targets for achieving and implementing financial inclusion and to sharing implementation outcomes among members.[73] Nigeria's target was to drive down financial exclusion from 46.3 per cent in 2010 to 20 per cent by 2020.[74] In line with the Maya commitments, the bank set up the National Financial Inclusion Strategy (NFIS) in 2012 to facilitate financial access and usage by 2020.[75] The CBN considered as a strategic objective of the NFIS, the input, concerns, roles and responsibilities of all stakeholders before defining regulatory policies.[76]

According to the strategy, financial inclusion is achieved when adult

Nigerians can easily access varied, affordable and suitable formal financial services including payments, savings, loans, insurance, and pension products.[77] A secretariat was established in 2012 to monitor and evaluate data from stakeholders, develop key performance indicators, compare results with targets, analyse gaps and trends, suggest measures to meet set targets, coordinate stakeholder activities and report on progress.[78] The secretariat is further responsible for 'coordinating the activities of working groups and committees in the implementation of the National Financial Literacy Framework'.[79] For the proper functioning of the strategy, various working groups and committees were established. The working groups shoulder the responsibility of implementation for the committees.[80] The technical committee is specifically charged with the responsibility of providing technical advice on implementation and disbursement of approved funding to the secretariat while the steering committee oversees strategy direction in relation to the secretariat's activities.[81]

The set goal for achieving financial inclusion is pursued by the CBN through a number of initiatives including tiered approach to KYC, agent banking, mobile payments, cash-less policy, financial literacy, consumer protection, Micro, Small and Medium Enterprises support, agricultural lending, entrepreneurship development and credit enhancement programmes.[82] To advance these, the CBN introduced two enabling frameworks. First, the national consumer protection framework aims to establish channels of redress and provide guidance that ensures fairness in pricing and regulates the market conduct of financial services providers.[83] The Consumer Protection Framework seeks to ensure transparent product pricing, curb consumer exploitation by service providers, foster consumer confidence and promote a sound finance sector.[84]

Second, the National Financial Literacy Framework (NFLF) serves to drive economic growth by advancing financial literacy programmes that positively impact financial inclusion policies.[85] The NFLF further provides a prototype for financial literacy in maintaining financial system stability and implementing the NFIS.[86] The CBN is also driving financial literacy in primary, secondary and tertiary institutions.[87]

1.7 Regulatory initiatives since the Maya Declaration

In 2012, the CBN initiated the cashless policy to advance the payment system, reduce costs associated with banking services, offer better service options, improve reach and manage inflation by appropriately steering monetary policies to foster economic growth.[88] According to the CBN, cash dependency results in significant cost implications, risks of theft or loss, surplus funds circulating outside the formal economy, inefficiency of the payment system and corruption.[89] Again, the bank explains that a cashless policy is necessary to correct the unwarranted cost subsidisation foisted on the customers of the entire banking system by the 10 per cent minority that go over the ₦150 000 withdrawal mark.[90]

Thus, this policy introduced a limit on cash deposits, withdrawals and cheque encashment by introducing a fee when transactions go above the prescribed limits of ₦500 000 for individuals and ₦3 000 000 for corporate.[91] The pilot project was launched in Lagos in April 2012, followed by a trial set for July 2013 in one state in each of the six geographical zones, namely, Anambra, Abia, FCT, Kano, Rivers, and Ogun and a nationwide launch scheduled for July 2014.[92]

To further encourage the deployment and use of DFS, the Central Bank in 2014 initiated an industry-wide incentive scheme which featured cuts in merchant service charges, commission-on-turnover exemptions, purchase with cashback, mystery shopper rewards and other incentivising rewards based on the frequency of debit or credit card used by customers.[93] Similar to this, the NIBSS Electronic Funds Transfer (NEFT) and the real-time NIBSS Instant Payments have also been adopted to facilitate the payment system.[94]

The Nigerian government has also embarked on facilitating measures, identification management and the establishment of credit bureaux towards the goal of broadening access to financial services.[95] Nigeria has shifted to Europay, MasterCard, and Visa (EMV) chip and pin cards to improve security and has adopted the Nigeria Uniform Bank Account Number (NUBAN) to address the problems of automated direct credits.[96] The CBN additionally introduced the mCASH as an innovative solution leveraged on the Nigeria Inter-Bank Settlement System (NIBSS) and designed to facilitate low-value electronic retail payments, to a wider range of users including payers and merchants at the bottom-of-the-pyramid where cash usage is prevalent.[97] Mcash leverages on the NIBSS Instant Payments

In 2018, the Tradermoni Scheme and the Agri-Business Small and Medium Enterprise Investment Scheme (AGSMEIS) were initiated to offer graduated loan and credit facilities, respectively, to traders and small and medium enterprises (MSMEs), while the NIRSAL microfinance bank was initiated to facilitate financial access using NIPOST offices located in all the 774 local government areas in Nigeria.[98]

1.8 The CBN 2018 National Financial Inclusion Strategy (NFIS) refresh

Although the CBN had made some inroads into breaking barriers to financial access, no interim targets were achieved by 2016.[99] Challenges such as religious and cultural barriers to access, difficulties in profitably extending financial services to the excluded, the low level of unemployment, security challenges in some regions and the high levels of informal finance in the economy still plagued the goal of achieving access to finance.[100]

A review of the 2012 National Financial Inclusion Strategy was, therefore, necessary to address these concerns. This review was also in line with the goal of NFIS 2012 to carry out a backward- and forward-looking comprehensive review of existing research, reports and databases and to consult with a diverse spectrum of stakeholders after four years, in order to apply learnt lessons.[101] The fact that specific target groups such as formally uneducated persons, women, youth, northerners and rural dwellers were still largely excluded also demonstrated the need for an intervention.[102] Again, Nigeria was an early adopter of the Maya Declaration and set up a national financial inclusion strategy as early as 2012 and so it was important to do a review to reposition the course of financial inclusion for more Nigerians.

With the above reasons as a background, the CBN carried out an extensive review utilising industry data and research, as well as consultation with stakeholders to understand the state of financial inclusion and prioritise the most critical regulatory interventions.[103] The CBN additionally consulted widely with public sector institutions including regulators, government ministries, private sector institutions such as financial service providers and international and regional development partners to obtain wide perspectives.[104]

The CBN was also mindful in the review process to apply lessons on specific practices from other jurisdictions where financial inclusion strides had been made. For instance, in Bangladesh the use of flexible agent banking business models and pricing was impactful and was found suitable for Nigeria by enabling female agents and, by doing so, increasing the reach of financial services to women in Northern Nigeria where Islam is practised.[105] From India's experience where less formal proof of identity is accepted, third-party enrolment is utilised and enrolment data collection is reduced to address the barrier of lack of identification in account opening, Nigeria has recognised the need to adopt more inclusive identification enrolment methods.[106]

The findings from this NFIS review have ushered in some changes into the bank's approach to pursuing financial inclusion. The agenda for increasing access to and usage of quality and affordable financial services by 2020 has been set from the recommendations, and priorities and access strategies are being tailored to those with the potential to yield results.[107] CBN has indicated that it is necessary to create an innovative environment to deepen financial inclusion using DFS and microfinance and is also focused on encouraging investments in tailored products, digitising government payments and promoting digital literacy.[108] Significantly, DFS is now recognised as a simple and flexible alternative channel to reach remote and rural areas beyond the present use as an add-on feature for the banked and the need to develop products that appeal to low-income customers has become imperative to harnessing DFS potential.[109]

The CBN has committed to employing an appropriate risk-based regulatory approach to level the playing field for providers with a focus on the activity of all players as well as an understanding that actors should apply comparative advantages to engender high impact.[110] Additionally, the Bank is scaling back on the emphasis on the POS channel to drive agent banking and is considering the disadvantages that fixed fees, macroeconomic and security situations and cultural and religious perceptions have on exclusion.[111]

Religious bias towards formal finance in Northern Nigeria is now being addressed with the advancement of Islamic banking products as banks such as Jaiz Bank and Taj Banks now offer non-interest-bearing *Shariah*-complaint financial products.[112] Remarkably, financial exclusion was observed to be lowest in the North. A focus on financial products that are on par with the tenets of Islam, therefore, deserve projection. As these banks now offer products that comply with the prohibition of interest on loans by providers, this will likely advance access to finance in the North.

Financial literacy is also being aided by the National Youth Service Corps (NYSC) as peer educators drive account openings at the grassroots and educate on savings, credit, insurance, capital market and pension.[113] These group of youth, aged below 30 and fresh out of university are required to complete a year-long national youth service.[114] They are largely deployed as teachers in the primary and secondary schools as well as government ministries and thus provide the vital and diverse workforce necessary to drive rural financial literacy projects to their students and host communities.

By approving the Guidelines for the Licensing and Regulation of Payments Service Banks in Nigeria 2020, MNOs can now 'incorporate special purpose vehicles to provide payment and remittance services, issue debit and prepaid cards, invest in Federal Government and CBN securities and provide deposit products to micro and small businesses and low-income households, using existing mobile and digital services'.[115] The CBN has equally signed a memorandum of understanding in 2018 with the Nigerian Communications Commission to enhance the payment system and has drafted a regulatory framework for Unstructured Supplementary Service Data (USSD).[116] A further collaboration with the NIBSS is now in place to introduce a regulatory sandbox that permits the testing of digital solutions and products in a controlled environment by financial technology companies.[117]

The CBN is also looking to introduce interest earnings to mobile money and to exclude biometrics registration for Tier 1 mobile money accounts.[118] Tier 1 accounts are low-value accounts that require less documentation to open and operate. Account-holders are only required to provide a name, phone number and contact details to open these accounts.[119] There is also no need for further verification by an external organisation such as the Independent National Electoral Commission (INEC) in the case of voter cards or the National Identification Management Commission for national identity cards.[120]

The CBN notes that there are now more drivers for financial inclusion in Nigeria such as the introduction of no-frills savings accounts, USSD, multi-functional ATMs and micro-insurance, and the implementation of the NFIS at federal and state levels.[121] Ultimately, the Bank has set out 2024 for achieving 95 per cent financial inclusion using a five-year policy thrust (2019–2024) to prioritise the development of a robust payments system infrastructure that fosters access to financial services.[122] It is expected that with these measures in place, the Bank is on course to reaching set goals.

1.9 Legal landscape for financial inclusion in Nigeria

Nigeria's financial inclusion commitments necessarily imply the formulation of relevant and tailored legal framework. Some of the legal instruments related to financial inclusion include the Guidelines on Electronic Banking 2003, CBN Cashless Policy Framework 2012, CBN Three-Tiered KYC Regulations 2013, Guidelines for the Regulation of Agent Banking and Agent Banking Relations 2013, CBN Guidelines on Card Acceptance 2014, the Framework for Mobile Money Services in Nigeria 2015 and the CBN National Financial Literacy Framework 2015. Also in 2015, the Regulatory Framework for Licensing Super-Agents was initiated. The Nigeria Deposit Insurance Corporation (NDIC) Framework for the Establishment of Pass through Deposit Insurance for subscribers of Mobile Money and the CBN Guidelines on Transaction Switching were introduced in 2016.

The year 2017 witnessed the passing into law of the Secured Transactions in Movable Assets Act 2017 and the Credit Reporting Act 2017 by the National Assembly. Most recently in 2020, the CBN has initiated the Guidelines for Licensing and Regulation of Payment Service Bank 2020 the Regulatory Framework for the Use of Unstructured Supplementary Service Data (USSD) for Financial Services in Nigeria 2020 and the Guidelines on the Operations of Electronic Payment Channels in Nigeria 2020. The Regulatory Framework for Open banking in Nigeria, the Framework for Quick Response (QR) Code Payments in Nigeria and Framework for Regulatory Sandbox Operations have been introduced in 2021. The Regulatory Guidelines on the eNaira were also initiated in October 2021.

Although delving in-depth into the provision of each of these laws, policies, guidelines and regulations is outside the scope of this book, a combined reading of these instruments reveals many lessons. First, these instruments are varied in scope and extend and address numerous financial inclusion themes and concerns. These include access, usage, safety, consumer protection, identification, competition, insurance, cost, financial literacy, credit facilitation and payment system efficiency. Second, each instrument is tailored to a particular exclusion issue and attempts to unlock opportunities for improving financial inclusion by addressing specific barriers. The CBN Three Tiered KYC Requirements 2013, for instance, seek to dismantle the hurdle of lack of identification for the excluded class by requiring fewer conditions for account opening and introducing tiered accounts. Similarly, the Guidelines for the Regulation of Agent Banking and Agent Banking Relationships 2013 help to bring financial services closer to users, aiding the barrier of distance and providing guidance on available financial products to close the financial literacy gap.

A third lesson is that the instruments demonstrate the willingness of the CBN to fulfil the commitments to advance financial inclusion as per the Maya

Declaration by introducing legal instruments and regulatory policies that help dismantle access and usage barriers, including demand-side, supply-side and regulatory ones. A fourth lesson is that the bank rightly prioritises the safety of digital channels and security of funds. The NDIC Pass-Through Guidelines on Mobile Money 2016 and the Guidelines on Transaction Switching 2016 are two examples. This is laudable as trust in the digital payment system needs to grow for the adoption and usage of financial services to scale up. The dependency on cash by Nigerians could also decrease where there is an assurance of safety when dealing with alternative finance providers such as the newly introduced Payment Service Banks.

Some challenges however persist. For instance, the insistence on a ratio of rural deployment on Payment Service Banks by the Guidelines for Licensing and Regulation of Payment Service Bank 2020 without any such burden on traditional banks is at best discriminatory. Again, the provisions of some guidelines are unable to purposefully result in high-quality financial services because these are in conflict with others. For instance, while the CBN Three Tiered KYC Requirements 2013 were introduced to ease customer on-boarding by reducing identification documentation for persons lacking official legal documents, the 2014 CBN Bank Verification Number (BVN) policy requires accounts to be operable only upon completion of a biometric verification exercise. The BVN enrolment usually requires identification documentation and so ushers the same exclusionary effect that the tiered banking guidelines seek to dislodge. Although reduced KYC is offered by some banks to enable the use of these low-value accounts, restrictions as to value and volume of transactions are emplaced.

Furthermore, some guidelines are restricted in wording and, therefore, are unable to yield similar positive strides as observed in other jurisdictions. The agent banking guidelines, for instance, restrict agent banking to financial institutions, thus leaving out alternative providers and preserving the initial problem of banks' reluctance to engage with some rural populations.[123] Again, even the present model prohibits bank agents from opening accounts for users on behalf of the bank thereby missing the opportunity to erase concerns of distance and cost (of transportation).

There are also untapped territories such as the use of the extensive post office infrastructure existing in Nigeria and the collaborative deployment of ATMs in rural facilities to help customers surmount concerns around distance. The CBN, with the review of the NFIS, is trying to address some of these gaps with the proposals for the creation of mini-branches in rural areas. The PBS guidelines that enumerate courier companies and the Post as eligible promoters could also address this. The CBN earlier in April 2018 signed an MOU with the NCC to provide a framework for licensing payment service providers, reducing cash transactions, enhancing cashless operations and guiding stakeholders in both sectors to attain financial inclusion timely.[124] Collaborations such as these are needed and it is hoped that more such partnerships will be made to provide cooperation for the multi-faceted service.

Lastly, the gamut of laws for the advancement of DFS in Nigeria are found to overlap and can be collapsed into related themes for easier referencing. Relevant themes would include, building blocks for mobile money, competition, DFS channels, proportionate regulation, infrastructure, culture, regulation, consumer protection, digital and economic exclusion, rural and urban divide. The Guidelines on Electronic Banking 2003, Financial Literacy Framework, Cashless Policy Initiative, the NDIC Pass-Through Guidelines for Mobile Money, the USSD Guidelines and the Agent Banking and Super-Agent Guidelines can all be merged into one to serve as the building block for mobile money. In addition, provisions on infrastructure can be drawn from the Guidelines on Electronic Banking, cashless policy, the Card Acceptance Guidelines and the Guidelines for Licensing and Regulation of Payment Service Bank 2020.

As for competition, the Transactions Switching Guidelines, the Framework and Guidelines for Mobile Money 2015 and the Guidelines for Licensing and Regulation of Payment Service Bank 2020 are related. To assure proportionate regulation, the provisions of the Regulatory Framework for the use of Unstructured Supplementary Service Data (USSD) for financial services in Nigeria can be merged with those of the Guidelines on Electronic Banking 2003. Furthermore, channels for effectively deploying DFS can be addressed by consolidating the cashless policy initiatives, as well as the Guidelines on Electronic Banking, the USSD Guidelines, Card Acceptance Guidelines, Agent banking and Super-Agent Guidelines and the Guidelines on the Operation of Electronic Payment.

Changing customer perception and culture towards money can be addressed by lessons from the financial literacy framework to learn about consumer perspectives, the cashless policy to dislodge digital aversion, as well as the Secure Transactions in Movable Assets Act and the Credit Reporting Act to improve the loan culture. The cashless policy can also include provisions that help to bridge the rural/urban divide and forestall digital and economic exclusion. Collapsing these laws will serve the purpose of easier referencing and bring clarity to stakeholders. Compliance will also be simplified.

1.10 Institutional landscape for financial inclusion in Nigeria

The Central Bank of Nigeria as the chief regulator of the finance sector maintains prudential oversight over all financial institutions in Nigeria in all matters of banking and finance including DFS. By the powers vested in the Central Bank of Nigeria Act 2007 and the Banks and Other Financial Institutions Act (BOFIA) 2020, the bank is empowered to introduce rules that govern the adequate provision of financial services to the public. This role has been manifested in the introduction of numerous guidelines on financial inclusion, particularly post-2011 as discussed earlier. Significantly, the role of CBN as DFS regulator is diverse and needs careful deliberation to carry through. The Bank has to make the proper balance between protecting financial system stability and integrity, enabling provider innovation and ensuring consumer protection.

Rules and policies need to be communicated to stakeholders and consultation with other relevant regulators has to be sought continually as DFS requires competence and expertise from other sectors. Remarkably, the uniqueness of DFS regulation lies in the fact that the service cuts across several sectors besides the payment system to include telecommunications, insurance, consumer protection, competition and communications technology which in many cases are overseen by other regulators and crisscross several market concerns. The CBN thus necessarily has to collaborate with regulators in these sectors to ensure the efficient deployment of DFS. These collaborations ensure that DFS, like all other disruptive and fast-paced technological exploits gets the top-notch regulatory expertise needed to weave through the complexities of novel and unfurling issues within the sector.

Regulatory collaboration enables a broad spectrum of resources and specialist industry knowledge to make model, uniform, proportionate and efficient frameworks as well as providing a forum for robust convergence of ideas that considers all stakeholders and creates a level playing field for participants. Furthermore, this type of collaborative effort eliminates duplicity of laws and resources that could emanate from multiplicity of regulatory efforts and creates consistent rules across sectors. Scarce regulatory resources can therefore be meaningfully allocated to needed areas.

The following section outlines the relevant regulators whose ambits traverse DFS. The roles of these regulators and relationships or efforts towards financial inclusion are also highlighted.

1.10.1 Central Bank of Nigeria

The mandate of the CBN is derived from the CBN Act of 2007 as amended which vests the bank with the responsibility of administering and advising the government on financial and monetary policies, ensuring price stability, a sound financial system, issuing legal tender and maintaining external reserves.[125] The Bank is the chief financial regulator in Nigeria. The Bank administers the Banks and Other Financial Institutions Act (BOFIA 1991) to promote high banking standards and financial stability by optimising the payment system.[126]

In relation to financial inclusion, the CBN has been striving to introduce and implement viable policies. The bank has succeeded in rolling out the National Financial Inclusion Strategy in addition to inaugurating relevant committees, working groups and a designated secretariat to administer the strategy. The bank has also carried out geospatial mapping of financial access points in the country and commissioned the revision of the financial inclusion policies related to microfinance, bank charges, tiered KYC, mobile wallet and BVN.[127] Furthermore, the bank has initiated policies on the licensing of super-agents, financial literacy, cashless Nigeria, collateral registration, consumer protection and mobile money.[128]

With the introduction of the 2018 NFIS, the CBN expects to implement agent banking and tiered KYC, disseminate information to stakeholders on regulatory adjustments, advance cost-saving shared services, encourage the deployment of services to rural dwellers through the use of ATMs and drive financial literacy advocacy.[129]

1.10.2 National Insurance Commission (NAICOM)

NAICOM is the insurance regulator in Nigeria responsible for administering insurance policies and products. In relation to financial inclusion, NAICOM creates awareness, initiates guidelines for inclusive finance and consumer protection, advocates for the inclusion of alternative providers, the creation of halal insurance products, the deployment of microfinance banks and the offering of insurance products at banks.[130]

NAICOM expects in the near future to launch a micro-insurance framework to further the awareness about insurance, facilitate speedy dispute resolution, promote compulsory insurance products and encourage companies to develop micro-Islamic and index-based insurance services for rural and low-income earners.[131]

NAICOM has an important role to play in advancing financial inclusion as insurance products can guarantee that the formerly excluded have access to long-term financial products that provide insulation from economic shocks or family emergencies. Insurance can also improve the confidence of the financially excluded in taking up financial services and can foster better financial health.

1.10.3 Nigerian Communications Commission (NCC)

NCC is the chief regulator of the telecommunications industry in Nigeria. NCC is charged with the responsibility of creating the right environment for competitive provision of quality and efficient telecommunications services across Nigeria as well as the licensing of providers and formulation of a framework for the industry.[132]

The commission has contributed to financial inclusion by obtaining super-agent status for mobile network operators to provide mobile money.[133] The commission has also given permission for MNOs to operate special purpose vehicles (SPVs) as super-agents using mobile networks and USSD.[134] Additionally, the Commission has launched the Internet Exchange Points (IXPs), the Wire Nigeria Project (WIN) and the States Accelerated Broadband Initiative (SABI) for the benefit of excluded communities.[135] This can provide the needed infrastructure for DFS.

The NCC is currently working on driving investment in fibre optic cables for service providers, deploying mobile payments enabling bandwidth and releasing statistics on network downtime to encourage providers to ensure networks remain active.[136]

1.10.4 Nigeria Deposit Insurance Corporation

This corporation is the government agency vested with the responsibility of securing deposits and ensuring that insured funds are repaid to depositors when banks are unable to do so.[137] The corporation has the mission of contributing to a stable finance sector by effectively supervising insured institutions, providing the needed technical and financial support, paying deposits promptly and resolving disputes.[138] The corporation also oversees and guarantees deposit liabilities of financial institutions and assists monetary authorities in the issuing and implementation of suitable policies necessary to achieve the functions of the corporation.[139]

Beyond protecting deposits, the NDIC deposit insurance scheme serves as a risk minimiser to avoid financial system disruption and promote competition and innovation in the industry.[140] Implicitly, where deposits are guaranteed, bank runs will potentially be minimised thus reducing the opportunity for systemic risks that result in economic crisis. The NDIC, however, guarantees sums only to a tune of ₦500,000.00 per individual subscriber.

In terms of financial Inclusion, the NDIC administers the NDIC Pass-Through Guidelines on Mobile Money 2016, which mandates that providers must insure mobile money subscriptions as well as make mandatory savings of these funds at a deposit money bank, separate from those of the providers. By these guidelines, mobile money operators are only permitted to invest users' funds in safe assets such as federal government financial instruments.

1.10.5 National Pension Commission (PENCOM)

PENCOM is a creation of the 2014 Pension Reform Act with the mandate of overseeing and regulating the effective administration of matters relating to pension.[141] The Act was introduced to provide retirement savings for all public servants, simplify the process of pension payment and establish uniformity of rules on pension.[142] This commission has the power to issue a broad range of legal instruments to manage and investigate the management of funds.[143] PENCOM also has the power to stipulate sanctions and fines for administrative matters against employees of pension fund administrators including assigning funds or asset administration to a different custodian or administrator and license revocation.[144]

The commission issues guidelines for the investment of pension funds; approves licences for pension fund administrators, custodians and other institutions; maintains the national data bank for all pension matters; creates awareness and capacity building for stakeholders and investigates complaints on the administration of pension funds.[145]

In relation to financial inclusion, the commission is leading the introduction and revision of regulations to drive the adoption of pension schemes and has succeeded in the inclusion of 11 per cent of the working population.[146] The micro pension scheme initiated by the commission serves the informal economy which covers 70 per cent of the population and is revising pension rules to cater for small businesses that have less than five employees.[147]

PENCOM has indicated some interest in implementing a micro-pension framework for the benefit of low-income earners working in the informal sector and driving consumer protection programmes and extend knowledge on the importance of pensions across all states.[148]

1.10.6 Securities and Exchange Commission (SEC)

SEC is the principal regulator of the capital market and is administered by the Investments and Securities Act 29 of 2007. The Act vests SEC with the task of regulating the capital market to protect investors and re-organise the market to pave the way for a private sector-led economy.[149] SEC strives to improve market integrity by ensuring the registration of fit and proper institutions, inspection of sites of operators, surveillance of exchanges to deter breaches, investigation of breaches and enforcement of actions against defaulters.[150]

SEC has been able to initiate the publication of a capital market journal and school curriculum to drive awareness about the capital market and is seeking to formalise informal community-based cooperatives and savings programmes.[151] Presently, these funds are unregulated and deemed unsafe by the CBN. The commission has also introduced e-dividends to reduce the incidents of unclaimed dividends and increase investor confidence and has launched the first sovereign sukuk (Sharia compliant bond) which was oversubscribed by 6 per cent.[152] These measures ensure that communities that rely on indigenous savings systems, as well as persons in need of Islamic-compliant financial services, do not remain excluded from formal finance.

1.10.7 National Bureau of Statistics (NBS)

The NBS houses and collates data on Nigerian statistics. The NBS aims 'to generate, continuous and sustainable socio-economic statistics on all facets of development in Nigeria'.[153] In aid of financial inclusion, the bureau collects data and assists in research on the state of financial inclusion.[154] For instance, the bureau assisted the Enhancing Financial Innovation and Access in Nigeria (EFInA) in respondent selection for the 2016 access to finance survey, collaborated with the CBN to advance financial literacy and carried out research for the NIBSS on POS usage.[155] The bureau is further committed to including yearly household surveys on financial inclusion indicators and the publication of these indicators.[156]

1.10.8 The National Identification Management Commission

The NIMC is the body designated to create an authentic national identification system for citizens and legal residents.[157] By the provisions of Section 5 of the NIMC Act 23 of 2007, the Commission has the specific duty to assign a unique national identification number to Nigerians and permanent residents and to register births and deaths.[158] The commission also has the duty to administer and harmonise the national identity database in collaboration with relevant bodies.[159]

The national identity database created by the NIMC helps financial inclusion by providing the necessary identification documentation to access finance.[160] NIMC also issues payment cards enabled by Access Bank and MasterCard to help the financially excluded to access finance.[161] The commission provides verification services to financial service providers and is harmonising the national identity database in collaboration with the Nigeria Communications Commission and the NIBSS.[162]

1.10.9 The Nigerian Postal Service

NIPOST was established to provide efficient, effective and reliable postal services in Nigeria.[163] The agency engages in domestic post-transfer, international remittance, agency banking and offers payment services for utilities and school fees.[164] NIPOST also runs the NIPOST mobile money which is to provide cash-in and cash-out outlets for mobile payments.[165] The postal service has partnered with One Network (Super-Agent) to use post offices as money agents.[166]

The postal service holds great potential for rural financial inclusion. Significantly, all 774 local government areas in Nigeria have a post office and this wide branch network can effectively be utilised as agent outlets for financial services.[167] NIPOST is on course to obtain a super-agent licence with which to offer finance across the postal service on behalf of banks, mobile money operators and other financial service providers and serve as distribution centres to disseminate resources for financial literacy.[168] It is expected that, just as Brazil improved financial inclusion figures using postal correspondents, NIPOST can also facilitate access to finance for Nigerians.

1.11 How have we fared in the financial inclusion journey?

Although significant feats have been attained in respect of increased financial inclusion for excluded populations, studies still show that the most excluded class in Nigeria remains women, Northern Nigerians, rural dwellers and youth.[169] The EFInA 2020 survey reveals that the major barriers for these excluded segments include significant distance to financial access points, eligibility barriers such as cumbersome account opening requirements and documentation, low financial literacy, lack of income and high cost of financial services.[170] The financial inclusion gender gap persists as while 56 per cent of men are financially included, the figures drop to 44 per cent for women.[171] There is also a manifest gap in terms of regional exclusion which is skewed more to the North-West and North-East zones compared to the

South, recording as high as 68 per cent in the North-West and as low as 17 per cent in the South-West.[172]

Lower exclusion figures are also noticeable in rural areas. The survey shows that about two-thirds of the adult population size of 106 million Nigerians, 70 million are rural dwellers with about 81 per cent of the rural population being excluded compared to 19 per cent of the urban population.[173] Of these, only 38 per cent of rural adults reside close to a financial access point, 84 per cent are financial services agents while bank branches and other FSPs make up 4 per cent and 7 per cent, respectively, and 13 per cent represent MNOs.[174] Presently, 64.1 per cent of Nigerians are financially served while 50.5 per cent use formal financial services.[175] Specifically, the banked population total 44.8 per cent (47.6 million), 5.7 (6 million) and 13.6 (14.4 million) are formally and informally included, respectively, and 35.9 per cent (38.1 million) are excluded.[176]

The foregoing figures demonstrate that while financial inclusion has improved since the start of the journey in 2011, more still needs to be done to achieve universal inclusion, particularly for the most vulnerable members of the society that are in need of meaningful financial services.

1.12 Conclusion

This chapter provided an overview of financial inclusion, defining relevant themes, tracing Nigeria's journey to achieving financial inclusion through the national financial inclusion strategy and the ensuing laws and policies. The relevant regulators of DFS-related sectors including finance, telecommunications, pension, insurance, competition, securities and the postal service were delineated.

Notes

1 Asli Demirgüç-Kunt, Leora Klapper, Dorothe Singer et al, *The Global Findex Database 2017: Measuring Financial Inclusion and the Fintech Revolution* (2018) at 35, available at https://globalfindex.worldbank.org/, accessed on 16 April 2019. See also Ceyla Pazarbasioglu et al, 'Digital Financial Services', April 2020, available at http://pubdocs.worldbank.org/en/230281588169110691/Digital-Financial-Services.pdf, accessed on 30 January 2021. Asli Demirgüç-Kunt et al, *The Global Findex Database 2021: Financial Inclusion, Digital Payments, and Resilience in the Age of COVID-19*, 33, available at https://openknowledge.worldbank.org/bitstream/handle/10986/37578/9781464818974.pdf, accessed on 6 July 2022.

2 Asli Demirgüç-Kunt, Leora Klapper, Dorothe Singer et al note 1 at 5. Asli Demirgüç-Kunt et al, *The Global Findex Database 2021: Financial Inclusion, Digital Payments, and Resilience in the Age of COVID-19*, 35, available at https://openknowledge.worldbank.org/bitstream/handle/10986/37578/9781464818974.pdf, accessed on 6 July 2022.

3 Enhancing Financial Innovation and Access in Nigeria (EFInA), *Key Findings: EFInA Access to Financial Services in Nigeria* Survey (2020) at 44, available at https://a2f.ng/wp-content/uploads/2021/06/A2F-2020-Final-Report.pdf, accessed on 14 January 2021.

4 CBN, 2019 Annual Report National Financial Inclusion Strategy Implementation 13, available at https://www.cbn.gov.ng/Out/2020/CCD/2019%20Annual%20Report%20of%20the%20National%20Financial%20Inclusion%20Strategy%20Implementation.pdf. See also EFInA at 16.

5 Ibid at 64.
6 Enhancing Financial Innovation and Access in Nigeria (EFInA), Key Findings: EFInA Access to Financial Services in Nigeria (A2F) 2016 Survey (2017) at 37–48, available at https://www.efina.org.ng/wp-content/uploads/2019/03/Key-Findings-A2F-2016.pdf, accessed on 26 June 2019.
7 World Bank Group, *Financial Inclusion: Overview* (2018), available at http://www.worldbank.org/en/topic/financialinclusion/overview, accessed on 30 April 2019.
8 World Bank, *UFA2020 Overview: Universal Financial Access by 2020* (2018), available at http://www.worldbank.org/en/topic/financialinclusion/brief/achieving-universal-financial-access-by-2020, accessed on 14 April 2019.
9 Ibid.
10 ITU *Focus Group on Digital Financial Services*, available at https://www.itu.int/en/ITU-T/focusgroups/dfs/Pages/default.aspx, accessed on 12 April 2019.
11 Ibid.
12 Bill and Melinda Gates Foundation, *Financial Services for the Poor,* available at https://www.gatesfoundation.org/What-We-Do/Global-Growth-and-Opportunity/Financial-Services-for-the-Poor, accessed on 14 April 2019.
13 Asli Demirgüç-Kunt et al, *Financial Inclusion, Digital Payments, and Resilience in the Age of COVID-19, XVII,* available at https://openknowledge.worldbank.org/bitstream/handle/10986/37578/9781464818974.pdf, accessed on 6 July 2022.
14 Columbia University Ibid.
15 Accion Centre for Financial Inclusion, *Mission and Vision*, available at https://www.centerforfinancialinclusion.org/about/mission, accessed on 30 April 2019.
16 Alliance for Financial Inclusion, *A Policy Leadership Alliance,* available at https://www.afi-global.org/about-us, accessed on 10 July 2020.
17 CGAP, *About CGAP*, available at https://www.cgap.org/about, accessed on 30 April 2019.
18 Central Bank of Nigeria *CPD FAQs* at 3, available at https://www.cbn.gov.ng/Devfin/CPD_FAQs.pdf, accessed on 12 May 2019.
19 Central Bank of Nigeria, *National Financial Inclusion Strategy* (2012) at 1, available at https://www.cbn.gov.ng/Out/2012/publications/reports/dfd/CBN-Summary%20Report%20of-Financial%20Inclusion%20in%20Nigeria-final.pdf, accessed on 10 April 2019.
20 Centre for Financial Inclusion, *Financial Inclusion Glossary* (2018), available at https://www.centerforfinancialinclusion.org/financial-inclusion-glossary>, accessed on 11 July 2020.
21 Carol Benson and Nils Clotteau, *Digital Financial Services Glossary ITU-T Focus Group on Digital Financial Services* at 6, available at https://www.itu.int/en/ITU-T/focusgroups/dfs/Documents/201701/ITU_FGDFS_DFS-Glossary.pdf, accessed on 11 July 2020.
22 Financial Action Task Force, *FATF Guidance: Anti-Money Laundering and Terrorist Financing Measures and Financial Inclusion* (2013) at 38, available at http://www.fatf-gafi.org/media/fatf/content/images/Updated-2017-FATF-2013-Guidance.pdf, accessed on 18 May 2018.
23 Alliance for Financial Inclusion, *Basic Terminology* Guideline Note No. 19, August 2016, available at https://www.afi-global.org/sites/default/files/publications/2016-08/Guideline%20Note-19%20DFS-Terminology.pdf, accessed on 11 July 2020.
24 Carol Benson and Nils Clotteau note 21 at 6.
25 Central Bank of Nigeria, Regulatory Framework for Mobile Money Services in Nigeria, Regulation 3.0 of 2015.
26 Carol Benson and Nils Clotteau note 21 at 20.
27 Ibid.
28 Techopedia, *Definition: What Does Mobile Network Operator (MNO) Mean?* available

at https://www.techopedia.com/definition/27804/mobile-network-operator-mno, accessed on 12 May 2019.

29 Ibid.

30 ADA Microfinance *Definition of Inclusive Finance,* available at https://www.ada-microfinance.org/en/about-ada/definition-inclusive-finance, accessed on 7 March 2022.

31 Julia Kagan *Microfinance,* Investopaedia, 4 January 2022, available at https://www.investopedia.com/terms/m/microfinance.asp, accessed on 7 March 2022.

32 International Bank for Reconstruction and Development/World Bank, *ID Enrollment Strategies: Practical Lessons from Around the Globe* 8, 9, available at http://documents1.worldbank.org/curated/en/539361582557916734/pdf/ID-Enrollment-Strategies-Practical-Lessons-From-Around-The-Globe.pdf, accessed on 11 May 2021.

33 Ibid.

34 Elisabeth Rhine *Measuring Financial Health: What Policymakers Need to Know,* April 2020 at 3, available at https://www.afi-global.org/Measurement_framework/Downloads/Measuring%20Financial%20Health.pdf, accessed on 14 May 2021.

35 Ibid.

36 UNCFD, *What is Financial Health?* available at https://www.uncdf.org/gfh/global-financial-health, accessed on 13 May 2021.

37 Ibid.

38 EFInA 2020 note 3 at 57.

39 Financial Health Institute, *Financial Health & Financial Stress in Human Services,* available at https://financialhealthinstitute.com/learn/financial-stress/, accessed on 14 May 2021.

40 Ibid.

41 John A. Sturgeon et al. *The Psychosocial Context of Financial Stress: Implications for Inflammation and Psychological Health* (2017), available at https://www.ncbi.nlm.nih.gov/pmc/articles/PMC4738080/, accessed on 14 May 2021.

42 Corporate Finance Institute, *What Is Financial Literacy,* available at https://corporatefinanceinstitute.com/resources/knowledge/finance/financial-literacy/, accessed on 13 May 2021.

43 Elisabeth Rhine note 33 at 12.

44 EFInA 2020 note 3 at 43.

45 EFInA 2016 note 6 at 12.

46 Ibid.

47 Ibid.

48 EFInA 2016 note 6 at 12.

49 Asli Demirgüç-Kunt et al, *The Global Findex Database 2021: Financial Inclusion, Digital Payments, and Resilience in the Age of COVID-19,* 10 and 143, available at https://openknowledge.worldbank.org/bitstream/handle/10986/37578/9781464818974.pdf, accessed on 6 July 2022.

50 EFInA 2020 note 3 at 44.

51 Asli Demirgüç-Kunt et al, *The Global Findex Database 2021: Financial Inclusion, Digital Payments, and Resilience in the Age of COVID-19,* 33, available at https://openknowledge.worldbank.org/bitstream/handle/10986/37578/9781464818974.pdf, accessed on 6 July 2022.

52 McKinsey Global Institute, *Digital Finance for All: Powering Inclusive Growth in Emerging Economies,* September 2016 at 6, available at https://www.mckinsey.com/~/media/McKinsey/Global%20Themes/Employment%20and%20Growth/How%20digital%20finance%20could%20boost%20growth%20in%20emerging%20economies/MGI-Digital-Finance-For-All-Executive-summary-September-2016.ashx, accessed on 13 March 2018. See also See Carol Coye Benson et al *The Digital Financial Services Ecosystem,* ITU-T Focus Group on Digital Financial Services, May 2016 at 1, available at https://www.itu.int/en/ITU-T/focusgroups/dfs/Documents/09_2016/FINAL%20ENDORSED%20ITU%20DFS%20Introduction%20Ecosystem%2028%20April%202016_formatted%20AM.pdf, accessed on 11 July 2020.

53 See George Obulutsa, 'M-Pesa helps drive up Kenyans' access to financial services', 03 April

2019, available at https://www.reuters.com/article/kenya-banking/m-pesa-helps-drive-up-kenyans-access-to-financial-services-study-idUSL8N21L2HK, accessed on April 2019.

54 See Gareth van Zyl 'Why Vodacom M-Pesa has flopped in SA', 05 September 2016, *fin24tech,* available at https://www.fin24.com/Tech/Companies/why-vodacom-m-pesa-has-flopped-in-sa-20160509, accessed on 9 May 2019. See also Lerato Mbele 'Why M-Pesa failed in South Africa', *BBC Africa Business Report*, Johannesburg, 11 May 2016, available at http://www.bbc.com/news/world-africa-36260348/, accessed on 11 May 2018.

55 M-Pesa, M-Pesa Send Money Home, TV Commercial, available at https://www.youtube.com/watch?v=nEZ30K5dBWU, accessed on 28 February 2022.

56 EFInA 2020 note 3 at 7 and 62.

57 Ibid at 7. See also Nigerian Communications Commission, *Industry Statistics,* available at https://www.ncc.gov.ng/statistics-reports/industry-overview#view-graphs-tables-2, accessed on 6 July 2022.

58 See Carol Coye Benson et al note 52 at 1, available at https://www.itu.int/en/ITU-T/focusgroups/dfs/Documents/09_2016/FINAL%20ENDORSED%20ITU%20DFS%20Introduction%20Ecosystem%2028%20April%202016_formatted%20AM.pdf, accessed on 11 July 2020.

59 Central Bank of Nigeria, *National Financial Inclusion Strategy* (2012) note 19 at 9–10.

60 Central Bank of Nigeria, *National Financial Inclusion Strategy* (2012) note 19 at 8.

61 Ibid at 6.

62 Ibid at 8.

63 Ibid.

64 Ibid.

65 Ibid at 7.

66 Ibid at 8.

67 Ibid at 7.

68 Ibid.

69 Ibid at 5.

70 Ibid at 4.

71 Ibid at 3.

72 Ibid at 4.

73 Alliance for Financial Inclusion, *Maya Declaration: Commitments You Can Bank On,* available at https://www.afi-global.org/maya-declaration, accessed on 11 April 2019.

74 Alliance for Financial Inclusion, *Maya Declaration: Central Bank of Nigeria,* 27 Nov 2011, available at https://www.youtube.com/watch?v=CX7sx-7ykxs&feature=youtu.be, accessed on 10 July 2020.

75 Central Bank of Nigeria, *National Financial Inclusion Strategy* (2012) note 19 at 1.

76 Ibid at 1.

77 Ibid at vii.

78 Ibid at ix, 34 and 41.

79 Central Bank of Nigeria, *Financial Literacy Framework* (2015) at 25, available at https://www.cbn.gov.ng/out/2016/cfpd/financial%20literacy.pdf, accessed on 18 May 2019.

80 CBN, *Financial Inclusion Newsletter,* (2016) (1), available at https://www.cbn.gov.ng/Out/2016/CCD/JANUARY%202016%20Volume%201,%20Issue%201%20Web.pdf, accessed on 21 April 2017.

81 Central Bank of Nigeria, *Financial Literacy Framework (2015)* note 79 at 22.

82 Central Bank of Nigeria, *National Financial Inclusion Strategy Implementation* (2018) at vi and 45, available at https://www.cbn.gov.ng/out/2019/ccd/national%20financial%20inclusion%20strategy.pdf, accessed on 8 July 2020.

83 CBN, National Financial Literacy Framework note 79 at 1.

84 Central Bank of Nigeria, *National Financial Inclusion Strategy* (2012) note 19 at 27.

85 CBN, *Financial Literacy: Overview*, available at https://www.cbn.gov.ng/Devfin/finliteracy.asp>, accessed on 28 February 2017.
86 CBN, National Financial Literacy Framework at xi.
87 Central Bank of Nigeria, *National Financial Inclusion Strategy* note 79 at 28.
88 Central Bank of Nigeria, *Cash-less Nigeria*, available at https://www.cbn.gov.ng/cashless/, accessed on 10 January 2018. Unfortunately, this exercise was suspended and re-scheduled. See Central Bank of Nigeria, *Financial Inclusion Newsletter,* July 2019, Volume 4, Issue 2 at 1, available at https://www.cbn.gov.ng/Out/2019/CCD/Q2%202019%20Financial%20Inclusion%20Newsletter_Final_08.08.19.pdf, accessed on 5 May 2020.
89 Ibid.
90 Ibid.
91 Ibid.
92 Ibid.
93 Central Bank of Nigeria, *Electronic Payments Incentives Scheme and Awareness Campaign Directive BPSD/DIR/GEN/CIR/012* (2014), available at https://www.cbn.gov.ng/Out/2014/BPSD/CIRCULAR%20ON%20EPAYT%20INCENTIVES%20SCHEME.pdf, accessed on 11 July 2020.
94 Central Bank of Nigeria, *Payments System Vision 2020* at 15, available at https://www.cbn.gov.ng/icps2013/papers/nigeria_payments_system_vision_2020%5bv2%5d.pdf, accessed on 25 March 2019.
95 Ibid at 12.
96 Ibid at 13.
97 NIBSS, *Mcash*, available at https://www.nibss-plc.com.ng/images/api/mCASH_Press_Release.pdf, accessed on 11 July 2020.
98 CBN Financial Inclusion Secretariat, *The National Financial Inclusion Strategy 2018 Annual Report*, (2019) 39 and 47, available at https://www.cbn.gov.ng/Out/2019/CCD/Annual%20Report%202018%20Financial%20Inclusion.pdf, accessed on 8 July 2020.
99 Central Bank of Nigeria, 2017 *Annual Report National Financial Inclusion Strategy Implementation* (2018) at 16. Available at https://www.cbn.gov.ng/Out/2018/CCD/FINANCIAL%20INCLUSION.PDF, accessed on 8 July 2020.
100 Central Bank of Nigeria, *National Financial Inclusion Strategy Implementation* (2018) at 14 and 15, available at https://www.cbn.gov.ng/out/2019/ccd/national%20financial%20inclusion%20strategy.pdf, accessed on 8 July 2020.
101 Ibid at v.
102 Ibid at viii. Generally, some mainstream financial products such as interest bearing loans and some women may not have the permission from their families, particularly their husbands, to own and operate accounts.
103 Central Bank of Nigeria, *National Financial Inclusion Strategy Implementation* (2018) at note v, available at https://www.cbn.gov.ng/out/2019/ccd/national%20financial%20inclusion%20strategy.pdf, accessed on 8 July 2020.
104 Ibid.
105 Ibid at 59.
106 Ibid at 60.
107 Central Bank of Nigeria, *National Financial Inclusion Strategy* (2018) note 82 at 1. The target has now been moved up to 95 per cent with a new target date of 2024. See Central Bank of Nigeria, *Financial Inclusion Newsletter* note 88 at 1.
108 CBN Ibid at 16.
109 Ibid at 17 and 65.
110 Ibid at vii.
111 Ibid at vi.
112 Jaiz Bank, *About Islamic Banking,* available at https://jaizbankplc.com/about-jaiz-bank/

about-islamic-banking/, accessed on 2 September 2021. See also Taj Bank, *Home*, available at https://www.tajbank.com/, accessed on 2 September 2021.
113 CBN, *Financial Inclusion Newsletter*, note 88 at 15.
114 National Youth Service Corps, *About the Scheme*, available at https://www.nysc.gov.ng/aboutscheme.html, accessed on 28 July 2021.
115 CBN, Financial Inclusion Secretariat 82 at 62, 47.
116 Ibid at 15. This framework has now been released.
117 CBN *National Financial Inclusion Strategy* note 82 at 8.
118 Ibid at 62.
119 Central Bank of Nigeria, *Anti-money Laundering and Combating the Financing of Terrorism in Banks and Other Financial Institutions in Nigeria Regulations* (2013) 100:65 O.G., Reg. 45.
120 Ibid.
121 CBN note 82 at 8.
122 CBN, *National Financial Inclusion Strategy Annual Report 2019*, 56, available at https://www.cbn.gov.ng/out/2020/ccd/2019%20annual%20report%20of%20the%20national%20financial%20inclusion%20strategy%20implementation.pdf.
123 This concern could be addressed by the deployment of Payment Service Banks to rural communities.
124 Adeyemi Adepetun, 'NCC, CBN sign MoU on mobile money, financial inclusion', 12 April 2018, *Guardian*, available at https://guardian.ng/business-services/ncc-cbn-sign-mou-on-mobile-money-financial-inclusion, accessed on 27 February 2019.
125 Section 2 Central Bank of Nigeria Act 2007. See also, CBN *About CBN*, available at https://www.cbn.gov.ng/AboutCBN/Coremandate.asp, accessed on 20 July 2020.
126 Ibid.
127 Central Bank of Nigeria. National Financial Inclusion Strategy (2018) note 82 at 9.
128 Ibid.
129 Ibid at 50
130 Ibid at 9.
131 Ibid at 51.
132 NCC, *About the NCC*, available at https://www.ncc.gov.ng/about-ncc/who-we-are, accessed on 2 February 2019.
133 Central Bank of Nigeria, National Financial Inclusion Strategy (2018) note 82 at 9.
134 Ibid.
135 Ministry of Communication Technology, *National Information and Communications Technology (ICT) Policy* (2012) at 22, available at https://www.researchictafrica.net/countries/nigeria/Nigeria_National_ICT_Policy_(draft)_2012.pdf, accessed on 22 April 2020.
136 Central Bank of Nigeria, National Financial Inclusion Strategy note 82 at 52.
137 Section 2 of the NDIC Act 2006. See also NDIC *About NDIC*, available at https://ndic.gov.ng/about-ndic-3/, accessed on 2 August 2019.
138 Ibid.
139 NDIC, *Mandate, Powers & Functions*, available at https://ndic.gov.ng/about-ndic-3/mandate-powers-functions/, accessed on 2 August 2019. See also Nigeria Deposit Insurance Corporation Act 2 of 2006. See also Section 2, NDIC Act, 2006.
140 Ibid.
141 Section 17 Pension Reform Act 2014.
142 Ibid at Section 1.
143 Ibid at Section 23.
144 Ibid at 64 and 76.
145 Ibid at 23.
146 Central Bank of Nigeria, National Financial Inclusion Strategy (2018) note 82 at 10.
147 Ibid.

148 Ibid at 52.
149 Securities and Exchange Commission, *About*, available https://sec.gov.ng/about, accessed on 2 August 2019.
150 Securities and Exchange Commission, *What We Do*, available at https://sec.gov.ng/about/what-we-do/, accessed on 2 August 2019.
151 Central Bank of Nigeria, National Financial Inclusion Strategy (2018) note 82 at 10.
152 Ibid.
153 National Bureau of Statistics, *Vision and Mission*, available at https://nigerianstat.gov.ng/page/vision-mission, accessed on 2 August 2019.
154 Central Bank of Nigeria, National Financial Inclusion Strategy (2018) note 82 at 10.
155 Ibid.
156 Ibid at 53.
157 National Identification Management Commission, *Vision and Mission*, available at https://www.nimc.gov.ng/vision-mission/, accessed on 2 August 2019.
158 National Identification Management Commission Act 5 of 2007.
159 NIMC, *Functions and Powers*, available at https://www.nimc.gov.ng/functionspowers/, accessed on 2 August 2019.
160 Central Bank of Nigeria, National Financial Inclusion Strategy (2018) note 82 at 10.
161 Ibid.
162 Ibid.
163 Nigerian Postal Services, *Vision and Mission*, available at http://www.nipost.gov.ng/Vision_Mission, accessed on 2 August 2019.
164 NIPOST *Financial Services*, available at http://www.nipost.gov.ng/Financial_Services, accessed on 2 August 2019.
165 Ibid.
166 Central Bank of Nigeria, National Financial Inclusion Strategy (2018) note 82 at 10.
167 Ibid.
168 Ibid at 52.
169 EFInA note 3 at 64.
170 CBN, 2019 Annual Report National Financial Inclusion Strategy Implementation 13, available at https://www.cbn.gov.ng/Out/2020/CCD/2019%20Annual%20Report%20of%20the%20National%20Financial%20Inclusion%20Strategy%20Implementation.pdf.
171 EFInA note 3 at 62.
172 EFInA 2020 note 3 at 56.
173 Ibid at 7 and 62.
174 Ibid at 54.
175 Ibid 44.
176 Ibid.

2 Financial Inclusion in the Context of Law and Development

2.1 Introduction

This chapter sets out the conceptual framework using the law and development theory in the context of financial inclusion in Nigeria, with a particular focus on legal transplants. Theorised in it is the role of law in development studies broadly and, more specifically, in the formulation of financial inclusion policies that foster economic growth of the financially excluded. At the beginning of the chapter, a background to the general theory of law and development is discussed before an analysis of the legal transplantation of financial inclusion laws and practices from other jurisdictions by the CBN is developed.

2.2 The law and development moments

The law and development discourse has since engaged scholars. A crucial point in this discussion has been to determine whether and to that extent, law, is imperative for development. The theory has recently been applied specifically to sectors such as the finance sector where regulators are seeking to balance the application of legal rules with economic policies that lead to the advancement of excluded populations. While this quest for balance has taken various shapes in jurisdictions around the world, it is important to note that the relationship between law and development, in general, has been in evidence since the 1960s.

This field, termed 'law and development' has witnessed different moments and drawn the attention of numerous writers. Lizarro-Rodriguez traces the origin of this field to the teaching of law in Asian and African colonial contexts and the US cooperation programmes of the 1960s followed by the United Nations recognition of the right to development in 1986 and the introduction of the human development index (HDI).[1] Trubek and Santos trace the origins of the field to the classical thinking of Marx and Weber as well as post-World War II methodical reformation of legal systems and incorporation into the work of international development agencies.[2]

More specifically, the first moment heralded by the modernisation theorists of the 1950s sought to support the importance of adopting the laws of

DOI: 10.4324/9781003217886-2

advanced countries to improve the capacity for rule making by adopting states and corporate in more advanced countries.[3] Theorists in this moment, viewed development as 'a process of convergence of the institutions of modern Western societies defined by free markets, a bureaucratic welfare state, a multiparty electoral system and the existence of civil and political rights'.[4] Modernisation theorists stressed that conformity with Western laws was the clear path to development without giving any consideration to the impact of this on local customs and the societal peculiarities of developing countries.

Trubek and Santos note that the theorists of this era assumed that law could produce economic impacts and social change by focusing on the role of the intervention by the state to manage economies and transform traditional societies.[5] These assumptions soon became less relevant as it became more evident that 'markets do not create conditions of operation without institutional reform'.[6] Tamanaha criticises the moment for being 'ethnocentric, evolutionary, falsely teleological, naive and lacking the political or civic culture in the developing countries, necessary to maintain western institutions'.[7] According to Baderin, the emphasis placed by modernisation theorists on the need for the transformation of societies to 'modernity' as a prerequisite for development had led to the under-exploration of the crucial role that customary and Islamic law could play in the development of regions such as Africa.[8]

The collapse of the modernisation theory led to the emergence of the dependency theory, named the second moment in law, which grew to prominence in the 1970s. Dependency theorists sought to dislodge the notion that countries, though different, should experience development in similar ways and supported the notion of varied and complex forms of development arising from economic, political and cultural dealings with developed economies.[9] Thus the moment featured 'a neo-liberal market and the pursuit of the growth of private markets through fair pricing, fiscal discipline, removal of disruptions in the market occasioned by regulatory interventions, market distortions created by intervention, promotion of free trade and foreign investment'.[10] Theorists also emphasised the need for enforcement of contracts, rights in property and a strengthening of the role of the judiciary to restrain the state and facilitate the markets.[11]

Although severely critical of the modernisation theory, the dependency theory also failed to produce the promised results as investments in reformist legal education, did not result in better economic growth or improved social relations for developing countries.[12] To Tamanaha, 'underdevelopment and the reliance of developing countries on Western produce, technology, foreign investment and capital, emanates from the history and structure of the global capitalist system and the colonial exploitation carried on into the global market system'.[13] Trubek and Santos note that around the 1980s the failure of this line of thinking to yield the expected result of state-led growth led to a call to empower the private sector.[14]

Ordor writes that with the fall of these two theories, the 1990s birthed a third moment with a mix of ideas both from the first two moments and a combination of other elements.[15] The new moment aimed at 'gaining preferential treatment and development assistance such as trade preferences, debt relief, low-interest loans or outright grants and low-cost transfer of technology for developing countries'.[16] Specifically, the Third World Approaches to International Law (TWAIL) promoted the need for new international mechanisms to solve problems of poverty and global wealth as against the imperialist definition of civil and political rights that fail to address the ills of colonialism.[17]

2.3 Law and development intersections

The moments discussed above, though not proving to be a total success individually, have altogether led to a deeper study of law and development as a composite field of study. Ordor describes this field as 'ideas that seek to connect law and development by creating a framework within which the role of law in development may be better understood and recommended to governments as a way of advancing development'.[18] Trubek also defines this field as 'the organised efforts to transform legal systems in developing countries to foster economic, political and social development and the academic projects associated with these efforts'.[19] Furthermore, Lee describes the field of study more simply as 'an area of enquiry into the interrelationship between law and development'.[20]

Some authors have highlighted the need to study the two pillars of law and development both separately and as a unit, expanding each field to construe scope, and application and then drawing a correlation. According to Lee, law is relevant to development, yet subject to separate analysis and determines the successful implementation of policy.[21] Ordor stresses that there is no single path to establishing the role that law plays in development, for this depends on the different perceptions about development including norms and facilitating structures as well as the feasibility and barriers to development which must then be contextually fed into the process of rulemaking.[22]

According to Lee, law includes statutes adopted by legislature, regulations adopted by regulatory agencies, ordinances passed by municipalities, binding judicial precedents and informal norms observed with an opinion juris.[23] Law is also described by Baderin as 'a powerful normative system, an effective tool of social order and socio-economic development'.[24]

Development on the other hand is defined by Lee as 'economic and social progress including economic values that enhance human lives such as political participation, the right to property, gender equality, access to clean and safe environment and the rule of law'.[25] Development has received significant expansion to include economic performance and social development. Ohnersorge argues that development in terms of economic performance is determined by law, legality and non-legal factors such as education, technology, demographics, natural resources, geography, domestic and international politics, institutions and economics and social and cultural norms.[26]

The social dimension of development is highlighted by Baderin, who asserts that, in defining development, the scope should not be limited to economic growth measured by increased gross national product (GNP) as this excludes human and social levels of development.[27] To Lee, social and economic development, though not totally separate are able to bear influence on each other given that social issues can emanate from the different distributive effects of economic development from different population groups.[28]

The social dimension to development was popularised by the introduction of the United Nations Declaration on the Right to Development (UN Resolution 14/128) which bestows on humankind the 'inalienable universal right to participate in, contribute to, and enjoy economic, social, cultural and political development, in which all human rights and fundamental freedoms can be fully realised'.[29] Likewise, the World Bank's comprehensive development framework (CDF) of 1999 calls for 'greater attention to the social, structural and human dimensions of development including human rights, gender equity, poverty alleviation, democracy and access to justice'.[30]

Authors also stress the need to make the connection between the law and these social dimensions of development. To Lee, law needs to be adapted to socioeconomic conditions as development changes socioeconomic conditions and creates regulatory gaps that require legal adjustment and reinforcement to fill.[31] Ayua asserts that the law is important to foster social development and distributive justice and improves both the standard of living and participation of people in economic development.[32]

Although the study of law and development has garnered substantial debate and growth, this is not without some resistance as a number of writers still decry the capacity of law to bring about development. Lee, for example, dismisses the capability of law to generate developmental solutions besides implementing those initiated by others and further warns that resort to law to solve social and political problems is, in a sense, an attempt to conjure a social agenda into reality by insisting that the law requires it.[33] Ohnersorge gives support to this stance by alluding to the North-East Asian experience where economic success was recorded in the absence of hallowed legal principles such as 'the judiciary, private litigation, laws on insolvency and competition, intellectual property rights, competition law and the legalisation of state-private sector relations through constitutional and administrative law'.[34]

Writing from the African experience, Baderin maintains that although this field of study has not been a complete success, law is apparent in development but is only undermined by the failure to put the law to use for development.[35] Baderin, therefore, recommends an enquiry that transcends law, economics, politics, sociology and development studies to promote cooperation between countries, both developed and developing.[36] In addition, Baderin advocates for a two-pronged self-reliant theory that encourages individual responsibility by African countries to employ domestic laws to foster country-level development and utilise regionally harmonised laws to develop the continent.[37]

Ordor also recommends that 'separate entry points such as the rule of law or legal empowerment of the poor are needed for all countries, regions, communities or cultures, even without coherence with one or more of the law and development theories'.[38] Ordor thus asserts that people's multiple realities should be recognised and the changes in development ushered by activities, values and responses of communities need to be understood to garner legal evolution and sustainable participation of developing countries in the discipline.[39] Finally, Lee proposes the 'analytical law and development model to systematically assess the organisation of LFIs and regulatory structure without entrenching to a best practice model from developed countries.[40]

2.4 Law and development theory in the context of financial inclusion

The role of financial inclusion in the economic development of citizens is currently receiving significant attention. Developing countries, development organisations such as the World Bank and the African Development Bank as well as the non-profit organisation, financial institutions and academia have all weighed in on the topic. Each of these entities emphasises the proven use of financial inclusion to improve the economic wellbeing of excluded persons, especially women, urban slum dwellers, rural populations and the poor. For instance, in recognition of the role of financial inclusion as 'a building block for both poverty reduction and opportunities for economic growth', the World Bank has adopted the Universal Financial Access initiative to address the barriers to financial inclusion.[41]

It is remarkable, however, that although financial inclusion has long been considered an economics topic, the use of law to tackle barriers to financial inclusion specifically and finance in general is a more recent endeavour and the role of the law in this regard is still unfurling. This captures the assertion of Trubek that economists, although they paid little attention to the law in the 1960s and 1970s, began in the 1980s to recognise the importance of law in the creation of financial markets.[42] This is typified in Nigeria where, before the signing of the Maya Declaration, the CBN tackled the topic mainly from a credit enhancement and finance channel distribution perspective with little regard for the impact of legal rules and policies. Accession to this Declaration has now led to the introduction of numerous laws, guidelines, regulations and policies as the importance of legal rules to facilitate and implement the financial regulator's policies becomes more evident.

Remarkably, even now that the role of law has become apparent to development studies, financial regulators still grapple with balancing suitable best legal practices with economic solutions in the specific sphere of financial inclusion. Kenya has buttressed this empirical association between financial inclusion and economic growth with the introduction of mobile money products, such as Mpesa, which have contributed to pushing financial inclusion figures to about 83 per cent.[43] This means that more people have gained access to finance and can better navigate their economic activities.

Despite the success recorded in this regard, it is notable that national regulators are still reworking suitable models to address the real needs of the excluded as the success of a model or financial product in one market has not historically guaranteed favourable results in another. The experience related to the deployment of Mpesa in Kenya and South Africa is illustrative. The rapid take-up and usage of Mpesa in Kenya could not be replicated on the same scale in South Africa where socio-economic and financial landscapes and expectations were different.[44]

Accordingly, the CBN has recently had to review the 2012 National Financial Inclusion Strategy (NFIS) to mirror the circumstances of the financially excluded as different take-up and usage patterns of financial services by Nigerians are manifested. The emphasis on point-of-sale devices to drive inclusion, the insistence on agent exclusivity and exclusion of mobile network operators from leading mobile money provision are topics that have been revisited to conform to user demands. Also, the CBN has now introduced the Guidelines for Licensing and Regulation of Payment Services Banks of 2020 to align with the calls for the inclusion of a wider range of alternative finance providers including mobile network operators.

2.5 Legal transplants

To facilitate the process of adopting laws for financial inclusion, it is imperative to note that the CBN adopted policies and practices from select peer countries by applying the concept of legal transplantation. This section traces the background of legal transplants, starting from the time of Watson, the originator. While whole frameworks can be imported to serve as the body of laws for a country, it can sometimes be more practical to cherry-pick aspects of the laws that are attuned to local contexts. This not only aids the acceptance of the laws in the destination country but additionally ensures that these laws are adhered to. The background to legal transplants and the motivating factors for transplantation of laws from originating jurisdictions to destination countries are outlined below.

2.5.1 Background to legal transplants

The foregoing has demonstrated that law is relevant to development. However, in formulating laws that usher development, legislators also have to decipher the rules which are pertinent and determine how to implement these rules. Besides the time and expertise that rulemaking involves, the cost of engaging in this process can also be daunting. This is especially so when laws are needed for germane or emerging fields. One easy fix that legislators have historically resorted to, is legal transplantation.

The concept of legal transplants was first proposed by Alan Watson referred to as the father of legal transplants and has been espoused by many authors. Legal transplantation according to Mousourakis involves ‘the incorporation of a legal rule, institution or doctrine from one legal system to another and could either be the reception of an entire legal system or occur in a centralist way’.[45]

In the view of Garoupa and Ogus, 'legal transplants are usually perceived as unilateral changes of a legal order by which one jurisdiction imports legal norms from another jurisdiction'.[46]

It is noteworthy that the possibility of this concept was in any case, severely doubted and criticised in its early days by authors and failed to make much of an impact until the 1980s. A leading sceptic of legal transplants is Pierre Legrande who completely denounces the possibility of transplants stating that integration into another legal order changes the understanding of the law by the host culture as a different culture which is at variance with the earlier one as it emerges.[47] Legrande insists that this change in meaning implies that transplants do not survive the passage from one legal order to the next as the ideas, language, rationality and moral interpretation are effectuated using new standards of justification of the receiving state and thus result in a new law.[48] Although conceding that law is defined in diversified terms based on socio-cultural norms, Mousoukaris points out that successful transplants have occurred historically and there is rather an importance to strike the delicate balance between the seemingly contrasting viewpoints.[49]

Significantly, renewed interest for legal transplants grew from the attempts of new law and development movements to promote the rule of law, good governance and reform.[50] This period coincided with the destruction of the Berlin Wall and the collapse of the Soviet Empire, leading to the emergence of new states in need of modern legal rules and thus the rebirth of Watson's philosophies.[51] Legal transplants are now more common and the motivations for adopting laws for other jurisdictions are explained in the next section.

2.5.2 The motivating factors for legal transplants

Legal transplants are common in situations where legislators are faced with a problem that other jurisdictions have had to grapple with and positive results are evident. Mousourakis notes that these transplanted laws are adopted to save legislators from guessing possible solutions at the risk of less appropriate results where there already exists an expansive body laws in other jurisdictions.[52] According to Watson, borrowing is much easier than thinking as this saves time and effort and aids acceptability of the transplanted laws.[53] For instance, in the sphere of financial inclusion, though still evolving, success has been recorded in specific respects in jurisdictions such as Brazil, Kenya and India and these are increasingly serving as models for adoption in other countries including Nigeria.

Legislators are motivated by different reasons to engage in legal transplantation including reasons such as efficiency, quality of the law, cost of transplantation versus legislation and cultural affinity. To these factors, Grajzl and Dimitrova-Grajzl add heterogeneity of interest, elitist law reforms, legal maturity, ability to complement local reality and the degree of adaptability of the legal system.[54]

On the point of efficiency, legislators could be motivated to transplant from specific jurisdictions based on the efficiency and the robustness of those laws especially where this lessens the stress of drafting legal rules from scratch. Here, motivation is also measured in terms of economic efficiency and the associated cost of adjustment of selected transplants. Mousourakis argues that willingness to adopt foreign laws by lawmakers is mostly considered in relation to economic efficiency.[55] Transplants are more likely to occur according to Garoupa and Ogus when the costs of importing and adjusting laws are justifiably low for the destination country.[56] Where, however, the cost of transplanting legal rules and adjusting these to recipient country needs outweighs the cost of legislating from scratch, the prospects of transplanting may become bleak.

Another motivation for transplants is the reputation that the originating jurisdictions have, often emanating from an imperialist proclivity. For instance, in the sixth century, the Justinian codification of Roman law became the foundation for Western legal cultures and was transplanted to regions in South America, Asia, and Africa, remaining relevant till the nineteenth century.[57] There are also considerations for social, economic and political factors, internal pressure from society, legal tradition and the legislative expertise and legal acumen of local and international law.[58]

Transplantation based on an imperialist predisposition often favoured laws of states with so-called super power status. However, this imperialist motivation for transplants is coming under scrutiny. Scholars argue that development for these supposed super nations was sustained by an economic model built on slavery and colonialism carried forward without remission into the global trade market. In the United States and Britain, for instance, industrialisation and ascension to the status of world power became possible as a result of the imposition of forced labour on enslaved persons who produced textiles such as cotton and other agricultural products including sugar, tobacco and rice.[59]

Remarkably, once former world powers began to lose supremacy, the imperialist motivation for legal transplants began receding as the perception of superiority of so-called super powers is now being threatened by emerging world powers such as China and Japan. The increasing influence of these emerging world powers in the global development discourse can no longer be ignored or discarded.

A replacement for this motivation seems to be emerging from gravitation towards cultural affinity and the adaptation of laws to local circumstances, social norms and the economic realities of the receivers. Cultural affinity is increasingly becoming acknowledged, because engaging in legal transplantation without the necessary consideration of local contexts could result in a completely unexpected and undesired outcome. Transplants are typically more likely where transplanted laws are able to fit in with the cultural nuances of the recipient states. As noted by Mousourakis, to determine if transplants will be accepted and applied properly, it is important to consider the different cultural, socio-economic and political contexts of these laws.[60] He adds that transplants could be prevented by the ethno-cultural, political and socio-economic distinctions in the originating and destination legal orders but could result in different outcomes depending on the capacity of the destination country to incorporate the transplants.[61]

According to Boulanger, law is about the stability of expectations necessitating the assurance that models adapted globally are suitable for the local needs of the destination community.[62] To Torpman and Jörgensen, adaptation to local conditions is important to foster legal effectiveness and build a strong relationship between what has been defined as legal effectiveness and the process of transplantation.[63] Grajzl and Dimitrova-Grajzl also acknowledge that transplants will more often fail where transplanted laws do not suit local contexts and adjustment costs are unjustifiable in comparison to home-grown laws.[64] The authors insist that the choice between transplants and home-grown laws is dependent upon local contexts as well as legal, political and socioeconomic considerations.[65]

In relation to the preceding point, another motivating factor is acceptance by the host country. Some factors that increase acceptance of transplants include shared linguistic tradition, reputation of the originating legal order and the educational background and legal expertise in the destination jurisdictions.[66] Importantly, transplants need to mirror the needs of the local communities who are expected to apply these laws. This aids acceptance as the adoption of foreign laws without consideration for local norms may fail for lack of conformity with beliefs and customs.

This is exemplified by the implementation of a Western-style financial system policy to economic initiatives that are unfamiliar to the receiving nation. In Nigeria, the insistence on stringent Know-Your-Customer (KYC) compliance as well as the relegation of indigenous savings systems such as the *esusu* and *ajo* by the CBN, buttresses this point. These indigenous savings systems, for example, have been in existence for several decades and enable users to access financial products such as savings and loans but are still not promoted by the regulators. Meanwhile, stringent KYC requirements such as the use of utility bills in proof of identification which is considered strange to local people more accustomed to identification by family or community recognition are required by the regulators to be requested by banks to open and operate an account.

It is therefore important for legislators to make the right considerations in employing transplants to ensure that transplanted laws will not only be accepted by the people but also complied with. Acceptance can ensure that the affected segment of the society accept and apply the policy initiatives aimed at addressing their concerns. For instance, where the rules for specific services lack the needed acceptance, subscriptions may not occur significantly as people may find other ways to get around the law and avoid compliance.

According to Del Duca and Levasseur, successful transplants are possible where there is some degree of correspondence with the general and legal culture of the recipient country.[67] In agreeing with this point, Torpman and Jörgensen observe that legal application by a layman tends to occur only if the layman feels confident that legal communications will be validated by reason of availability of law enforcement and the familiarity with law.[68] The writers opine that the applicability of transplants is predicated first on trust in the system and second on personal ability to engage with the system.[69]

Adding to this, Lee alludes to South Korea in observing that compliance with regulation flows from the general quality of law, design and implementation of laws in tandem with the socioeconomic conditions of the people.[70] According to the author, South Koreans complied with government economic initiatives that encouraged savings and strong work ethics as there was trust in government rewards in terms of higher interest rates, pay rise and increased employment opportunities.[71]

Penca, however, rejects this notion, insisting rather that a blueprint about how to ensure legal acceptance in the transnational context is futile, and requires legitimacy which is impossible to inherit or easily replicate from an originating jurisdiction.[72] Penca, therefore, recommends that attention must be paid to efforts directed at attuning legitimacy to communities and their local contexts and relationships.[73] In summary, Niglia stresses the imperativeness of considering the substantive agenda driving each intended legal transplant as well as the feasibility of persisting in the adopted strategy.[74]

2.6 Financial inclusion transplants in Nigeria

Nigeria has, like many nations since the signing of the Maya Declaration in 2011, sought to improve financial inclusion using a target-based strategy set out in the 2012 National Financial Inclusion Strategy (NFIS) as recommended by the Alliance for Financial Inclusion (AFI). The NFIS according to AFI is 'a comprehensive public document that presents a strategy developed at the national level to systematically accelerate the level of financial inclusion'.[75] This is often usually developed by widely consulting with private and public stakeholders of the finance industry to garner information on industry status, barriers, measurable goals, strategies, timelines and the key performance index for measuring the progress of the strategy.[76]

Nigeria's NFIS was set up to drive financial service access and usage by the year 2020, deliberate on relevant stakeholders' input and outline a framework for improving formal financial inclusion from the 2010 figure of 36.3 per cent of the adult population to 80 per cent by 2020.[77] Remarkably, at the time of setting up the NFIS, Nigeria had no dedicated regulatory policies to improve financial inclusion aside some regulations and policies such as the ATM and POS regulations and credit enhancement interventions.[78] The CBN as financial regulator thus assumed the role of drafting laws, guidelines, policies and regulations to address the many barriers.

As the use of legal rules was a relatively new approach, it was practical for the CBN to seek international best practices and legal rules from other jurisdictions.[79] The transplantation of legal rules and practices from these jurisdictions in the case of Nigeria was not affected as legislative acts of the House of Assembly but through the CBN governor's power to introduce relevant financial services regulations for the finance sector. This power is enshrined in

Section 2 (d) of the Central Bank of Nigeria Act, 2007 and Section 57 (2) of the Banks and other Financial Institutions Act (BOFIA) 2020.[80]

By drawing on legal frameworks from a wide array of jurisdictions, the local context in Nigeria was considered as these legal transplants were not imported wholesale but only select practices were adopted from individual countries to avoid the imposition of whole frameworks. South Africa and Kenya were to represent sub-Saharan Africa, and Indonesia and Mexico were selected as top twenty economies.[81] Best practices were also adopted from Malaysia, Brazil, India, the Philippines, Ghana, Pakistan and Uganda.[82] These countries were selected 'to set specific targets for each financial product and channel in areas relating to product use, channel penetration, gender and youth inclusion, and enablers for financial inclusion'.[83] Another reason for the selection was the recognition by the CBN that growth in these jurisdictions has been driven by competition, tiered KYC regulation, branch expansion and branchless banking initiatives, thus the regulations adopted by the CBN mirrored some of these models.[84]

Specifically, Uganda, India and Pakistan were selected as model countries to address the gap in Nigeria's national identification. In Uganda, even though the National Security Information System (NSIS) project was only implemented as recently as 2014, the programme already covers 99 per cent of the target population of 16 years and above.[85] India has a large population size of more than 1.4 billion and is, therefore, a beacon for the possibility of effectively registering Nigerians despite the large country population of more than 200 million.[86] Pakistan like Nigeria also had to grapple with the dynamics of the unique geography of the country and culture of the people. Here, mobile registration was adopted using van drivers, bikers, hikers, mountaineers and skiers to reach remote places and cover the entire breadth of the country.[87] The exercise attained a coverage rate of 98 per cent of the target population including rural and tribal groups, women, undocumented children, the poor, disadvantaged groups, tribal/rural minority groups, orphaned children, transgender persons, persons in the Diaspora and refugees.[88] Mobile registration which is now being adopted in Nigeria as confirmed by the participants in the empirical study set out in Chapter 4 of this book, accounts for the increasing number of voter card and national identity number procurements.

Examples for improving financial inclusion by enabling a diverse array of digital finance service providers were drawn from Ghana and the Philippines. The Philippines was one of the first countries in the world to adopt mobile money, while Ghana was a forerunner in the mobile money legislation in Africa, adopting Branchless Banking Guidelines as early as 2008 to extend banking transactions beyond conventional bank branches.[89] The Central Bank of Ghana's license a varied array of financial services providers including both traditional and alternative finance providers such as commercial banks, rural and community banks, licensed mobile finance institutions, mobile network operators, non-bank financial institutions (NBFIs) and licensed thrift collectors (*susu*).[90] Nigeria has now adopted the PSB Guidelines to admit a wider range of providers namely agent banks, courier companies, retail outlets and MNOs to provide finance.

Like Ghana, financial inclusion in the Philippines has been able to reach excluded populations due to the acceptance of a range of providers comprising conventional banks, pawnshops, remittance agents, money changers/foreign exchange dealers, non-stock savings and loan associations (NSSLAs), money service business, cooperatives and credit companies'.[91] This model was introduced in response to the observed tendency of banks to locate branches in most populated urban centres.[92] This remains a challenge in Nigeria.

Financial integrity is guaranteed in the Philippines by the introduction of corresponding prudential scrutiny by the Bangko Sentral ng Pilipinas (BSP). For instance, pawnshops have to comply with anti-money laundering (AML) and internal control rules as well as strict standards of corporate governance.[93] In like manner, banks are allowed to open extension offices, banking offices and microfinance units subject to capitalisation and documentary requirements.[94] MSBs are similarly charged with overseeing remittance networks, accrediting agents and maintaining transaction trails for large cash transactions and AML registration.[95] It is remarkable that one of the wins of financial inclusion efforts in the Philippines is that women have a higher probability of having a financial institution account than men, a departure from the global gender bias in favour of men in the World Bank Global Findex.[96]

Agent banking was adopted from Brazil, Mexico and Bangladesh to reach rural populations as rural/urban exclusion in Nigeria still shows a stark gap at 19 and 81 per cent, respectively.[97] The agent banking model permits 'banks to provide financial services through non-bank agents, such as grocery stores, retail outlets, post offices, pharmacies or lottery outlets, in rural areas that offer insufficient incentive or capacity to establish a formal branch'.[98] As shown from the difficulties which the participants in the empirical study set out in Chapter 4 experienced to get to banks, the need for bank branches in local communities is re-emphasised.

Agent banking has been successfully practised in Brazil, Bangladesh and Mexico and has served as bedrock for financial inclusion. These countries leverage on the expansive network of the post asserted by the Universal Postal Union (UPU) to have about 663,000 physical contact points around the world.[99] According to the UPU, the Postal Service has the capacity to serve about 1.5 billion financial service customers using a combination of electronic, financial and physical dimensions to deliver efficient, reliable, secure and affordable electronic payment services such as payment, transfers and savings.[100] In Brazil, postal banks, named correspondents are permitted to provide the necessary distribution channels for the deployment of DFS in Brazil with outlets spread across unserved municipalities.[101] In addition, supermarkets, pharmacies, bakeries and hardware stores are permitted to serve as correspondents.[102] These correspondents receive payments and deposits, enable withdrawals, accept applications for savings accounts and facilitate disbursement and repayment of loans.[103]

From Mexico's example, the use of new entities such as chain stores was significant. Here, agent banking is dominated by chain stores such as Walmart and other large entities with the advantage of already existing structures and resources to oversee the network, train staff, provide technical support and manage cash flow.[104] Agents are permitted to accept deposits, offer utility payment platforms, perform cash-checking and balance enquiries, execute cash transfers and issue bank statements.[105] In Bangladesh, agents are permitted to execute cash deposits, cash withdrawal remittance payments and small loans.[106] The CBN asserts that the flexibility of the agent network and pricing model and the inclusion of female agents was exemplary for Nigeria for reaching women in Northern Nigeria debarred from formal finance by religious norms.[107]

Kenya is the leading example of successful mobile money deployment in the world with its flagship Mpesa product launched in 2007 by Safaricom, the dominant mobile network provider. Mpesa grew from 'a basic SIM card-based money transfer application into a fully-fledged financial service, offering loans and savings in conjunction with local banks and merchant payments services'.[108] A unique feature that drives the Mpesa model in Kenya is that mobile accounts offered by MNOs are not necessarily linked to financial institution accounts.[109] It has been observed that many financial account holders also own a mobile money account and about 40 per cent of the adult population uses these mobile money accounts, and the usage rate of mobile money and digital payments is widespread at 97 per cent which is on par with figures in high-income countries.[110]

One reason for this widespread adoption and usage of mobile money is the use of diverse class of agents such as local shops, schools and post offices across the country and particularly in rural areas to reach clients. Mpesa has also served as a platform for additional financial products such as Lipa na Mpesa used for buying goods and settling utilities.[111] Industry collaborations equally fuelled this growth. In conjunction with Equity Bank, Safaricom offers a co-branded interest-bearing savings account called MKesho for funds transfer, savings, credit and insurance.[112] Similarly, the collaboration between Safaricom and the Commercial Bank of Africa (CBA) birthed MShwari in Kenya in 2012, a product that enables customers of the two companies to apply for loans, top-up the Mpesa wallet and a build credit history.[113]

South Africa's appeal as a model country is its adoption of the Mzansi low-level account and insistence on rural bank branch locations. Like Nigeria, the sophistication of the financial sector and the existence of large banks in urban areas seemed to mask pervasive rural financial exclusion.[114] The account was introduced by the big four banks (Standard, FirstRand, Absa and Nedbank) in conjunction with Postbank as a voluntary financial services charter in 2004, to improve racial inclusiveness and avoid government intervention.[115] Participating banks were able to share financial and reputational risks, cost and infrastructure.[116] Although the banks reported losses in maintaining these accounts, the needs of numerous clients were met.[117] The Mzansi account is still notable as a historical success as this social initiative by the banks brought financial access to the unserved.[118] This also served as a gateway for the excluded to sign up for other financial products and services.

2.7 Conclusion

Demonstrated in this chapter are financial inclusion transplants in Nigeria. The law and development moments were traced and the role that law has been acknowledged to play in development initiatives. It is notable that the CBN regulatory initiatives on financial inclusion are aimed at improving the economic wellbeing of Nigerians. Thus the application of the law and development theory served to detail the impact that law has on the development of citizens, particularly in relation to improving economic wellbeing through financial inclusion. There is also the corresponding effect of development exploits to influence advances in the law. Thus, as more people adopt financial services due to progressive laws, the financial lives of citizens improve. Likewise, the patterns of adoption and usage and the choice of financial services determine further innovations in the legal framework. The transplantation of these laws from other jurisdictions while being easier on the legislative process must be aptly applied to conform to the local context of destination countries.

Notes

1 Liliana Lizarazo-Rodriguez, 'Mapping law and development' (2017) 4 (4), *Indo. J Int'l & CompL* 764–5, available at https://heinonline-org.ezproxy.uct.ac.za/HOL/Page?lname=&public=false&collection=journals&handle=hein.journals/indjicl4&men_hide=false&men_tab=toc&kind=&page=761, accessed on 22 July 2020.
2 David Trubek & Alvaro Santos, *The Third Moment in Law and Development Theory and the Emergence of a New Critical Practice* (2006) at 1, available at https://scholarship.law.georgetown.edu/facpub/2105.
3 Ibid at 5.
4 Kevin Davis & Michael Trebilcock, 'Legal reforms and development' (2001), *Third World Quarterly* 22(1) at 22, available at https://www.jstor.org/stable/3993343, accessed on 10 June 2019.
5 David Trubek & Alvaro Santos note 2 at 2.
6 Ibid at 10.
7 Brian Tamanaha, 'The lessons of law and development studies' (1995), *American Journal of International Law* at 472, available at https://www-jstor-org.ezproxy.uct.ac.za/stable/pdf/2204226.pdf, accessed on 29 April 2019.
8 Mashood Baderin, 'Law and development in Africa: Towards a new approach' (2011), *NIALS Journal of Law and Development* at 20, available at https://www.researchgate.net/publication/256086798_Law_and_Development_in_Africa_Towards_a_New_Approach, accessed on 12 May 2019.
9 Kevin Davis & Michael Trebilcock, 'Legal reforms and development' (2001), *Third World Quarterly* 22(1) at 22, available at https://www.jstor.org/stable/3993343, accessed on 10 June 2019.
10 David Trubek & Alvaro Santos note 2 at 5.
11 Ibid at 6.

12 Jan Torpman & Fredrik Jörgensen, 'Legal effectiveness: Theoretical developments on legal transplants' (2005) (4), *Archives for Philosophy of Law and Social Philosophy* 91 at 515, available at https://www.jstor.org/stable/23681578, accessed on 14 June 2019.
13 Brian Tamanaha note 7 at 477.
14 David Trubek, 'The political economy of the rule of law: The challenge of the new developmental state' (2009), Hague, *Journal on the Rule of Law* 1 at 29, available at https://link-springer-com.ezproxy.uct.ac.za/content/pdf/10.1017/S1876404509000281.pdf, accessed on 22 July 2020.
15 Ada Ordor, 'Tracking the law and development continuum through multiple intersections' (2015) 8(2), *Law and Development Review* at 335.
16 Brian Tamanaha note 7 at 479.
17 Liliana Lizarazo-Rodriguez note 1.
18 Ada Ordor note 15.
19 David Trubek, 'Law and development 50 years on', Legal Studies Research Paper Series Paper No. 1212, International Encyclopedia of Social and Behavioural Sciences at 2.
20 Yong-Sik Lee, *Law and Development Theory and Practice* (2019) at 3.
21 Ibid at 4 and 5.
22 Ada Ordor note 15 at 345.
23 Yong-Sik Lee note 20 at 6 and 7.
24 Mashood Baderin, note 8 at 3.
25 Yong-Sik Lee note 20 at 11–2.
26 John Ohnesorge, 'Developing development theory: Law and development orthodoxies and the Northeast Asian experience' (2007) 28 (2), *U Pa JInt'l Econ L* at 226.
27 Mashood Baderin note 8 at 22, 24 and 28.
28 Yong-Sik Lee, 'General theory of law and development' (2017) 50, *Cornell International Law Journal* at 430.
29 UN Declaration on the Right to Development Resolution 41/128 of 4 December 1986, Article 1.
30 David Trubek & Alvaro Santos note 2 at 11 and 12.
31 Yong-Sik Lee, *Law and Development Theory and Practice* (2019) at 48.
32 I Ayua, 'Law and Development in Africa' (1998) 3(1), *International Journal on World Peace* at 78–9.
33 Brian Tamanaha note 7 at 480 and 486.
34 John Ohnesorge note 26 at 290.
35 Mashood Baderin note 8 at 4.
36 Ibid at 12.
37 Ibid at 34.
38 Ada Ordor note 15 at 347.
39 Ibid at 348.
40 Yong-Shik Lee, 'General theory of law and development' note 26 at 442–3.
41 World Bank, *UFA 2020 Overview: Universal Financial Access by 2020*, available at https://www.worldbank.org/en/topic/financialinclusion/brief/achieving-universal-financial-access-by-2020, accessed on 28 December 2019.
42 David Trubek note 19 at 8.
43 George Obulutsa, 'M-Pesa helps drive up Kenyans' access to financial services', 3 April 2019, available at https://www.reuters.com/article/kenya-banking/m-pesa-helps-drive-up-kenyans-access-to-financial-services-study-idUSL8N21L2HK, accessed on 14 May 2019.
44 Gareth van Zyl, 'Why Vodacom M-Pesa has flopped in SA', 05 September 2016, *fin24tech,* available at https://www.fin24.com/Tech/Companies/why-vodacom-m-pesa-has-flopped-in-sa-20160509, accessed on 9 May 2019. See also Lerato Mbele, 'Why M-Pesa failed in South Africa', *BBC Africa Business Report*, Johannesburg, 11 May 2016, available at http://www.bbc.com/news/world-africa-36260348/, accessed on 11 May 2018.

45 George Mousourakis, Legal transplants and legal development: A jurisprudential and comparative law approach', (2013), *Acta Jur. Hng.* 54 at 225.
46 Nuno Garoupa & Anthony Ogus, 'A strategic interpretation of legal transplants' (2006), *Journal of Legal Studies* 35 (2) at 344.
47 Pierre Legrand, 'The impossibility of legal transplants' (1997), *Maastricht J. Eur. & Comp. L.* 4 at 117.
48 Ibid at 117–8.
49 George Mousourakis note 45 at 236.
50 Randall Peerenboom, 'Toward a methodology for successful legal transplants' (2013), *Chinese Journal of Comparative Law*) 1(1) at 4.
51 John Cairns, 'Watson, Walton, and the history of legal transplants' (2013), *Ga. J. Int'l & Comp. L.* 41 at 676.
52 George Mousourakis note 45 at 220.
53 Alan Watson, 'The birth of legal transplants' (2013), *Ga. J. Int'l & Comp. L.* 41 at 605.
54 Peter Grajzl & Valentina Dimitrova-Grajzl, 'The Choice in the lawmaking process: Legal transplants vs. indigenous law' (2009), *Rev. L & Econ.* 5 at 646.
55 George Mousourakis note 45 at 227.
56 Garoupa & Ogus note 46 at 342.
57 George Mousourakis note 45 at 226.
58 Ibid at 232
59 Ronald Bailey 'The other side of slavery: Black labor, cotton, and textile industrialization in Great Britain and the United States' (1994), *Agricultural History* 68 (2) at 36–8, available at https://www.jstor.org/stable/3744401, accessed on 26 July 2019.
60 George Mousourakis note 45 at 229.
61 George Mousourakis note at 229.
62 Christian Boulanger, *Law and Development as Practice and as Theory: From Self-estrangement to Alienation*? available at https://barblog.hypotheses.org/832, accessed on 14 June 2019.
63 Jan Torpman & Fredrik Jörgensen note 12 at 530.
64 Peter Grajzl & Valentina Dimitrova-Grajzl note 54 at 617–8.
65 Ibid at 646.
66 George Mousourakis note 45 at 231.
67 Louis F Del Duca & Alain A Levasseur, 'Impact of legal culture and legal transplants on the Evolution of the U.S. legal system' (2010), *American Journal of Comparative Law*, 58 at 1, available at https://www.jstor.org/stable/20744530, accessed on 14 May 2019.
68 Jan Torpman & Fredrik Jörgensen note 12 at 528.
69 Ibid at 518.
70 Yong-Shik Lee note 20 at 51–2.
71 Ibid at 80.
72 Jemeja Penca, 'Transnational legal transplants and legitimacy: The example of clean and green development mechanisms' (2016), *Legal Stud.* 36 at 723–4.
73 Ibid at 724.
74 Leone Niglia, 'Of harmonization and fragmentation: The problem of legal transplants in the Europeanization of private law' (2010), *Maastricht J. Eur. & Comp. L.* 17 at 127.
75 Alliance for Financial Inclusion, *National Financial Inclusion Strategies: Current State of* Practice (2015) at 2, available at https://www.afi-global.org/sites/default/files/publications/fisplg-state_of_practice.pdf, accessed on 28 March 2019.
76 Ibid.
77 Central Bank of Nigeria, *National Financial Inclusion Strategy* (2012) at vi available at https://www.cbn.gov.ng/Out/2012/publications/reports/dfd/CBN-Summary%20Report%20of-Financial%20Inclusion%20in%20Nigeria-final.pdf, accessed on 10 April 2019.
78 Ibid at 9.

79 Central Bank of Nigeria (CBN), Ibid at vi. See also Alliance for Financial Inclusion, *National Financial Inclusion Strategies: Current State of Practice* (2015) at 11, available at https://www.afi-global.org/sites/default/files/publications/fisplg-state_of_practice.pdf, accessed on 28 March 2019.
80 Laws of the Federation of Nigeria (2004) Cap. B3.
81 Central Bank of Nigeria (CBN) note 77 at 23.
82 Ibid at vi. See also Alliance for Financial Inclusion note 79 at 11.
83 Central Bank of Nigeria (CBN) note 77 at 23.
84 Ibid at 2012 at viii and 17.
85 C Leigh Anderson et al. *Review of National Identity Programs ITU Focus Group Technical Report* (2016) at 25, available at https://www.itu.int/en/ITU-T/focusgroups/dfs/Documents/09_2016/Review%20of%20National%20Identity%20Programs.pdf, accessed on 13 August 2019.
86 World Population Review, *India Population 2022,* available at https://worldpopulationreview.com/countries/india-population, accessed on 28 February 2022. See also World Population Review, *Nigeria Population 2022*, available at https://worldpopulationreview.com/countries/nigeria-population, accessed on 28 February 2022.
87 C Leigh Anderson note 85 at 114 and 116.
88 Ibid at 116.
89 Kwadwo Boateng, 'Ghana's progress on reaching out to the unbanked through financial inclusion' (2018), *International Journal of Management Studies* V (Special Issue 2), at 3.
90 Financial Inclusion Insights, *Ghana,* available at http://finclusion.org/country/africa/ghana.html#overview, accessed on 10 July 2019.
91 Bangko Sentral ng Pilipinas, *National Strategy for Financial Inclusion* (2015) at 5, available at http://www.bsp.gov.ph/downloads/publications/2015/PhilippinesNSFIBooklet.pdf, accessed on 8 July 2019.
92 Ibid.
93 Anti-Money Laundering Council, Republic of the Philippines, *Towards Deepening Regulatory Compliance: An Assessment of the Development of Anti-Money Laundering Reporting Compliance of the Pawnshop and Money Service Business Industry: Strategic Analysis Report* at 6, available at http://www.amlc.gov.ph/images/PDFs/2018%20Strategic%20Analysis%20Report%20on%20Pawnshop%20and%20MSB.pdf, accessed on 13 July 2019.
94 Lawrence Agcaoili, 'Big banks establish more branch-lite units', October 9, 2018, *Philstar Global,* available at https://www.philstar.com/business/banking/2018/10/09/1858385/big-banks-establish-more-branch-lite-units, accessed on 1 July 2019.
95 Anti-Money Laundering Council note 93 at 6. See also Bankgo Sentral ng Philipinas, *BSP Adopts Enhanced Oversight Framework for Money Service Businesses,* 20 January 2017, available at http://www.bsp.gov.ph/publications/media.asp?id=4276&yr=2017, accessed on 20 July 2019.
96 Asli Demirgüç-Kunt, Leora Klapper, Dorothe Singer et al. *The Global Findex Database 2017: Measuring Financial Inclusion and the Fintech Revolution* (2018) at 23, available at https://globalfindex.worldbank.org/, accessed on 16 April 2019.
97 Enhancing Financial Innovation and Access in Nigeria (EFInA), *Key Findings: EFInA Access to Financial Services in Nigeria* Survey (2020) at 62, available at https://a2f.ng/wp-content/uploads/2021/06/A2F-2020-Final-Report.pdf, accessed on 14 January 2021.
98 Alliance for Financial Inclusion, *Agent Banking in Latin America: Discussion Paper* (2012) at 3, available at https://www.afi-global.org/sites/default/files/discussion_paper_-_agent_banking_latin_america.pdf, accessed on 22 July 2019.
99 Universal Postal Union, *About Financial Services,* available at http://www.upu.int/en/activities/postal-financial-services/about-postal-financial-services.html, accessed on 24 July 2020.
100 Ibid.

101 CGAP, *Branchless Banking Agents in Brazil: Building Viable Networks* (2010) at 6, available at https://www.gsma.com/mobilefordevelopment/wp-content/uploads/2012/06/agentnetworksinbrazilcgapfgv1_7.pdf, accessed on 16 July 2019.
102 Alliance for Financial Inclusion note 98 at 12.
103 Ibid at 8.
104 Ibid at 16.
105 Ibid at 8.
106 Shariful Islam, 'The rapid growth of agent banking in Bangladesh Dhaka', *Tribune Sunday*, Jun 09, 2019, available at https://www.dhakatribune.com/business/2018/06/03/the-rapid-growth-of-agent-banking-in-bangladesh, accessed on 17 July 2019.
107 Central Bank of Nigeria, *National Financial Inclusion Strategy Implementation* (2018) at 59, available at https://www.cbn.gov.ng/out/2019/ccd/national%20financial%20inclusion%20
strategy.pdf, accessed on 8 July 2020.
108 Reuters, 'M-Pesa helps drive up Kenyans' access to financial services', available https://www.reuters.com/article/kenya-banking/m-pesa-helps-drive-up-kenyans-access-to-financial-services-study-idUSL8N21L2HK, accessed on 16 June 2019.
109 Asli et al. note 96 at 7.
110 Ibid at 56 and 60.
111 Safaricom, 'What is Lipa Na M-Pesa', available at https://www.safaricom.co.ke/personal/m-pesa/lipa-na-m-pesa/what-is-lipa-na-m-pesa, accessed on 7 November 2020.
112 Alliance for Financial Inclusion, *Mobile Financial Services Regulatory Approaches to Enable Access* at 6–7, available at https://www.findevgateway.org/sites/default/files/mfg-en-paper-mobile-financial-services-regulatory-approaches-to-enable-access-nov-2010.pdf, accessed on 23 July 2019.
113 Rory Macmillan, *Digital Financial Services: Regulating for Financial Inclusion: An ICT Perspective* (2016), available at https://www.itu.int/en/ITU-D/Conferences/GSR/Documents/GSR2016/Digital_financial_inclusion_GDDFI.pdf, accessed 1 July 2018. See also Ken Macharia, 'CBA, Safaricom mark 5 years of M-Shwari with customer savings of Sh12.6Bn', *Capital Business,* December 6, 2017, available at https://www.capitalfm.co.ke/business/2017/12/cba-safaricom-mark-5-years-m-shwari-customer-savings-sh12-6bn/, accessed on 27 February 2019.
114 World Bank Group, *Achieving Effective Financial Inclusion in South Africa: A Payments Perspective* at 10, available at http://www.treasury.gov.za/publications/other/Achieving%20Effective%20Financial%20Inclusion%20in%20South%20Africa.pdf, accessed on 22 June 2019. See also Lydie Louis & Chartier Frederic, 'Financial inclusion in South Africa: An integrated framework for financial inclusion of vulnerable communities in South Africa's regulatory system reform' (2017), *Journal of Comparative Urban Law and Policy* 1 (1) at 179
115 Bankable Frontiers Associates, *The Mzansi Bank Account Initiative in South Africa: Final Report* (2009) at 3, available at http://www.finmark.org.za/wp-content/uploads/2016/02/Rep_MsanziBankAccInitiativeSA_2009.pdf, accessed on 24 July 2020. World Bank Group note 114 at 46 and 58.
116 Bankable Frontiers Associates Ibid at 4.
117 Ibid.
118 World Bank Group note 114 at 60.

3 Regulation of Digital Financial Services

3.1 Introduction

This chapter commences with the introduction of a review of the new NFIS strategy instituted by the Central Bank of Nigeria (CBN) in 2018. The drivers for the revision as well as the new targets set out by the CBN will be summarised. Also explored is the regulation of DFS in Nigeria and the relevant laws and regulators in the field. The chapter additionally addresses the regulatory model adopted by the CBN in the deployment of DFS and its adequacy for assuring effective competition in the industry. The chapter concludes by noting the role that regulatory sandboxes could play in advancing competitive DFS deployment.

3.2 The financial sector regulator

As noted above, the regulation of the DFS sector in many countries is a role taken on by the financial systems regulator or apex bank. In Nigeria, the CBN assumes this role and exercises the responsibility of electing a regulatory model for DFS deployment in Nigeria. In making this election, regulators should ideally employ a delicate balance between addressing the needs of the financially excluded and maintaining financial sector stability and integrity. This also determines the flexibility or rigidity of DFS rules. Getting this balance right is a core determinant of whether DFS would scale up.

In choosing a regulatory model for DFS, regulators should also be mindful of the environment for deploying financial services, including considerations such as the geographical location of users and the perception of users about the financial system and financial offerings. There should also be a consideration for the readiness of users to adopt digital finance, and the capacity or motivation of providers to reach financially excluded consumers. In Kenya, the non-bank-led model is observed to have thrived as a result of the flexibility of the regulators, the size and customer base of Safaricom, (the parent company of Mpesa) and the need for low-value transfers and mobile money to bridge the dearth of banks in rural areas.[1] On a societal level, there was also evidence

DOI: 10.4324/9781003217886-3

of mobile phone ubiquity and a low level of financial inclusion that drove the adoption of mobile money.[2]

Before the introduction of the Guidelines for Licensing and Regulation of Payment Services Banks 2020 (the PSB guidelines) in Nigeria, only the bank-led and the corporation-led DFS models were recognised in Nigeria and alternative providers such as MNOs were largely excluded. For example, the Guidelines on Mobile Money Services in Nigeria 2015 defined the bank-led approach as one where a bank either alone or in partnership with other banks or approved organisations delivers banking services with the bank as the lead initiator.[3] MNOS were expressly exempted from providing finance under this model and could only do so in strict collaboration with banks. The corporation-led model, on the other hand, permits a corporate organisation duly licensed by the CBN to deliver mobile money services to customers as lead initiator.[4] While some corporations such as PAGA are taking up this space, it is observed that the reach of these entities is not yet widespread, particularly in rural areas.

The CBN Regulatory Framework for Mobile Money Services in Nigeria 2015 also laid out the two models for deploying mobile money services in Nigeria to be bank-led and non-bank-led models. The bank-led model applies where a bank or consortium of banks provides banking services as leverage on the mobile money system with the bank serving as lead initiator and accountable to the CBN and end users.[5] The non-bank-led model on the other hand allows a duly licensed corporate organisation to deploy mobile payment services to subscribers and acts as the lead initiator in the provision of mobile payment services.[6] Like the Guidelines on Mobile Money Services in Nigeria 2015, this provision also excludes MNOs.[7]

Similarly, the CBN Guidelines on Mobile Money Services in Nigeria 2015 outline limited roles for MNOs, including providing telecommunications network infrastructure, enabling secure communication channels, avoiding anti-competition and preferential treatment in terms of traffic and price.[8] MNOs were also prohibited from receiving deposits from the public unless where it is intended to be used as prepaid airtime but not for transfer of monetary value between customers.[9] Likewise, the Framework on Mobile Money Services in Nigeria 2015 restricts these entities to infrastructure provision to facilitate messaging in mobile payments transactions.[10]

Although the CBN acknowledged the critical nature of the MNO network infrastructure to mobile money services in Nigeria, it was maintained that the MNO-led model is rightly excluded to avoid wielding systemic risks on the national security system.[11] The CBN also asserted that MNO exclusion reduces the possibility of loss of customer funds when placed in the care of telecommunications companies.[12] According to CBN, the restriction of MNOs enables the bank to exercise full control over monetary policy operations, minimise financial risks and ensure that financial services are driven by organisations that have been licensed to do so.[13]

Although it is understandable that the lower degree of licensing requirements mandated by the CBN regarding alternative providers is one reason for these restrictions, it is argued that the focus on the activity rather than the entity providing finance has proved to be a better option in many jurisdictions. This allows a wide range of alternative providers including MNOs and the post to offer finance. MNOs for instance, have a wide customer base, network infrastructure and brand recognition needed to leverage into finance and can easily create niches in areas starved of financial access points. The success of MNOs at increasing financial inclusion in countries such as Kenya and Tanzania is notable. Similarly, postal banks can help reduce financial exclusion in geographically hard-to-reach communities as the postal service is present in most communities in Nigeria.

In jurisdictions where this bank-led model is favoured, the need to adhere to requirements such as rigorous licensing processes, capital adequacy and maintenance of financial systems security are cited. Banks, which are required to fulfil these requirements, are therefore given the prerogative to offer full banking services, intermediate customer funds and invest in a wide range of capital market securities. In contrast, non-bank entities are often only permitted to offer fewer services such as wallet savings, utility settlements and fund transfers without the sanction, in some cases, to intermediate or invest funds freely. Funds held by non-bank entities are mostly permitted to be stored in a trust account at a deposit money bank with customers as beneficiaries. Unlike the case with banks, these trust accounts scarcely yield interest for customers. Again, some providers are sometimes not permitted to charge clients but are expected to mainly profit from commissions on transactions. This mainly pertains to mobile money agents.

The bank-centred approach does some disservice to the excluded in view of the significant figures for financial exclusion, particularly in relation to rural exclusion due to stringent access terms and the unsuitability of channels of providers. A bank-centred regulatory model sometimes translates to urban saturation of banks while rural areas are bereft of access points. Significantly, rural banking in Nigeria seems to be sparse due to reasons such as the negative perception of the poor in relation to creditworthiness, a notion that the poor have no funds to save and the strain of KYC regulation which leads banks to cut off whole consumer groups in a bid to de-risk. The excluded who should really be the subject of financial inclusion initiatives are consequently being shunned by deposit money banks in spite of the opportunity to pool community funds.

Financially excluding poor communities increases the amount of money in circulation in the informal sector or shadow economy with attendant risks on the stability and integrity of the financial system as the excluded begin to patronise informal channels of finance at the risk of being drawn into the hands of unsafe finance providers such as loan sharks, payday lenders and other moneylenders. These entities often lend with usury, imposing stringent repayment plans, sinking the poor deeper into a cycle of debt.

Notably, even though economically disadvantaged people may have small earnings individually, it is interesting to note that bringing these small funds together within the formal sector can result in significant numbers. The Mpesa story in Kenya is proof of the fact that people with small means can be commercially viable when their small individual funds are pooled together to form a larger and more diversified pool of funds for service providers who dare to invest in this category of persons. Here, micro-payments drove MPesa to a position of dominance in mobile money provision in Kenya. The company's business strategy of targeting the 'shillings' in terms of bringing access to persons at the base of the pyramid in recognition of the commercial viability that could result from investing in these persons, was instrumental to achieving success.[14]

A similar situation is evident in Bangladesh where the Grameen Bank financial inclusion model aided the inclusion of numerous excluded and vulnerable persons by providing microcredit without collateral.[15] This feat won the founder, Yunus Muhammad and the Grameen Bank the Nobel Peace prize in 2006 for their efforts in creating economic and social development.[16]

Financial services providers need to recognise the business opportunity in serving economically disadvantaged persons including the opportunity for expanding customer base and revenue stream from finance products and more importantly as an income-generating medium to receive social transfer payments for the poor.[17] Again, network effects are possible, particularly with regard to persons sending remittances to dependent relatives. In Nigeria, remittances are huge and account for $14.2 billion as of 2021.[18] EFInA notes that remittances contribute 25 per cent of bank growth in Nigeria alongside payment savings, agent networks, income and loans.[19] Therefore, a bank-centred approach in the face of clear potential for increased inclusion; misses the opportunity to reach the rural population that resides too far away from banks.

One can observe how the introduction of agent banking by the CBN to reach rural areas has not proved successful as banks which have been given the mandate to drive this channel continue their practice of concentrating on customers in urban centres, leaving swathes of rural populations unserved. Agent banking currently accounts for only 19 per cent, although a significant rise from the 3 per cent recorded in 2018 according to EFInA.[20] Nigeria is a diverse nation both in terms of geography, religious beliefs and cultural bias regarding money and, additionally, grapples with a significant level of financial exclusion that necessitates embracing as many channels as are feasible to reach more people. Making several channels available for the provision of finance not only offers viable alternatives that the excluded can choose from but also ensures that adoption is based on the financial needs of the users to sustain usage.

Interestingly, the Guidelines for Licensing and Regulation of Payment Services Banks 2020 could change the bank-centred approach of the CBN by allowing courier companies, retail outlets, MNOs and similar alternative providers to offer financial services independently. Approval-in-principle has been granted to three entities.[21] At present, however, the bank/alternative provider ratio is still significantly skewed. In addition, with the CBN NFIS review of 2018, banks are now encouraged to set up mini-branches in rural areas.[22] But this is curious given that the PSB Guidelines mandate alternative providers which are the newcomers to the industry to deploy 25 per cent of their branches in rural areas.[23]

While this provision will clearly drive rural deployment of finance, it is odd that banks which have a seemingly better chance of reaching rural areas in terms of possessing the reputation as recognised finance providers, the facility to offer cash-inand cash-out functions nationwide and the financial capacity to build local branches are not being compelled to expand financial services to rural communities as a pre-condition to operate. The place of providing a level playing field for healthy competition to thrive as an indispensable ideal in the provision of finance is buttressed below.

3.3 Regulation and market competition

Market collaboration in the finance sector entails some degree of cooperation or facilities sharing by industry players. Collaboration between providers has some positive aspects such as sustaining meaningful partnerships and fostering the interoperability of systems with the potential to lower costs and reduce customer charges.[24] Also collaboration could enable synergies and increase the chances of wider customer adoption of products and services.[25] Collaboration opens up niche markets representing different consumer interests with profound positive implications for rural financial inclusion. Agent banking presents an example as there could be a better chance of including the DFS sceptics using close-to-door local agents such as kiosks, gas stations and schools known to and domiciled closed to users as practised in Kenya.

Collaboration between financial services providers equally creates an ecosystem where customers can use financial services in a frictionless manner.[26] Typically, collaborative products develop faster than products created by individual providers.[27] This is because combined expertise and customer base can lead to faster scale. An example can be found in the collaboration between Safaricom and the Commercial Bank of Africa (CBA) which birthed MShwari in Kenya in 2012, a service that enables customers of the two companies to apply for loans, receive transfers into the Mpesa wallet and build credit history.[28] A similar example is the collaboration between Safaricom, CBA group and KCB where deposit and loan services are offered to customers on the Mpesa platform.[29]

Again, while banks can offer access to bank branches, MNOs provide the IT infrastructure and customer base for advancing mobile money. Both entities are thus able to reach their full potential by focusing on areas of strength and relying on effective partnerships for other aspects. With these collaborations, more products can be offered, leading to sustainability of DFS as more services become available to consumers and alternative sources of revenue are created for providers.[30]

However, the practice of mandating collaboration as a business model for a set of entities without any collaboration obligation on others creates market imbalance at best and could lead to investment apathy and market exit for disadvantaged providers. The erstwhile practice of the CBN in mandating MNOs to collaborate with banks without the corresponding imposition on the banks to negotiate fairly or collaborate opens the door for a lopsided direction for the market. This was also unwholesome for the business case for MNOs. Moreover, the unmatched proportion of four main MNOs to about 22 deposit money banks in Nigeria buttresses the challenges of this forced collaboration and heralds harrowing consequences for unhealthy competition and a lower quality of DFS.

Mandating collaboration scarcely allows for the realisation of individual company goals, especially where the burden to collaborate is foisted on one party alone. For one, the business models of providers would ordinarily be varied because while non-bank entities customarily seek a niche in excluded markets with specific financial needs, banks provide a fuller suite of financial services from payment to savings, investment, credit and some offer special packages such as pension and insurance services.

In Nigeria, for instance, banks have been observed gravitating more to the urban areas probably with the notion of the potential to serve more profitable consumers. Aside from this urban attraction, it has also been observed that services offered mainly improve the financial experience of the persons that are already financially served. Fewer entry-level products are innovated for the financially excluded and it is no wonder that only 19 per cent of the rural adult population in Nigeria is financially included.[31] This obvious disinterest of banks in serving the financial needs of the excluded persons has been decried by authors for making collaboration a less dynamic and less developing system.[32]

Therefore, the restrictive approach to providing finance, particularly through forced and one-sided collaboration is not ideal. In its stead, regulators can set minimum standards of eligibility for providers and then watch out for anti-competitive practices perpetrated. For instance, in a collaboration arrangement, MNOs should not be allowed to over-price or downgrade the quality of mobile communication components such as SIM cards, voice, SMS and USSD to lock out bank competition.[33] Banks that are also able to reduce the cost of delivering financial services by offering digital finance options in place of building out bank branches cost-effectively and operating low-value accounts should collaborate on these services on fair terms with MNOs.

By moving the market in this direction, regulators can thus encourage the honing of the competitive advantages of individual finance providers as the basis for collaboration so that providers endeavour to provide quality and innovative services at a competitive price to users. The place of healthy competition by encouraging the exhibition of the competitive advantages of providers towards the goal of achieving greater innovation is explored in the next section. It is notable that although banks and MNOs are used as the main examples, similar arguments can be made for other alternative providers.

3.4 The place of competitive advantages for DFS providers

Healthy competition in every industry is essential as this drives innovation and leads to improved consumer protection. Enabling alternative providers to offer mobile money independently will usher in the needed competition to drive provider efficiency in the DFS sphere. Notably, every DFS provider, no matter how small, has some competitive advantages in relation to other providers which, if properly harnessed, largely dispense with the need for regulatory restrictions. Exhibiting these competitive advantages thereby naturally invites collaboration that is freely entered into without regulatory imposition.

For instance, MNOs have the advantage of owning mobile gateway systems.[34] This advantage also extends to less exposure to strict regulations such as KYC compliance compared to banks.[35] Again, MNOs supply vital components and could compete directly with banks by seamlessly leveraging market power from core telecommunications services to mobile money.[36] Further, MNOs can succeed in creating niche markets in simple transactions such as small-value transfers and bill payments in places where banks have not established significant footprints. MNOs usually have a wide base of telecommunications service clients, numbers, spectrum and access to network infrastructures. MNOs also control crucial mobile networks that are relied upon by other mobile financial services providers as these cannot be easily or cost-effectively duplicated.[37] Even though lacking the legal backing in most cases to engage in intermediation, MNOs are able to leverage ubiquitous low-cost network infrastructure to process transactions.[38]

For banks, the network of branches with the potential for widespread customer reach creates a competitive edge. Banks also benefit from brand recognition by reason of a deeper historic reputation with finance and long-running relationship with urban clients who can extend network effects to rural dependents through remittances. Banks can thus exert leverage on this trusted brand recognition to grow their customer base. Similarly, banks benefit from first-mover advantage, having been in the business of providing financial services longer than other alternative providers and as a result easily amass a larger market share of loyal clients. Banks have the option of building their own network operations or engaging the services of mobile virtual network operators (MVNO).

As dominant entities in cash reticulation with direct access to the national currency from the central banks and the relevant infrastructure for moving cash around, banks can easily deploy cash-in-cash-out (CICO) services nationwide.[39] Furthermore, banks are able to offer broader, longer-term and more robust financial services such as loans, pensions, trusts and retirement packages as a result of possessing more sophisticated banking licences. These licences also enable broader mobile banking offerings to long-standing clients that additionally require DFS. Deposit and insurance facilities are also available. Banks equally offer over-the-counter (OTC) services free of cost for CICO unlike MNOs that charge commissions.

These competitive advantages set the stage for the promotion of vigorous competition in the industry which can lead to better innovative products, higher consumer protection and the achievement of financial inclusion goals. Once the environment for effective competition is in place, regulators can be rest assured that competitive advantages will be employed strategically. Collaboration will also be more likely. A safeguard for creating this environment for competition will be for regulators to closely watch the market in order to detect signs of abuse of competitive advantages, particularly by an entity in a dominant position.

Significantly, the Federal Competition and Consumer Protection Act 2019 makes provisions for competition and the provisions of this Act in relation to competitive advantages and the abuse of dominance will be elucidated in the following section.

3.5 Determining dominance and anti-competition in DFS

Dominant companies can wield anti-competition in a sector and drive the market towards individual company gains with detrimental effects on competitors, consumers and the industry. Regulators thus try to curb this by intervening in the market to jettison abuse. In determining anti-competition, regulators first have to ascertain the relevant market and further determine whether a firm is in a dominant position or possesses a significant market power (SMP) to exercise anti-competitive practices. Defining the relevant market helps to identify relevant products and services as well as the relevant geographic coverage pertaining to competitors. 'A relevant market is a collection of products or services in respect of which a hypothetical monopolist would be able to charge a price significantly above the notional competitive price'.[40]

Generally, a relevant market is determined by considering the demand-side substitutes. These assess the ease of customer switching to the services of a competitor.[41] Another method is the determination of supply-side substitutes, useful in assessing the ease of a supplier entering into new markets within a reasonable time.[42] This increase can be jettisoned by changes in supply methods or volumes of other suppliers. Lastly, the small but significant and non-transitory increase in price (SSNIP) test weighs the ability and willingness of consumers to switch to a competitor where the hypothetical monopolist increases the price of goods by 5 to 10 per cent above the prevailing competitive price of a product.[43] The test considers the profitability and sustenance of price of this hypothetical monopolist after the price increase and if clients will be retained nonetheless.

Notably, the Federal Competition and Consumer Protection Act 2019 (FCCP) Act provides in Section 71 that regulators in defining a market must consider geographical boundaries that identify groups of buyers and sellers of defined products and services where competition may be restrained.[44] The Act further considers the availability of alternative suppliers and substitutes for goods or services with consideration for characteristics, price and intended use to measure the possibility of dominant companies abusing their position by increasing the price of goods and services or wielding detriments on consumers.[45] These metrics are deemed to place a company in a position of likely abuse of dominance.

After determining the relevant market, the next step is therefore the determination of the existence of a dominant company or one with a significant market power. A dominant company is defined by Section 70 of the Act as 'one that is able to act without taking account of the reaction of customers, consumers or competitors'. Section 70(2) provides that

> A dominant position in a relevant market exists where an undertaking enjoys a position of economic strength to prevent effective competition and possesses the power to behave to an appreciable extent independently of competitors, customers and ultimately, consumers.

A dominant firm can also set a price above prevailing market price, decrease innovativeness and offer goods of inferior quality.[46] Therefore, without the right regulation in place, a company in a dominant position can exhibit anti-competitive practices that bring adverse effects to the market by attempting through illegal means to take control of the market.

In assessing market dominance the regulator considers the relevant company's financial power, market share, market/supplier access, market entry barriers both legal and real, connections with other companies, supply/goods switching abilities and the capacity of the opposite market side to deal with other companies.[47]

The third step in determining anti-competition is to analyse if the conduct of the dominant company amounts to abusive practices. Before this third step is discussed, it is important to note that a mere determination of dominance is not necessarily tantamount to anti-competition, but is a call to regulators to watch out for exclusionary behaviour that ushers in anti-competition. As a matter of fact, dominant companies must adopt imaginative business strategies to remain relevant as history is replete with narratives of dominant companies that experienced shrinkage of their customer base and even market exit in the face of stiff competition from new and smaller entrants, especially in the disruptive space. The 2001 introduction of the Global System for Mobile Communications (GSM) in Nigeria is a telling example.

Here, even though the Nigeria Telecommunications Limited (NITEL) enjoyed the status of being a government-funded monopoly with years of experience and a wide customer base, the licensing of two private corporations, namely, MTN and Airtel (both foreign corporations) changed the course of history in the telecommunications sector. These two companies which came through on the prospect of a communication device in the hands of every Nigerian were able to trigger a mass migration of users from the conventional landline to a disruptive GSM.[48] Even the belated move of the telecom giant to deploy MTEL, the GSM component to retain customers failed to impress.[49] Patronage continued to plummet until its eventual liquidation and sale.[50]

This example illustrates that regulators should not only focus on the dominance of an entity, large market size or a wide scale of customers. The focus should also extend to the capacity of an entity to successfully use its dominant position to carry out anti-competitive acts to the disadvantage of market competitors or consumers.

The third step to ascertaining anti-competition after determining the relevant market and dominance of players is to analyse the conduct of dominant firms to determine abusive practices that amount to anti-competition. Anti-competition occurs when companies charge excessively, restrict access to crucial facilities without the excuse of economic feasibility, restrict dealings with competitors, refuse to supply scarce goods, place unrelated conditions on transactions, sell below the marginal or average cost or buy up limited market supplies required by a competitor.[51]

The FCCP Act specifically prohibits exclusionary acts such as price-fixing, dividing the market by allocating consumers, suppliers, territories, goods or services, reducing or placing controls on manufacture and distribution, collusion in tenders and imposing unrelated obligations as conditions for concluding an agreement.[52] However, abuse of a dominant position does not include conducts that improve the production or distribution of goods or services, promotion of technical or economic progress which benefits consumers and helps attain objectives and acts that do not eliminate competition in the goods or services concerned.[53]

Importantly, in the DFS sphere, both banks and alternative providers can be anti-competitive even in a small sense where dominance has been attained. On the one hand, MNOs can drive other providers out of the market or make the provision of services more daunting by leveraging dominance from mobile handsets to mobile payments.[54] MNOs can also abuse their dominant position in mobile networks by bundling services (merging products or services for sale as a single unit) and other complementary goods including mobile payments together as a unit.[55] Similarly, MNOs can refuse or make it difficult or expensive to interoperate network systems with rival firms.[56] This can in turn restrict customers' ability to send money to users on other platforms and effectively result in dominance and lock-in.[57] These entities can further refuse to provide USSD to competitors and could discriminate in pricing or engage in margin squeeze to reduce/eliminate profits of competitors by citing the lack of capacity or technical readiness.[58]

Banks on the other hand can refuse to share credit and identification data (collected for KYC), making it more difficult for MNOs to identify credible customers for financial transactions such as loans, insurance and pensions. Banks can also offer access to deposit and insurance services to MNOs on revised terms. For example, additional rules could be foisted on MNOs for opening and operating trust accounts for mobile money subscribers stipulated in regulations such as the NDIC Framework for the Establishment of Pass through Deposit Insurance for subscribers of Mobile Money 2016. Banks may also refuse to collaborate with MNOs interested in building scale through physical branches of bigger banks.

Whatever the type of anti-competitive behaviour, regulators should reserve the power to examine market competition, jettison both monopoly and oligopoly, penalise collusive behaviour and object to price structures that are uncompetitive.[59] In Zambia, MTN was given a fine by the regulator for limiting a competitor's access to the USSD of Zoona.[60] Similarly, in Zimbabwe, the Competition and Tariff Commission (CTC) probed Econet for setting access cost to banks at a higher rate than those charged to customers of the Econet's mobile money service (EcoCash).[61] In Uganda also, the commercial court in *EzeeMoney v MTN,* fined MTN to the tune of UGX 2.3 billion (USD$ 662000), for threatening Yo!Uganda Ltd. over the supply of MTN's USSD connection to the plaintiff.[62]

3.6 Regulatory sandboxes and prospective use cases in Nigeria

As noted in Section 3.2, the bank-led model was before the introduction of the PSB Guidelines 2020 favoured in Nigeria to the exclusion of the MNO-led model and MNOs were only permitted to provide DFS in strict collaboration with banks. The scepticism of the CBN to allow MNOs to provide DFS independently did not take into account the competitive advantages outlined in Section 3.4 and the opportunity for a healthier and more innovative market. Explored in this section, therefore, is the prospect of using a regulatory sandbox. Sandboxes are increasingly being deployed in novel and fast-paced spaces to avoid the provider/user burden that could emanate from making laws based on predictions or disrupting a market when detriments ushered in by technology manifest. With the use of sandboxes, the scepticism of regulators could be allayed as DFS offerings by alternative providers are tested out in a controlled space to monitor market effects before eventual product launch.

Fundamentally, a regulatory sandbox is

> a framework set up by a financial sector regulator to allow small scale, live testing of innovations by private firms in a controlled environment (operating under a special exemption, allowance, or other limited, time-bound exception) under the regulator's supervision.[63]

Sandboxes can be regulatory or industrial. 'A regulatory sandbox is driven by regulators to increase the adoption of innovations which deliver superior consumer outcomes'.[64] 'An industry or virtual sandbox, on the other hand, is supplementary, enabling industry players to self-organise and provide a knowledge-sharing and communication forum, as well as an optional certification facility'.[65]

In a sandbox experiment, regulators could adjust rules, weigh up the regulatory impacts of these adjustments and then introduce these into the policy-making process.[66] The regulator then concentrates on monitoring key metrics, adjusting regulatory parameters on a periodic basis and providing guidance for product launch.[67] Furthermore, the regulator may relax certain legal requirements and other licensing challenges.[68] Regulators are also able to create an ad hoc framework with safeguard and performance indicators using a test-and-learn approach to observe how an innovation evolves before intervening in the market.[69]

Sandboxes offer businesses a shorter time to product launch as well as provide easier access to funding and avoid systemic risks from product failure.[70] They also help to mitigate risk for firms by providing closer regulatory oversight and helping with the adoption of regulations that keep pace with innovation.[71] Again, these experiments have the potential to lessen regulatory requirements for providers, lower entry barriers and improve transparency of licensing by offering regulatory guide.[72]

The sandbox experiment has been used in various countries including Singapore, the United Kingdom and Australia to various degrees.[73] In the United Kingdom, the regulators note that the experiment has helped to decrease the cost and time taken to innovate new ideas into market, a record of about 90 per cent of wider market launch and improved access to finance for Fintech firms as participation in the programme provides some degree of assurance to investors that projects are backed by regulators.[74]

In the specific sphere of financial inclusion, sandboxes have the capacity to measure the potential impact of innovations and to intervene in the market in a manner that is beneficial and diminishes risks.[75] Again, because the finance sector is innovative and fast-paced, sandboxes help with compliance, thereby reducing penalties for parties and costs to consumers.[76] Significantly, this holds prospects for improved results as more products and services can be offered at a lower price and providers can gain better access to finance.[77]

The sandbox experiment in Nigeria has been adopted by the Central Bank of Nigeria and the Nigeria Interbank Settlement System (NIBSS) with the specific aim of giving regulatory support to Fintech companies engaged in innovative exploits to attain wider financial inclusion.[78] This initiative is managed by the Financial Service Innovators Association of Nigeria (FSI) and supervised by the CBN and NIBSS.[79] Although it is still too early to measure the impact of this initiative, it is expected that sandboxes will enable industry players and new entrants to test new products under regulatory supervision.

In spite of the opportunities outlined above, regulators must utilise sandboxes cautiously as challenges such as inadequate resources both in terms of human capacity and financial resources to choose proposals, offer guidance, supervise tests and appraise innovations could manifest.[80] Again, setting the wrong parameters for these experiments (such as eligibility for candidacy, appropriate duration, accepted levels of innovativeness and mechanisms for evaluating effectiveness of the sandbox could occasion risks and the quest to achieve first-mover status can lead to regulatory capture.[81] Further, acquiring a customer base, especially for small firms and surmounting the complex conditions for authorisation have been observed as other core challenges.[82]

3.7 Conclusion

A brief introduction of the regulation of digital finance began this chapter. This was followed by the prospects for creating an enabling regulatory environment for exhibiting competitive advantages and the approach to detecting the abuse of dominance. Lastly, the potential for employing sandbox experiments to efficiently test DFS deployment by alternative providers was analysed. An investigation of the barriers to accessing finance will be conducted in the next chapter.

Notes

1 Safaricom, the parent company of the dominant MNO was the biggest telecommunications provider with nationwide presence and a wide customer base and so could leverage these advantages into mobile money provision. Significantly, Safaricom was launched in 2007 with a market share of 80 per cent in active SIM cards and specialised in the niche area of providing low-cost, simple financial products for the poor without any competition from banks in the first two years of its launch. See Joseph Kariuki Nyaga, 'Mobile banking services in the East African Community (EAC): Challenges to the existing legislative and regulatory frameworks' (2014), *Journal of Information Policy* 4 at 275, available at https://www-jstor-org.ezproxy.uct.ac.za/stable/pdf/10.5325/jinfopoli.4.2014.0270.pdf?refreqid=excelsior%3Ac9ec4f90e7b2eb489c31cd6e04dd1188, accessed on 1 June 2018.
2 Ibid at 275.
3 Central Bank of Nigeria Guidelines on Mobile Money Services in Nigeria of 5.0 (a) of 2015.
4 Ibid at 5.0 (b).
5 Central Bank of Nigeria Regulatory Framework for Mobile Money Services in Nigeria 3.0 of 2015. As with the regulatory framework on mobile payment systems discussed above, some of these provisions have been made obsolete by the introduction of the PSB Guidelines.
6 Ibid.
7 Ibid.
8 Central Bank of Nigeria note 3 at 8.4.
9 Ibid 5.0 (a).
10 Central Bank of Nigeria Framework on Mobile Money Services in Nigeria 4(c) of 2015.
11 Ibid at 1.0. See also Mondato, *Do Bank-led Models Stall Progress*? (2018), available at https://blog.mondato.com/do-bank-led-models-stall-progress/, accessed on 20 June 2018. See also CBN Central Bank of Nigeria note 5 (*Framework Objectives*).
12 Chima Nwokoji, 'We chose bank-led mobile money to protect users from losses – CBN', *Nigerian Tribune,* 5 June 2018, available at http://www.tribuneonlineng.com/chose-bank-led-mobile-money-protect-users-losses-cbn/, accessed on 10 August 2019.
13 Central Bank of Nigeria note 3 at 1.0.
14 Kieron Monks, 'M-Pesa: Kenya's mobile money success story turns 10', *CNN* 24, February 2017, available at https://edition.cnn.com/2017/02/21/africa/mpesa-10th-anniversary/index.htm, accessed on 6 May 2018.
15 *The Nobel Peace Prize for 2006* (2006), available at https://www.nobelprize.org/nobel_prizes/peace/laureates/2006/press.html, accessed on 6 May 2018.
16 Ibid.
17 Lydie Louis & Frederic Chartier, Financial inclusion in South Africa: An integrated framework for financial inclusion of vulnerable communities in South Africa's

regulatory system reform' (2017), *Hult International Business School Journal of Comparative Urban Law and Policy*, 1 (1) at 174, available at https://www.researchgate.net/publication/317095597_Financial_Inclusion_in_South_Africa_An_Integrated_Framework_for_Financial_Inclusion_of_Vulnerable_Communities_in_South_Africa's_Regulatory_System_Reform, accessed on 21 July 2020.

18 Babajide Komolafe, Nigeria's diaspora remittances may beat World Bank's projection, rise 10 per cent to $14.2bn, January 11, 2022, available at https://www.vanguardngr.com/2022/01/nigerias-diaspora-remittances-may-beat-world-banks-projection-rise-10-to-14-2bn/#:~:text=Nigeria's%20diaspora%20remittances%20inflow%20is,post%2DCOVID%20economic%20recovery%20measures, accessed on 23 January 2022.

19 Enhancing Financial Innovation and Access in Nigeria (EFInA), *Key Findings: EFInA Access to Financial Services in Nigeria* Survey (2020) at 15, available at https://a2f.ng/wp-content/uploads/2021/06/A2F-2020-Final-Report.pdf, accessed on 14 January 2021.

20 Ibid at 15.

21 Obinna Chima, CBN Grants Approval-in-Principle to Three PSBs, September 19, 2019, available at https://www.thisdaylive.com/index.php/2019/09/19/cbn-grants-approval-in-principle-to-three-psbs/, accessed on 24 July 2020.

22 Central Bank of Nigeria, *National Financial Inclusion Strategy Implementation* (2018) at 50, available at https://www.cbn.gov.ng/out/2019/ccd/national%20financial%20inclusion%20strategy.pdf, accessed on 8 July 2020.

23 Central Bank of Nigeria, Guidelines for the Licensing and Regulation of Payment Service Banks in Nigeria Guideline 3 of 2020.

24 Rory Macmillan, *Digital Financial Services: Regulating for Financial Inclusion: An ICT Perspective: GDDFI Discussion Paper 57* at 50, available at https://www.itu.int/en/ITU-D/Conferences/GSR/Documents/GSR2016/Digital_financial_inclusion_GDDFI.pdf, accessed on 1 July 2018.

25 Accion, *Smart Campaign* (2014) at 5, available at http://www.smartcampaign.org/storage/documents/Tools_and_Resources/20140821_EoS_DfS_MFIs.pdf, accessed on 3 June 2018.

26 Ian Pollari, *The Rise of Digital Platforms in Financial Services* (2018) at 2, available at https://assets.kpmg.com/content/dam/kpmg/xx/pdf/2018/02/kpmg-rise-of-digital-platforms.pdf, accessed on 13 November 2018.

27 See GSMA Success Factors for Mobile Money Services: A Quantitative Assessment of Success Factors (2016) at 13, available at https://www.gsmaintelligence.com/research/?file=923539C02F5D39174BA09C6851EFC25A&download, accessed on 2 June 2018.

28 Rory Macmillan note 24 at 50. See also Ken Macharia, 'CBA, Safaricom mark 5 years of M-Shwari with customer savings of Sh12.6Bn', *Capital Business,* December 6, 2017, available at https://www.capitalfm.co.ke/business/2017/12/cba-safaricom mark 5-years-m-shwari-customer-savings-sh12-6bn/, accessed on 27 February 2019.

29 Duncan Miriri, 'Kenya's Equity Bank, Safaricom team up to expand digital banking' *Reuters,* April 29, 2019, available at https://www.reuters.com/article/us-kenya-equity-group-hol-safaricom/kenyas-equity-bank-safaricom-team-up-to-expand-digital-banking-idUSKCN1S51IC, accessed on 16 August 2019.

30 UNSW Digital Financial Services Research Team, *Regulatory Handbook: The Enabling Regulation of Digital Financial Services* (2015) at 20.

31 EFInA 2020 note 19 at 62.

32 Sandra Suárez, 'Poor people's money: The politics of money in Mexico' (2016), *Telecommunications Policy* 40 at 947, available at https://ac-els-cdn-com.ezproxy.uct.ac.za/S0308596116300027/1-s2.0-S0308596116300027-main.pdf?_tid=19f52bdc-de6d-4664-b420-133ea6c3422b&acdnat=1528174867_101c04ef5f82d09d39da45de9838f027, accessed on 12 May 2018.

33 Ignacio Mas, *What Is the Telecom Regulator's Role in Fostering Mobile Money?* (2012), available at http://www.cgap.org/blog/what-telecom-regulator%E2%80%99s-role-fostering-mobile-money#comments, accessed on 16 June 2018.

34 A Bara, 'Mobile money for financial inclusion: Policy and regulatory perspective in Zimbabwe' (2013) 5(5), *African Journal of Science, Technology, Innovation and Development* at 349, available at http://dx.doi.org/10.1080/20421338.2013.829287, accessed on 1 June 2018.

35 Ibid.

36 Ignacio Mas note 33.

37 Rory Macmillan note 23 at 40 and 43. Available at https://www.itu.int/en/ITU-D/Conferences/GSR/Documents/GSR2016/Digital_financial_inclusion_GDDFI.pdf, accessed on 1 July 2018.

38 Hennie Bester, Christine Hougaard, Jeremy Gray et al, *Mapping the DNA: Using Consumer Insights to Unlock the Potential of Financial Inclusion* (2016) note 6 at 10, available at https://cenfri.org/wp-content/uploads/2017/02/MAP-global-insight-note-6_Mapping-the-DNA_Cenfri-FinMark-Trust-UNCDF_2016.pdf, accessed on 21 April 2020.

39 Ibid at 13.

40 Desmond Rudman & Sima Ostrovsky, *Dominance Test: A Superfluous Jurisdictional Hurdle?* (2010) at 8, available at http://www.compcom.co.za/wp-content/uploads/2014/09/article-dominance-test.pdf, accessed on 9 June 2018.

41 Chris Doyle, Market Definition and Dominance (2002) at 9, available at https://www.itu.int/osg/spu/ni/competition/Presentations/Market%20Definition%20-CDoyle.pdf, accessed on 23 June 2018.

42 Ibid at 10.

43 Desmond Rudman & Sima Ostrovsky note 40 at 8.

44 Federal Competition and Consumer Protection Act 71 of 2018.

45 Ibid.

46 Concurrences, *Glossary of Competition Terms: Dominant Position*, available at https://www.concurrences.com/en/glossary/dominance-notion, accessed on 21 July 2020.

47 Federal Competition and Consumer Protection Act 72(3) of 2018.

48 MTEL was exempt from paying the $285 million licence fees imposed on the other competitors by inheriting NITEL's licence. See Samson Akintaro, Goodbye NITEL … Hello! NTEL: New Network Operator Raises Broadband Hope, (2015), available at https://ittelecomdigest.com/goodbye-nitelhello-nte, accessed on 27 June 2018.

49 Ibid.

50 Ibid.

51 Federal Competition and Consumer Protection Act 72(2) of 2018.

52 Ibid at 59(2).

53 Ibid at 60.

54 Marc Bourreau & Tommaso Valletti, *Enabling Digital Financial Inclusion through Improvements in Competition and Interoperability: What Works and What Doesn't*? at 16, available at https://www.researchgate.net/publication/284124402_Enabling_Digital_Financial_Inclusion_through_Improvements_in_Competition_and_Interoperability_What_Works_and_What_Doesn't, accessed on 21 July 2020.

55 See Stijn Claessens & Liliana Rojas-Suarez, *Financial Regulations for Improving Financial Inclusion* (2016) at 11, available at https://www.cgdev.org/sites/default/files/CGD-financial-regulation-task-force-report-2016.pdf, accessed on 17 July 2018.

56 Rafe Mazer & Philip Rowan, *Competition in Mobile Financial Services: Lessons from Kenya and Tanzania* (2016) at 20, available at http://www.cgap.org/sites/default/files/Working-Paper-Competition-in-MFS-Kenya-Tanzania-Jan-2016.pdf, accessed on 16 May 2018 20.

57 Ibid.
58 Rory Macmillan note 24 at 44–5.
59 Stijn Claessens & Liliana Rojas-Suarez note 55 at xvi and xii.
60 Rory Macmillan note 24 at 43.
61 Ibid
62 Ibid at 44.
63 Ivo Jenik and Kate Lauer, *Regulatory Sandboxes and Financial Inclusion* (2017) at 1, available at https://www.cgap.org/sites/default/files/Working-Paper-Regulatory-Sandboxes-Oct-2017.pdf, accessed on 21 July 2020.
64 Sustainable and Inclusive DFS *Innovation Sandboxes as a Tool for Driving Financial Inclusion in Nigeria. How Regulators can Foster Innovation without Destabilising the Entire Financial Services Ecosystem* (2017), available at https://medium.com/@SustainableDFS/innovation-sandboxes-as-a-tool-for-driving-financial-inclusion-in-nigeria-bdb26761944e, accessed on 20 June 2018.
65 Ibid.
66 Deloitte, *Regulatory Sandbox: Making India a Global Fintech Hub* (2017) at 6, available at https://www2.deloitte.com/content/dam/Deloitte/in/Documents/technology-media-telecommunications/in-tmt-fintech-regulatory-sandbox-web.pdf, accessed on 13 July 2019.
67 Ibid at 9.
68 Ibid.
69 Ivo Jenik, *Regulatory Sandboxes: Potential for Financial Inclusion?* (2017), available at http://www.cgap.org/blog/regulatory-sandboxes-potential-financial-inclusion, accessed on 23 June 2018.
70 Deloitte, *Regulatory Sandbox: Making India a Global Fintech Hub* note 66 at 9 and 16.
71 Khushboo Agarwal, Playing in the regulatory sandbox' (2018), *New York University Journal of Law & Business*, available at https://www.nyujlb.org/single-post/2018/01/08/Playing-in-the-Regulatory-Sandbox, accessed on 21 June 2018.
72 Mondato, *The Regulatory Sandbox* (2016), available at http://blog.mondato.com/the-regulatory-sandbox/, accessed on 7 July 2018.
73 Sue McLean, *UK: FCA's Regulatory Sandbox – Lessons Learnt* (2017), available at http://www.mondaq.com/uk/x/643458/fin+tech/FCAs+Regulatory+Sandbox+Lessons+Learnt, accessed on 17 June 2018. See also Chang-Hsien Tsai & Kuan-Jung Peng, 'The fintech revolution and financial regulation: The case of online supply chain financing' (2017), *Asian Journal of Law and Society*, 4, (1) at 127–8. See also Australian Securities and Investment Commission, *Regulatory Sandbox*, available at https://asic.gov.au/for-business/your-business/innovation-hub/regulatory-sandbox/, accessed on 27 February 2019 and Monetary Authority of Singapore, *FinTech Regulatory Sandbox*, available at http://www.mas.gov.sg/Singapore-Financial-Centre/Smart-Financial-Centre/FinTech-Regulatory-Sandbox.aspx, accessed on 18 April 2019.
74 Sue McLean note 73.
75 Ivo Jenik note 69.
76 Khushboo Agarwal note 71.
77 Herbert Smith Freehills, *Hong Kong Launches Regulatory Sandbox in Wake of Developments in Australia, Malaysia, Singapore, and the UK* (2016), available at https://sites-herbertsmithfreehills.vuturevx.com/103/12430/landing-pages/2016.09.30-apac-fintech-briefing.pdf, accessed on 13 July 2018.
78 Babajide Komolafe, 'CBN, NIBSS unveil regulatory sandbox to empower fintechs' 26 March 2018, *Vanguard,* available at https://www.vanguardngr.com/2018/03/cbn-nibss-unveil-regulatory-sandbox-to-empower-fintechs/, accessed on 13 July 2018.

79 Ibid.
80 Ivo Jenik 69.
81 Mimi Zhou, *Law and Autonomous Systems Series: Innovation without Authorisation? The Regulatory 'Black Box of Cryptocurrencies in China'*, 2018, available at https://www.law.ox.ac.uk/business-law-blog/blog/2018/04/law-and-autonomous-systems-series-innovation-without-authorisation, accessed on 18 April 2019.
82 Sue McLean note 73.

4 Dislodging the Barriers to Accessing Financial Services in Nigeria

4.1 Introduction

Globally, the push for financial inclusion has resulted in the decline in exclusion figures from 2.5 billion in 2014 to 1.7 billion in 2017 and 1.4 billion in 2021, led by digital technology and mobile money.[1] Commencing in 2015 and continuing into 2016, Nigeria witnessed an economic recession due to the reduction in global oil revenue which wielded a negative effect on household consumption, increased inflation and reduced the purchasing power of the populace.[2] Furthermore, the uprising in North-East Nigeria resulted in the closure of some financial institutions and a general decrease in patronage of banking services due to security concerns.[3] North-Central states such as Abuja, witnessed a significant decline in the usage of financial institutions as insufficient funds hardly justified using a bank account.[4] Many of the bottom-of-the-pyramid (BOP) population, having no means to cushion against these socio-economic shocks, had to resort to saving at home.[5]

The financial exclusion was as high as 41.6 per cent in 2016; the majority being women, youth aged 18 to 25, rural dwellers and residents of the Northwest and Northeast geo-political zones.[6] Financial exclusion in these two zones was as high as 70 and 62 per cent, respectively, and both regions made up 56.6 per cent of the total national exclusion.[7] Excluded persons in these regions are mainly debarred from accessing finance due to religious and cultural barriers, high unemployment rate, the lack of security due to the insurgency, the use of informal financial services and exclusion by profit-driven finance providers.[8]

The goal of the CBN in carrying out the NFIS 2018 refresh was therefore to address the challenges in the 2012 strategy and effectively reduce financial exclusion.[9] By reviewing the NFIS, the bank has committed itself to creating an enabling environment for innovation, expanding finance models and deepening inclusion through tailored offerings, DFS and digitised government payments.[10] The efforts of the CBN have been complemented by improvement in the macroeconomic environment including monetary, financial and exchange rate stability which could drive financial inclusion, especially among

DOI: 10.4324/9781003217886-4

underserved populations.[11] It is expected that this progressive state of affairs will influence positively on financial inclusion before long.

In this chapter, the barriers to accessing finance in Nigeria are examined. The seven core barriers to accessing finance identified by the Enhancing Financial Innovation and Access (EFInA) 2018 survey are discussed. These barriers include- irregular income, unemployment, distance to banks, the complexity of documentation, cost of accessing finance, cash preference, literacy and lack of an identity document.

4.2 Barriers to financial inclusion in Nigeria

Through the years, surveys by EFInA have shown a trend in the barriers to finance. Notably, recurrent barriers to accessing finance in Nigeria are irregular income and unemployment, distance to banks, the complexity of documentation, the cost of accessing finance or reaching a bank, cash preference, literacy and lack of an identity document to open an account.[12] While some of these barriers affect access, others affect usage. Access barriers are those that debar people from opening accounts for reasons such as prohibitive costs or stringent eligibility requirements. For instance, irregular income and the lack of employment may not justify owning an account, especially where the cost of banking is considered to be too expensive. Additionally, the lack of required documentation for opening an account serves as an access barrier.

Usage barriers such as financial illiteracy limit the understanding of financial products, terms of use and the technical skills to utilise providers' platforms, including digital channels. Distance can equally serve as a usage barrier where financial access points are remotely located and users are not keen on using digital platforms to transact. These barriers can also be shared. For example, lack of employment, irregular income and cost of banking can both debar people from opening and using an account. In other words, these constitute both access and usage barriers. The same applies to financial illiteracy, inadequate digital sophistication and cash preference. These barriers are discussed below.

4.2.1 Irregular income and unemployment

There is a strong link between irregular income, unemployment and financial exclusion. The EFInA study shows that irregular income, lack of access and unemployment all constitute major hindrances to the use of deposit money banks.[13] Persons at the bottom-of-the-pyramid have been shown to be the most affected by unemployment and a reduced disposable income.[14] Unemployment rate was 33.3 per cent as of the fourth quarter of 2020 according to the National Bureau of Statistics.[15]

Furthermore, as noted earlier, North-Central states such as Abuja and Niger, have witnessed a reduction in the banked segment as well as an increase in the excluded segment as decreasing consumer incomes failed to justify the continued patronage of financial institutions.[16] Similarly, in Kano and Jigawa, unemployment occasioned by massive job losses and inflation has led many without sufficient income to abandon existing accounts.[17] This spate of account abandonment resulting from unemployment and the lack of funds is understandable because where funds are insufficient to fulfil essential personal and household needs such as food, shelter and energy, the chances of having leftover funds to bank is slim.

Therefore, to adequately serve the excluded, there is a need to develop financial products that match the economic circumstances of specific users. Since excluded populations already grapple with poverty, unemployment and, in general, survival and marginal economic activities, it is important to design tailored products such as savings, micro pension and insurance offered through digital and non-digital means.[18] For example, the predominantly agrarian rural population in Nigeria could be served better by adapting products that mirror seasonal needs. Agriculture (comprising crop production, livestock, forestry and fishing), contributed 26.57 per cent to the nominal GDP and 29.9 per cent to the overall GDP in Q3 2021.[19] Targeted financial inclusion initiatives in the agricultural sector could therefore help and include economically disadvantaged farmers.

4.2.2 Cost of financial services

Another major barrier to accessing finance is cost. A total of 15 per cent of adults in Nigeria do not have financial access because it costs too much and another 8 per cent cite that it is too expensive to own a bank account while a further 5 per cent assert that charges are too high.[20] Cost relates not just to the charges imposed by providers but also to the cost of transportation and other inconveniences associated with getting to a bank. The EFInA survey reveals that while bank charges do not immediately lead to a drop in exclusion figures, mandatory charges for transactions largely hinder usage of products and result in the migration to alternative sources of finance.[21] Banks in Nigeria apply various charges to consumers ranging from third-party transfers and current account maintenance fees to ATM charges.[22] In practice, some banks still insist on a minimum balance (about ₦1,000 Nigerian naira) to be maintained on accounts and stipulate minimum account opening amounts. E-wallet users still earn no interest and third-party cash withdrawal is limited to ₦150,000 daily.[23]

In relation to the charges imposed by the regulator for financial services as contained in the CBN Guide to Bank Charges 2019, rates are in some cases still prohibitive even though a downward review was done to ameliorate the hardship of the 2017 version. The explanation by the Central Bank that these charges were necessary as cost recovery of banking services has also been criticised as writers argue that cost recovery needs to be holistic and leveraged across other banking services to lower customer charges.[24] Again, although these charges were beneficial to government agencies and financial services providers, poor customers could potentially withdraw funds from the formal financial sector to avoid costs.[25]

In 2016, as revealed by the EFInA study, the stamp duty fee, current account maintenance fee, ATM withdrawal charge and withholding tax charged on fixed deposits impacted negatively on customer acquisition, retention and experience.[26] This is reflected in statistics for the following year which reveal that four commercial banks, namely Zenith Bank Plc, Guaranty Trust Bank Plc, Access Bank Plc and United Bank for Africa Plc generated about ₦49 billion from clients as maintenance charges on savings, current and term deposit accounts.[27] Access Bank earned ₦6.45 billion; Zenith earned ₦27.7 billion; GTBank got ₦9.4 billion; and UBA charged ₦5.4 billion in addition to a ₦1 billion commission on turnover.[28] This does not come as a surprise as GTB, for instance, was charging clients ₦50 commission plus ₦2.50 VAT per fund transfer to other banks' accounts and ₦20 for same bank transfers.[29]

The argument that some of these costs such as ATM charges are necessary to migrate to digital banking does not take into account the fact that banks, like other companies, need to spend on technological upgrades to stay abreast of competition and market innovations. This cost of going digital should not warrant a prerogative to impose digitalisation on clients. To support this view some writers complain that the practice of imposing ATM charges is akin to billing clients for self-service even though this reduces the strain on bank staff in a banking hall.[30]

Furthermore, it is notable that the fact that bank clients are permitted to make three withdrawals per month free of charge is not satisfactory as this only encourages bulk withdrawals and increases the propensity for cash dependency contrary to the cashless Nigeria initiative being canvassed by the CBN. Even the argument that one can withdraw from one's own bank ATM free of charge defeats the purpose of interoperability as bank clients should be able to withdraw from the most conveniently accessible ATM, irrespective of provider. Encouraging interoperability can also bring benefits to excluded populations that reside in communities served only by a few banks. Again, banks would be incentivised to deploy banking services to un-served and under-served areas in the interest of financial inclusion if the opportunity to maximise profit by serving a wide range of clientele exists.

The exhortation of the Nigerian Senate to banks to suspend ATM maintenance charges and enable people to withdraw as much as ₦40,000 has not been heeded by some banks as many still peg withdrawals to as little as ₦10,000 to 20,000.[31] This low maximum means that customers quickly reach the number of withdrawals limit and then have to pay charges or struggle to withdraw from own bank despite the inconveniences to avoid charges. Consequently, it is not an uncommon sight to observe long ATM queues at banks as customers try to avoid withdrawal charges by sticking to banks they operate accounts in spite of the proximity of other banks, thereby demonstrating the burden of cost on the populace.

The CBN Guide to Bank Charges 2019 ushered in the reduction of some bank charges and the removal of others. Fewer charges are now imposed on clients.[32] For instance, the ₦50 monthly charge on accounts is now charged at ₦50 per quarter in the 2019 guide and charges for third-party transfers are now tiered, starting at ₦10 for transactions below ₦5,000 to ₦50 for charges above ₦50,000.[33] ATM charges have equally been reduced to ₦35 in the 2019 guide from ₦65 in the 2017 guide after the third withdrawal in other banks in a month.[34] According to the Guide, current account maintenance fee formerly charged at ₦1 per ₦1,000 is now negotiable subject to a maximum of ₦1,000. Monthly current and savings accounts charges of ₦50 have been reduced to ₦50 quarterly maintenance fee only for bank cards. Charges for current accounts are exempt.

In relation to debit and credit card issuance and replacement which was ₦1,000 in addition to negotiable interest charge, the 2019 revision has set a once-only charge of ₦1,000 irrespective of card type whether regular or premium card. Digitised government payment of salaries and dividends charged in 2017 at ₦50 per beneficiary has now been removed. Lastly, mandatory SMS alerts set at ₦50 per SMS have been revised. Cost recovery is charged on customer-induced transactions while bank-induced transactions can no longer be charged to customers.

4.2.3 Illiteracy

Lack of the needed level of literacy to use financial services debars 10 per cent of the adult population from accessing finance.[35] In general, the figures for educational levels in the country are still growing. About 29.0 per cent of respondents to the CBN baseline survey have no formal education and only 32.5 per cent have basic education, meaning that at least half of the adult population had no or only basic education with a 10 per cent gender gap in favour of men.[36] In terms of financial skills, men with basic literacy and numeracy skills have a better probability of being banked and accessing formal finance than women.[37]

Presently, knowledge about financial services such as current and savings accounts, pension and insurance is still low. From a digital finance perspective, it is observed that awareness of micro pension plans, micro insurance, and mobile money are still low at eight, 12 and 22 per cent, respectively.[38] In general, not knowing about financial services as well as access to these services has been indicated as the greatest barrier to adopting mobile money in the country.[39] Even with a high national mobile penetration rate of 75 per cent for telephone subscribers, mobile money usage is still low.[40] More so, many users happen to be educated urban dwellers while this remains largely out of the reach of the excluded class. Statistically, about 82 per cent of the mobile money users in Nigeria are urban dwellers who already have accounts at deposit money banks and are educated beyond the secondary school level with 74 per cent of this population having a university and post-university degree.[41]

This clearly indicates that much work is needed to bring knowledge of digital financial products to the excluded class as the lack of knowledge about these services is still a huge bar to usage. Accordingly, digital finance has not been able to achieve its full potential and only a few products specifically target excluded groups.[42]

On a positive note, however, there are reassuring signs of the advancement of digital financial inclusion in Nigeria. For instance, though adoption of mobile money services is still low, usage level is transitioning from mainly airtime purchases to remittances.[43] Again, increasing consumer confidence, trust and knowledge of utilising the digital channels is giving rise to a corresponding increase in transaction value and volume on different DFS channels including POS, mobile, ATM and Internet with ATM being the most frequently used channel.[44]

In relation to financial capability, participants of the baseline survey demonstrate an impressive level of competence in relation to budgeting. About 60 per cent of the adult population indicated that they have a personal or household budget.[45] Short-term planning was also impressive, as about 90.9 per cent always or mostly keep to budget.[46] Not having a budget for many was as a result of income pressures and not poor planning or over-spending.[47] Two-thirds of Nigerian adults have devised financial goals in the long-term and 92 per cent indicate plans to achieve these goals including retirement strategies (97.8 per cent) and strategies for dependent's future (83 per cent) though above half of the respondents have concerns that these plans may not be sufficient.[48] Interestingly, most respondents were willing to obtain information or be trained on planning and budgeting in the long-term, insurance and management of risks as well as knowledge of financial products and services.[49]

There is likewise an appreciable level of competence in numerical skills with many respondents providing correct answers to basic addition, subtraction, division and multiplication.[50] According to the study, 72.9 per cent and 72.7 per cent are proficient in addition and subtraction, respectively.[51] The survey also shows an equally impressive rate at 70.8 per cent and 69.8 per cent for division and multiplication.[52] In terms of language skills, the baseline survey reveals varying levels of competence in the speaking and reading components of English and other local languages, emphasising the opportunity to incorporate local language to further financial education initiatives.[53] According to the Lagos Business School's State of the Market Report, one's ability to communicate in other indigenous tongues is an additional indication of literacy.[54]

Some skills, however, still need to be learned. It has been observed that skills in keeping track of income are not impressive, as 53.4 per cent of adult Nigerians could not tell or could only estimate their spending in the previous week and as much as 50.8 per cent could not tell or estimate their daily spending.[55] Also, respondents did not have a risk management strategy; as 58 per cent have not devised plans for large unforeseen expenses, even though about half worried about the occurrence of these expenses.[56] Again, respondents approach mainly family and friends (61.1 per cent), religious leaders (9.5 per cent) and their children (9.4 per cent) for financial advice while only

4.3 per cent approach a finance provider office or websites or have a personal tax or financial advisor.[57]

Presently, 44 per cent of men compared to 56 per cent of women are excluded.[58] The Lagos Business School State of the Market Report notes that gender bias around financial inclusion needs to be addressed and that 'women will only need targeted financial literacy skills and the right financial products to bring them into the formal financial system'.[59] The CBN equally notes that to increase financial knowledge and capability across the socio-demographic populations in the country, there is a need to address the areas of concern through financial education interventions.[60] One such initiative is the introduction of financial literacy to the school curriculum and the engagement of national youth corps members as peer educators to drive literacy.[61] The CBN has also introduced the national financial literacy framework 2015 which among other things is intended to equip Nigerians with the skillset to choose from a growing and increasingly sophisticated and complex array of new financial services and reduce risk exposure.[62]

These initiatives need to be diversified as methods that work for one segment of the population may not be fitting for another. For instance, the CBN Baseline survey finds that 'upper middle income and wealthy consumers with formal education need information on advanced financial products such as insurance, the capital market and electronic banking and are better reached using print media, websites, radio, workplace programmes, seminars, in-branch flyers and audio-visual'.[63] According to the survey, rural farmer segments, on the other hand, being less likely educated could find it more useful to obtain information on microfinance, savings and credit that is customised to agricultural risk and presented on media such as radio, TV and mobile phones.[64] In summary, in conceptualising initiatives for the excluded, peculiar needs of each class should serve as a driving force.

4.2.4 Distance

Distance to banks affects 27 per cent of adult Nigerians according to the EFInA 2020 survey.[65] Significantly, rural users unlike their urban counterparts grapple with non-proximity to banks and thus have to make long journeys to reach a financial access point. Finance providers tend to locate branches in urban centres where profits seem more likely. Banking services are sparse in some rural areas and many rural adults are more likely to rely exclusively on informal financial services than urban dwellers.[66] While 66 per cent of urban dwellers are banked, 34 per cent in the rural areas are banked and excluded population show a significant contrast at 20 and 44 per cent, respectively.[67] Again, 81 per cent of the excluded are rural compared to an urban exclusion rate of 19 per cent.[68] This stark variance in urban/rural financial inclusion buttresses a missed opportunity to mop up some funds circulating in informal unregulated sectors and under mattresses in communities unserved by banks in some rural communities.

As the CBN does not insist on the location of bank branches, many urban neighbourhoods in Nigeria are brimming with the presence of banks, while rural dwellers that are most in need of financial inclusion initiatives have to cover significant distances to access a simple banking service. Significantly, for an adult population of 106 million (18 years and above), roughly two-thirds, accounting for 70 million adults, reside in rural areas.[69] To curb this, regulators in other jurisdictions are introducing policies that mandate a more encompassing geographical distribution of bank branches as practised in South Africa, the use of agent banking in Brazil and the deployment of mobile money agents in Kenya. These practices are discussed in the next section in a Nigerian context.

4.2.4.1 Geographical spread of financial access points

A financial access point is defined as 'a regulated access point where cash-in (including deposits) and cash-out transactions are performed and includes traditional bank branches, agents of regulated entities and automated teller machines (ATMs)'.[70] To achieve financial inclusion it is important to have a strong network of financial access points comprising commercial bank branches, microfinance bank branches, ATMs, point-of-sales (POS) terminals, agent banking outlets and mobile money agents.[71]

The number of financial access points across Nigeria is still low, particularly in rural areas where informal financial services predominate.[72] Rural exclusion is glaring with about 81 per cent of the rural population being excluded compared to 19 per cent of the urban population and only roughly 38 per cent of adults in rural areas live in close proximity to a financial access point.[73] Of this segment, 84 per cent are financial services agents, 4 and 7 per cent are bank branches and other FSPs, respectively, while MNOs account for 13 per cent.[74]

Available data also demonstrate more widespread distribution of financial services in the South and higher figures for financial exclusion in the North. In the South-West and South-East, exclusion is as low as 17 and 26 per cent compared to the North-West and North-East at 68 and 50 per cent, respectively.[75] In the South-South and North-Central, exclusion stands at 26 per cent.[76] The North which has been ravaged in recent years by insurgency, leading to the massive closure of banks and invariably increasing the distance to the remaining ones, is lagging behind in terms of inclusion rates. In the North-West, for instance, about 68 per cent of the populace does not have access to finance and in 2016 alone, financial exclusion increased by 12 per cent in three states including Kano, Jigawa and Kebbi.[77] In contrast, the South-West states have already achieved the 2012 NFIS target of reducing exclusion by 20 per cent by 2020.[78]

With the review of the NFIS in 2018, the CBN has asked banks to extend mini-branch networks to reach underserved customers but this is still fraught with concerns over the necessary capital outlay to comply with this mandate.[79]

The CBN has also conducted a geospatial mapping survey of the finance sector to provide a visual representation of active and inactive financial access points as an indication to determine suitable places to locate services.[80] It is necessary to deploy finance, particularly with the use of DFS to rural areas.[81]

4.2.4.2 Agent banking/network

Agent banking is 'the provision of financial services to customers by a third party (agent) on behalf of a licensed deposit-taking financial institution or mobile money operator (principal)'.[82] Since 2013, the CBN has held out agent banking as one panacea for financial exclusion in Nigeria. In 2013, the CBN initiated the Guidelines for the Regulation of Agent Banking and Agent Banking Relationships and subsequently the Regulatory Framework for Licensing Super-Agents in Nigeria. Super-Agents are expected to facilitate the deployment of finance by banks and other regulated providers of finance to unserved and underserved communities.[83] The use of super-agents has been proposed by the CBN to drive agent recruitment on a large scale and scale-up these services in rural and peri-urban areas, manage liquidity and help resolve customer complaints timely.[84]

Additionally, the CBN in conjunction with the bankers' committee launched the shared agent network expansion facility (SANEF) to drive nationwide agent banking growth and achieve the target of deploying 476 agents for every 100,000 adults.[85] Member banks have agreed to merge resources to rollout new financial access points nationwide and improve financial inclusion, especially in the North where there are about 40 million unserved low-income Nigerians.[86]

Agent networks hold the potential to aid liquidity management by facilitating cash-in-cash-out (CICO). Agents bring financial services closer to users and reduce the distance and cost of travelling to financial access points. Agent banking equally helps providers to build brand awareness, educate customers on finance and improve users' confidence in the service.[87]

In spite of these projected positive benefits, agent banking has been unable to scale up in Nigeria. Some reasons for the low level of agent banking activities are indicated to include inadequate capital, difficulty in managing liquidity, unattractive commissions and return on investment, insufficient knowledge of DFS, poor patronage, inadequate network connectivity leading to frequent transaction downtimes and complex sign-up documentation.[88]

Agents are also impeded by stringent entry conditions. An applicant for an agent banking licence has to be a company doing legitimate business for at least 12 months and must furnish the CBN with information regarding the name and contact address of the company as well as documentary evidence of company registration and the qualifying criteria for engaging agents.[89] An eligible agent can be a limited liability company, sole proprietorship, partnership, cooperative society, public entity and trust.[90] Faith-based, non-profits, educational institutions or bureau-de-change which by law are not allowed to make a profit must first seek consent before offering agent banking services.[91]

Like the agent banking requirements, super-agents applications to the CBN must be accompanied by documentary evidence such as board approval, certificate of incorporation, company profile and contact information, memorandum and articles of association, shareholding structure, return on allotment of shares, particulars of Directors, curriculum vitae of board and management of company and feasibility Report.[92] Applicants must also be registered by the CAC for at least 12 months and must have a minimum shareholders' fund of ₦50 million and 50 agents.[93] This magnitude of requirements by the CBN can deter prospective market entrants from applying for the license.

Another limiting factor for agent banking is the fact that the agent banking guidelines mandate financial institutions intending to employ the use of agents to carry out due diligence on agents and ensure compliance with the guidelines.[94] Both the Guidelines for the Regulation Agent Banking and Agent Banking Relationships in Nigeria 2013 and the Regulatory Framework for Licensing Super-Agents' 2014 place the responsibility for monitoring and supervising the activities of the agents in relation to stipulated thresholds on the principal.[95] In other words, financial institutions and super-agents deploying agent networks are vicariously liable for the acts of these agents. This could, however, be discouraging especially since, by the provisions of the guidelines, financial institutions cannot demand exclusivity of agents. For instance, Guideline 7 of the Guidelines for the Regulation of Agent Banking and Agent Banking Relationships 2013 permits agents to work for as many banks as possible to open the market to interoperability and competition.

Following the recent NFIS amendment, the CBN has decided to reverse the rule on agent exclusivity.[96] This move should incentivise the recruitment and training of agents and reduce the trend of free-riding where first-mover financial institutions that bear the burden of training agents, enjoy no advantages in the services of these agents but are rather compelled to share with other providers without financial compensation.

But agent exclusivity is not the global norm in view of the difficulty of achieving universality of services where individual agents serve single providers with the potential to duplicate agent services in some areas and cause slow entry into others. A better solution could be to have a central agent training and recruitment fund sponsored by all banks. Certified agents can thus set up shop in their local communities and provide any-to-any services across all financial institutions to clients. The Nigerian interbank settlement system and the Bank Verification Number exercise are two of the successfully run centrally funded collaborations by the bankers' committee and agent training can also be like modelled.

A further limiting factor to agent banking is the financial reward paid to agents. The Guidelines on Agent Banking and Agent Banking Regulations 2013 stipulate the sharing formula for interchange fees between the NIBSS, issuer, acquirer, agent and super-agent. Cash-in transactions are deemed to be free to encourage client patronage but a minimum interchange fee of ₦50 to ₦100 is charged for inter-scheme cash-out transactions to incentivise agents.[97] Agents are observed to overcharge customers with attendant negative effects on adoption and usage of financial services.[98] This could be in a bid to compensate for low fees. Better pricing structures are therefore needed. The CBN has also committed to developing mechanisms to help agents in detecting and curbing fraud by engaging in agent training.[99]

Also discouraging is the fact that agents are restricted to some permissible activities. Guideline 6.2 of the Guidelines on Mobile Money in Nigeria 2015 permits activities such as accepting deposits and withdrawal of cash, bill payments, fund transfers, balance enquiry and printing of mini-statements, cash payout and loan repayment, request and collection of cash books or bank correspondence and payment of retirement benefits and salaries.[100]

Agents are prohibited from operating and carrying out transactions when there is a communication failure with the financial institution or where a receipt and acknowledgement of transaction cannot be generated.[101] Agents are not also permitted to open accounts, charge customers fees, give guarantees, undertake cheque deposit and encashment, provide cash advances or offer any banking services not sanctioned by the financial institution.[102] The prohibition from opening accounts is particularly worrisome as this misses the opportunity to bring banking services to remote areas lacking access points. This also implies that agents only serve the already banked population without any room to accommodate the excluded.

The potential for agent banking to usher gains such as reducing distance, costs, inconvenience and achieving simpler access to financial services which have been witnessed in other jurisdictions has therefore not been felt by the excluded population in Nigeria. As trusting agents is still a hurdle, it is important to imbibe practices that improve consumer confidence, particularly in rural areas. In this regard, agents can 'create viable agent distribution channels by on-boarding trusted agents with a long-term view of the venture'.[103] Explaining financial offerings to users in their local language or demonstrating an understanding of their culture and perception towards finance holds high prospects for adoption and usage. This was a major driving factor for Mpesa in Kenya where effective agent network management was instrumental to driving usage.[104]

Additionally, adequate agent distribution should also be strategically offered to areas in need of the service to avoid flooding some markets with too many agents who are then unable to make a profit, to the disadvantage of customers.[105] The Shared Agent Network Expansion Facility (SANEF) initiated by the CBN, banks, mobile money operators and super-agents are expected to employ 'a network of 500,000 agents to offer basic financial services including cash-in-cash-out, fund transfers, bill payments, airtime sales, Bank Verification Number enrolment services and government payments'.[106] It is hoped that these efforts will culminate in deepening financial inclusion through a more effective agent banking model.

4.2.5 Cash preference

Cash remains the predominant means of payment in Nigeria.[107] Even though the use of POS and USSD for remittances and bill payments are helping to reduce cash dependency, cash still remains king as shown below in the empirical study in Chapter 5. This is especially so in the informal sector and in small-scale retail transactions; indeed, it would sound strange to ask a petty trader in a Nigerian market to accept digital payment for low-cost wares or non-capital goods such as perishable food items – pepper, vegetables, locust beans.

The CBN initiated the Cashless Policy in 2012 to drive down banking costs and effectively advance the nation's monetary policy by reducing the amount of cash circulating in the economy.[108] The cashless policy was also intended to curb corruption, reduce cash within the informal economy and correct the high subsidy of cash transactions above ₦150,000 (which is incurred by 10 per cent of the population but subsidised by all).[109] For consumers, the initiative promises convenience, more low-cost and less risky options and for providers, increased access to capital, less leakage of funds and lower cash-handling costs.[110] It was projected that the government would gain in this way from more revenue from taxes, improved financial inclusion and economic development.[111]

A daily limit on cash withdrawal of ₦500,000 for individuals and ₦3,000,000 for companies was set by the bank irrespective of channel (counter, ATM and third-party cheques), subject to a cash-handling charge borne by account holders.[112] The pilot launched in Lagos State in January 2012 and in July 2013 was extended to Rivers, Anambra, Abia, Kano and Ogun states as well as the Federal Capital Territory (FCT).[113] The CBN, however, called for the suspension of the nationwide implementation of the policy in the other 30 states, 21 days after commencement.[114] Notably, the use of digital media in many settings could be impractical or expensive for some persons. For instance, roadside vendors and petty traders will hardly accept transfers or offer POS machines as payment options for small transactions. More so, the cost of these channels does not economically justify usage, particularly in the case of low-cost transactions and could serve as a deterrent.

There is a need to develop low-value products that offer small transfers conveniently without imposing an off-putting charge on users. Additionally, trust needs to be built around digital payment platforms including POS devices and ATMs to discourage cash dependency. Building efficiencies around ICT infrastructure, driving digital literacy, reducing Internet data pricing and ensuring access to low-cost gadgets are also important. Furthermore, there should be clear information on financial products and redress mechanisms that offer consumers multiple channels to make complaints and obtain reliefs including for small claims.

The failure to be intentional about achieving a paradigm shift from the present prevalence of cash could slow the prospect of achieving a completely cashless society in the near future. This is especially so as cash preference has been found to decrease the use of formal finance as typified in Nigeria where even though DFS is growing, cash remains the preferred medium of transacting.[115] Measures such as the cashless policy initiative, put in place by the CBN which are to redress cash dependency nationwide have not progressed as expected. The CBN, therefore, has a significant amount of work to do both in lowering the cost of using digital channels of finance and changing mindsets towards alternatives to cash. Whatever measures are chosen, these must prove cheaper and more efficient and convenient than cash. The value provided by alternatives to cash must offer superior value to displace cash. Otherwise, from a consumer perspective, what is the point of going digital?

4.2.6 Identification documentation

The lack of identification documentation (ID) is another barrier to financial inclusion in Nigeria. There are four main ID documents required by banks in Nigeria to open accounts, namely, the National Identity Number (NIN) card, permanent voter card, driver's licence and international passport. These documents are assigned by different government agencies, which apply varying rules. The international passport is mostly sought by persons who intend to travel abroad while the driver's licence is mainly applied for by persons who either have cars or can drive. A fee for these documents is charged to applicants. Since this text focuses on financially excluded persons who are often at the bottom-of-the-pyramid, only the NIN and voter cards will be considered in this section. This is because these documents can be obtained free of charge and are less prohibitive to obtain by the excluded compared to the other two above.

4.2.6.1 The National Identification Number

In Nigeria, the body responsible for assigning the NIN is the National Identification Management Commission (NIMC). This agency was instituted by the Federal Government in 2007 to set up a comprehensive national identification database of citizens and permanent residents and register citizens and lawful residents on the national identity database.[116]

To assign the NIN, the authority collects information on demographic data, fingerprints and other biometrics, head-to-shoulder facial picture and digital signature and afterwards, issues a chip-readable general multipurpose card (GMPC).[117] The 11-digit identification number becomes for its owner, a foundational piece of identification to access various forms of services including obtaining a driver's licence, applying for visas, accessing the National

Health Insurance scheme and for bank transactions.[118] The NIN can also be used to pay taxes, access pension and government welfare and dealing in land transactions.[119]

The NIMC Act 2007 makes it an offence to perform any of the above-listed acts without an NIN and offenders are liable to a fine of not less than ₦50,000 or imprisonment for not less than 6 months for an individual offender and in the case of a corporate offender, a fine of not less than ₦1,000,000 for the corporate body with an additional ₦1,000,000 charged to the chief executive officer, line manager or any other officer deemed to be guilty.[120]

However, with 805 enrolment centres in 556 Local Government Areas (LGAs) and the additional use of mobile vans, the commission has been able to register 82.73 million Nigerians of the 106 million adults.[121] One trend that could be responsible for this low number of registered users is the time and inconvenience it takes to obtain the card. Besides the fact that some people have to travel a significant distance to reach designated registration centres (since some local governments are only served by one registration centre), users also need to make repeat visits and wait a significant amount of time to finally obtain a permanent GMPC.[122]

On the first visit, applicants are registered in the database and asked to return in about one to five working days after which the initial NIN slip is printed, while the e-ID card is issued after a month.[123] These repeat visits put a strain on the excluded and could be a reason for the abandonment of the process halfway by some applicants. Significantly, some LGAs have no enrolment centres and others are only served by one centre.[124] This means that applicants from several communities, towns and villages have to queue up to get registered. There is no doubt that many Nigerians will find it rather off-putting to travel significant distances to get registered.

On a positive note, however, the NIMC is harmonising and integrating the commission's data with that of other agencies across Nigeria including the biometric verification number data with already evident results.[125] In four years of the harmonisation exercise, the number of registered persons grew from 7 million in 2015 to 30 million in 2017 and presently 77 115 343 million.[126] The NIMC projects universal registration in the central database by 2025.[127] To achieve this, 100 million Nigerians will have to be registered in the next three to five years, meaning a monthly enrolment rate of 2.5 million people, a feat which the NIMC states is already being attained at the present record of 2.6 million persons monthly.[128]

4.2.6.2 Permanent voter card

The Independent National Electoral Commission (INEC) is the body responsible for registering and issuing voter cards in Nigeria.[129] Applicants are first issued the temporary voter cards and afterwards, the permanent voter cards (PVC). This agency was established in 1999 to organise elections into various political offices in the country, register and monitor the activities of political parties, register persons qualified to vote, revise the register of voters and conduct voter and civic education.[130]

The PVC is used to vote at elections and protects user information from unauthorised access by only allowing access via designated card readers.[131] The PVC is one of the identification documents requested by banks to open an account and is now accessible to more than 84 million adults registered in the commission's 119,973 polling units across local government areas in the country.[132]

This significant registration feat for an adult population the size of about 106 million can be attributed to some degree to political rallies by politicians to gain popularity among voters during national and local election seasons by lobbying for the establishment of polling units in local constituencies. As will be shown in the succeeding Chapter 5, these units are often set up to ease the process of obtaining the card and by extension increase the chances of obtaining local votes. A universal coverage is, however, still desired to ensure that everyone has access to identification. Financial literacy will also help the excluded understand how to access financial services using this identification document.

4.2.7 *Complexity of account opening*

The last barrier discussed is the complexity of opening accounts. About 11 per cent of Nigerians note that the account opening procedures put in place by financial institutions are complex.[133] While some of these complexities flow from regulatory policies, others are imposed by financial services providers. In this section, the Know-your-customer compliance and Bank Verification Number registration imposed by the CBN as well as the insistence on proof of address by providers are examined.

4.2.7.1 *Know-Your-Customer compliance*

The CBN's insistence on Know-Your-Customer compliance implemented by the Central Bank of Nigeria Introduction of Three-Tiered Know Your Customer (KYC) Requirements and its review constitutes a significant regulatory hurdle to accessing finance. Although these guidelines usher a tiered-accounting system, giving the opportunity for all without identity documents to open low- or medium-value accounts, the purpose of inclusion seems to wane by the restrictions imposed on these accounts.

The low-value account for instance is opened by providing basic information such as name, address, gender, date and place of birth, passport and phone number without the need for additional verification.[134] The medium-value account on the other hand, requires the same information as the low-value accounts but these have to be verified against records held by the NIMC, the INEC or the Federal Road Safety Commission (FRSC) depending on the document.[135] These accounts are strictly savings accounts, and transactions outside Nigeria are prohibited.[136] Again, single deposits must be kept at ₦50,000 and ₦100,000, respectively, for low- and medium-value accounts while cumulative balance at all times cannot exceed ₦300,000 and ₦500,000 for each account.[137]

Therefore, while low- and medium-value accounts are opened with limited documentation, the restrictions placed on thresholds in terms of value and volume of transactions as well as geographical limitations, diminish the quality of financial services offered to account holders. But obtaining a high-value account comes at a cost as prospective clients must present one of the four compulsory documents: voter card, driver's licence, international passport or the NIN card and at times a utility bill in addition, to evidence address.[138]

As noted above in Section 4.2.6, these compulsory documents are in some cases, especially for the first two, outside the reach of the average financially excluded person. While obtaining the voter card and NIN card is relatively simpler and cost free, the distance and inconvenience associated with getting these documents is daunting. The absence of an identity document could very well promote unsafe informal savings channels such as moneylenders and under-the-mattress savings among the excluded if left unaddressed.

4.2.7.2 Bank Verification Number

In 2014, the Bank Verification Number (BVN) was initiated by the CBN as a precondition to opening and operating any account in Nigeria. Applicants can obtain a unique number within 24 hours of presenting particulars, fingerprints and facial image.[139] The CBN states that the BVN also serves as a security measure against unauthorised access, identity theft and exposure to fraud, helps to lessen waiting time at banks and standardises efficiency of banking operations.[140] The BVN has the potential to eliminate the practice of opening accounts in fictitious names across multiple banks as biometrics is used to verify user identity.

Again, by tying all customer digital financial footprints across all banks to one number, the BVN will likely decrease financial risk in the banking sector. So far, the CBN database now houses about 54,651,086 as of 3 July 2022.[141] A limiting factor to the BVN is the non-availability to the number to the unbanked as one must have a bank account to obtain one.

4.2.7.3 Proof of address

Proof of address is usually requested by banks as a prerequisite for opening an account in Nigeria. Notably, the CBN recommends that in the interest of financial inclusion, documentation such as a letter or statement from a person in a position of authority (including solicitors, doctors, teachers and ministers of religion) can be substituted to prove the identity and address of prospective bank clients.[142] However, this has not been observed to be the practice. Banks rather obligate prospective clients to provide a utility bill from designated state water, power or waste management bodies such as the Water Corporation and the Electricity Distribution Companies (EDCs) in different states to verify their address.

But demanding utility bills as evidence of address does not necessarily provide the best evidence of residence as there is no comprehensive database to verify the claimed address against. Similarly, the insistence on the presentation of utility bills as proof of address does not consider persons who reside in regions without conventional street addressing systems such as clan-based localities which still rely on the family house addressing arrangements. Again, the specification of the utility receipts of specific corporations such as the water or waste management bodies ignores the fact that not every community is served by these entities. For instance, a number of villages in Nigeria are observed not to be connected to the national electricity grid and many communities still rely on natural water sources such as rain, wells and streams.

New technologies such as the what3words and the snoocode are currently being deployed around the world and could be good substitutes for utility receipts as proof of address. What3words, for example, 'helps locate unique addresses by dividing the world into 57 trillion 3 m × 3 m squares and assigning three random words' such as '///readily.fencepost.lumpiness' so that each square represents a definite address.[143] With offline capabilities and connection to navigation maps such as Google and Navmii, this application (app) provides a viable solution to prove user address and could additionally aid communities without conventional addresses to access healthcare, letter and parcel delivery and e-commerce at no cost to the user.[144] The Nigerian postal service has already signed up for this service and hopefully banks will also follow suit.[145]

Snoocode is a related free mobile app developed in Ghana and used in countries such as Ghana, Kenya, Gabon and Nepal that generates a six- to seven-digit alphanumeric code to identify a person's location and equally serves as an alternative address.[146] It is hoped that Nigerian banks will adopt such trends in order to lessen the burden of accessing finance for the excluded.

4.3 Conclusion

The core barriers to financial inclusion in Nigeria were identified in this chapter. These include irregular income, unemployment, illiteracy, distance, cash preference, a lack of identification documentation and the complexity of account opening. Exploring these barriers was necessary to shed some light on areas in need of regulatory consideration. Additionally, the discussion of these barriers serves as groundwork to the empirical study conducted by the author in the next chapter to understand how communities without bank presence cope with accessing finance.

Notes

1 Central Bank of Nigeria, 2017 *Annual Report National Financial Inclusion Strategy Implementation* (2018) at 13, Available at https://www.cbn.gov.ng/Out/2018/CCD/FINANCIAL%20INCLUSION.PDF, accessed on 8 July 2020. Asli Demirgüç-Kunt et al, *Financial Inclusion, Digital Payments, and Resilience in the Age of COVID-19*, 33,

available at https://openknowledge.worldbank.org/bitstream/handle/10986/37578/9781464818974.pdf, accessed on 6 July 2022.

2 Ibid at 72.

3 Ibid.

4 EFInA, *Key Findings: EFInA Access to Financial Services in Nigeria (A2F) 2016 Survey*, available at http://www.efina.org.ng/assets/A2F/2016/Key-Findings-A2F-2016.pdf at 38, accessed on 26 May 2019.

5 Ibid at 16.

6 Central Bank of Nigeria note 1 at 16.

7 Ibid.

8 Ibid.

9 Central Bank of Nigeria, *National Financial Inclusion Strategy* (Revised 2018) at 28, available at https://www.cbn.gov.ng/out/2019/ccd/national%20financial%20inclusion%20strategy.pdf, accessed on 8 July 2020.

10 Central Bank of Nigeria note 1 at 16

11 CBN Financial Inclusion Secretariat, *National Financial Inclusion Strategy 2018 Annual Report* (2019) at 8, available at https://www.cbn.gov.ng/Out/2019/CCD/Annual%20Report%202018%20Financial%20Inclusion.pdf, accessed on 13 July 2020.

12 EFInA, *Key Findings: EFInA Access to Financial Services in Nigeria (A2F) 2018 Survey*, available at https://www.efina.org.ng/wp-content/uploads/2019/01/A2F-2018-Key-Findings-11_01_19.pdf at 52, accessed on 2 May 2020. See also EFInA Access to Financial Services in Nigeria 2020 Survey, June 3, 2021 at 16, available at https://a2f.ng/wp-content/uploads/2021/06/A2F-2020-Final-Report.pdf, accessed on 19 September 2021.

13 EFInA note 4 at 52.

14 Central Bank of Nigeria op 1 at 72.

15 National Bureau of Statistics, Home, available at https://www.nigerianstat.gov.ng/, accessed on 28 February 2022.

16 EFInA note 4 at 38.

17 Ibid.

18 Ibid at 26.

19 Nigeria National Bureau of Statistics, *Nigerian Gross Domestic Product Report (Q3 2021)* (2019) at 9, available at file:///C:/Users/nnn/Downloads/GDP%20Q3%202021_Report.pdf

20 EFInA 2020 note 12 at 16.

21 EFInA, *Review of Policies That May Adversely Impact Financial Inclusion in Nigeria: Key Findings* (2016) at 15.

22 Ibid at 7.

23 Ibid.

24 Chris Enyinnaya, 'Lapses in guide to bank charges', *Guardian,* 01 January 2019, available at https://guardian.ng/opinion/lapses-in-guide-to-bank-charges/, accessed on 11 September 2019.

25 EFInA note 21 at 30.

26 Ibid at 19 and 26.

27 Oyetunji Abioye, 'Four banks earned N49bn from maintenance charges in 2017' *The Punch,* 1 April 2018, available at https://punchng.com/four-banks-earned-n49bn-from-maintenance-charges-in-2017, accessed on 12 May 2019.

28 Ibid.

29 Guaranty Trust Bank, *Instant Transfer FAQs,* available at https://www.gtbank.com/personal-banking/services/e-banking/instant-transfer-faqs, accessed on 11 September 2019.

30 Enyinnaya note 24.

31 Oladeinde Olawoyin, 'How bank charges hinder financial inclusion in Nigeria', *Premium Times,* 7 May 2019, available at https://www.premiumtimesng.com/business/financial-

inclusion/328817-how-bank-charges-hinder-financial-inclusion-in-nigeria.html, accessed on 31 August 2019.

32 Central Bank of Nigeria, *Guide to Bank Charges* (2017 and 2019).

33 Central Bank of Nigeria, *Guide to Bank Charges* (2019).

34 Central Bank of Nigeria, *Guide to Bank Charges* (2019).

35 EFInA 2020 note 12 at 16. The same was found in the 2018 survey.

36 Central Bank of Nigeria, *Nigeria Financial Literacy Baseline Survey Report* (2015) at 22.

37 Olayinka David-West, Immanuel Ovemeso, Umukoro, Olawale Ajai et al., *Digital Financial Services: State of the Market Report* 2018, available at http://sustainabledfs.lbs.edu.ng/FI-Resources/SoMR_Full_Report_2018.pdf, accessed on 16 May 2019 at 102.

38 EFInA 2020 note 12 at 19.

39 EFInA 2016 note 4 at 35.

40 Central Bank of Nigeria note 1 at 72.

41 Ibid at 55.

42 Ibid at 75.

43 EFInA 2016 note 4 at 33-4.

44 Central Bank of Nigeria note 1 at 28-9.

45 CBN Baseline survey note 36 at 34-5.

46 Ibid at 6.

47 Ibid.

48 Ibid at 7.

49 Ibid at 6.

50 Though these skills are crucial for simple financial services, arithmetic skills also need to be developed to help with calculating interest and budgeting. See Central Bank of Nigeria note 36 at 6.

51 Ibid at 6.

52 Ibid at 6.

53 Ibid at 21.

54 David-West, Olayinka, Olawale Ajai, Adedoyin Salami et al., *Digital Financial Services: State of the Market Report* (2017) at 67, available at https://www.researchgate.net/publication/322315266_Digital_Financial_Services_in_Nigeria_State_of_the_Market_Report_2017, accessed on 23 September 2019.

55 Ibid at 7.

56 Ibid.

57 Ibid at 48.

58 EFInA 2020 note 12 at 62.

59 Olayinka David-West et al note 37 at 102.

60 Central Bank of Nigeria note 42 at 1.

61 Central Bank of Nigeria note 36 1 at 14.

62 Central Bank of Nigeria, *National Financial Literacy Framework 2*.1 (2015).

63 Ibid at 4.2.

64 Ibid.

65 EFInA 2020 note 12 at 15.

66 Ibid at 53.

67 Ibid.

68 Ibid.

69 Ibid at 7.

70 EFInA, *Scoping Study on Super Agents* (2015) at 9, available at https://www.efina.org.ng/wp-content/uploads/2018/12/EFInA-Super-Agents-Scoping-Study.pdf, accessed on 14 July 2020.

71 Central Bank of Nigeria, *Financial Inclusion Newsletter* (2018) 3 (1) at 7, available at https://www.cbn.gov.ng/Out/2018/CCD/Financial%20Inclusion%20Newsletter_%20MARCH%202018_Volume%203%20Issue%201.pdf, accessed on 13 July 2020.

72 EFInA 2016 note 4 at 23.
73 Ibid at 62.
74 Ibid at 54.
75 Ibid at 56.
76 Ibid.
77 Ibid at 56. See also EFInA 2016 note 4 at 19.
78 Ibid.
79 Central Bank of Nigeria note 9 at 50.
80 CBN NFIS Secretariat, *NFIS Annual Report* (2019) note 11 at 48.
81 2017 Annual Report National Financial Inclusion Strategy Implementation note 1 at 17.
82 Central Bank of Nigeria Guidelines for the Regulation of Agent Banking and Agent Banking Relationships (2013) at 1.
83 EFInA, *Scoping Study on Super Agents* note 70 at 8.
84 Ibid at 20.
85 Central Bank of Nigeria note 9 at 24.
86 Olayinka David-West et al note 37 at 36.
87 EFInA note 70 at 6.
88 Ibid at 17.
89 CBN, *Guidelines on Agent Banking and Agent Banking Regulations* 2 of 2013.
90 Ibid at 4.1.
91 Ibid.
92 Central Bank of Nigeria, *Regulatory Framework for Licensing Super-Agents in Nigeria* (2016) 1 and 3.
93 Ibid at 2.
94 Central Bank of Nigeria note 82 at 3 and 4.
95 Ibid at 8 and 13. See also Central Bank of Nigeria note 92 at 4.
96 Central Bank of Nigeria note 9 at 59.
97 CBN note 92 at 7.
98 EFInA, *Scoping Study on Super-Agents* note 72 at 12.
99 Central Bank of Nigeria note 70 at 59.
100 Central Bank of Nigeria Guidelines on Mobile Money in Nigeria 2015 at 6.2.
101 Ibid at 6.3.
102 Ibid.
103 EFInA, *Scoping Study on Super-Agents* note 70 at 60.
104 Beth Cobert, Brigit Helms, and Doug Parker, 'Mobile money: Getting to scale in emerging markets' 4, available at https://www.mckinsey.com/~/media/McKinsey/Industries/Public%20and%20Social%20Sector/Our%20Insights/Mobile%20money%20Getting%20to%20scale%20in%20emerging%20markets/Mobile%20money%20Getting%20to%20scale%20in%20emerging%20markets.pdf, accessed on 28 February 2022.
105 EFINA, *Scoping Study on Agent Networks* note 70 at 20.
106 Central Bank of Nigeria note 9 at 8.
107 CBN, *Payment Modes in Nigeria,* available at https://www.cbn.gov.ng/Paymentsystem/Modes.asp, accessed on 16 September 2019.
108 Central Bank of Nigeria, *Cash-less Nigeria*, available at https://www.cbn.gov.ng/cashless/, accessed on 19 May 2019.
109 Ibid.
110 Ibid.
111 Ibid.
112 Ibid.
113 Ibid.
114 Oyetunji Abioye, 'CBN suspends cashless policy in 30 states', *The Punch,* 22 April 2017, available at https://punchng.com/cbn-suspends-cashless-policy-in-30-states/,

accessed on 26 June 2019. Notably, the CBN was to revive the policy effective from 1 April 2020 nationwide. See Central Bank of Nigeria, *Financial Inclusion Newsletter,* July 2019, 4 (2) at 1, available at https://www.cbn.gov.ng/Out/2019/CCD/Q2%202019%20Financial%20Inclusion%20Newsletter_Final_08.08.19.pdf, accessed on 5 May 2020.

115 Louis de Koker & Nicola Jentzsch, Financial Inclusion and Financial Integrity: Aligned Incentives? *World Development* Vol. 44, 2013, 268. See also CBN, Payment Modes in Nigeria note 107.

116 National Identification Management Commission (NIMC), Section 5 Act No. 23 of 2007.

117 National Identification Management Commission, *Why Your NIN Is Important,* available at https://www.nimc.gov.ng/nin-importance/, accessed on 22 August 2019.

118 National Identification Management Commission (NIMC) Act Mandatory Use of Identification Number Regulation, 9.

119 Ibid.

120 Ibid at Regulation 13.

121 Temitayo Jaiyeola, NIN registration surges over SIM ban, 10 million Nigerians captured – NIMC, available at https://punchng.com/nin-registration-surges-over-sim-ban-10-million-nigerians-captured-nimc/#:~:text=AT%20least%2010.3%20million%20Nigerians,as%20of%20May%2026%2C%202022, accessed on 6 July 2022.

122 For information on the enrolment centres across the country, see NIMC, *NIMC Enrolment Centres,* available at https://www.nimc.gov.ng/nimc-enrolment-centres/, accessed on 14 July 2020.

123 NIMC, *How to Enrol (Adults),* available at https://www.nimc.gov.ng/how-to-enrol-adults/, accessed on 15 August 2019. Applicants can, however, use the paper slips given as temporary cards until the GMPCs are ready for collection. It is important to note that the timelines envisioned by the commission vary with the practice at the enrolment centres. Anecdotal evidence reveals that the invitation to the second visit can be extended for up to two weeks while the eventual collection of the GMPC may be delayed by more than one year.

124 NIMC note 122.

125 National Identification Management Commission (NIMC), *About the NIN, available at* https://www.nimc.gov.ng/about-nin/. See also National Identification Management Commission (NIMC) Act S27 of 2007 and National Identification Management Commission (NIMC) Mandatory Use of Identification Number Regulation, 11 of 2015, available at https://www.nimc.gov.ng/docs/MandatoryNIN_Gazetted.pdf, accessed on 20 May 2019.

126 Emma Okonji, 'NIMC registered 21.4 million Nigerians in five years', *THISDAYLIVE*, 13, Sept. 2017, available at https://www.thisdaylive.com/index.php/2017/09/13/nimc-registered-21-4-million-nigerians-in-five-years/, accessed on 13 July 2020. See also, '30 million Nigerians get National Identity Number, *Vanguard Newspaper,* 4 March 2018, available at https://www.vanguardngr.com/2018/03/30-million-nigerians-get-national-identity-number/, accessed on 4 September 2019. See also NIMC, Enrolment Dashboard 2022, available at https://nimc.gov.ng/enrolment-dashboard-february-2022/#:~:text=NIMC's%20enrolment%20figures%20as%20at,across%20the%20North%20and%20South, accessed on 28 February 2022. National Identification Management Commission, Enrollment Dashboard 2022, available at https://nimc.gov.ng/enrolment-dashboard-march-2022/, accessed on 6 July 2022.

127 NIMC to conclude NIN Registration by 2025 June 4, 2020 3:34 am, available at https://www.thisdaylive.com/index.php/2020/06/04/nimc-to-conclude-nin-registration-by-2025/.

128 Thales Nigerian National ID Program: An Ambitious Initiative, available at https://www.thalesgroup.com/en/markets/digital-identity-and-security/government/customer-cases/nigeria-eid, accessed on 18 November 2021.
129 Independent National Electoral Commission, *About INEC*, available at https://www.inecnigeria.org/home/about-inec/, accessed on 14 July 2020.
130 The Constitution of the Federal Republic of Nigeria 1999 (as amended), Third Schedule, S15 Part 1. See also National Electoral Act of 2010 S2.
131 Independent National Electoral Commission, *About INEC* note 126.
132 INEC, *INEC Nigeria,* available at https://www.inecnigeria.org/, accessed on 21 July 2021. See also INEC, Total Registered Voters and PVC Collection, available at http://www.inec.gov.ng/, accessed on 21 July 2021. This figure should increase with the ongoing registration in preparation for the 2023 general elections.
133 EFInA 2020 note 12 at 16.
134 Central Bank of Nigeria, *Introduction of Three-Tiered Know Your Customer (KYC) Requirements*, available at https://www.cbn.gov.ng/out/2013/ccd/3%20tiered%20kyc%20requirements.pdf, accessed on 15 August 2019. See also Central Bank of Nigeria (CBN), Anti-Money Laundering/Counter Terrorism Financing Regulation 45 of 2013.
135 Ibid.
136 Central Bank of Nigeria, *Know-Your-Customer Guidelines* 3.0 of 2013.
137 Central Bank of Nigeria, *Review of Restrictions and Limits on Levels I and II of the Tiered Know-Your-Customer ("Kyc") Accounts,* Fpr/Dir/Cir/Gen/06/002.
138 Ibid at 50, 72 & sch 2. See also Central Bank of Nigeria, Anti Money Laundering and Counterfeiting of Terrorism Regulations sch 2 (2013). Besides the use of utility bills, this schedule additionally stipulates the use of tax assessment, letter from a person in authority and bank statements but utility bills remain the most requested documentation.
139 NIBSS, *About,* available at https://nibss-plc.com.ng/bvn/, accessed on 11 September 2019.
140 Ibid.
141 NIBSS note 139.
142 See Central Bank of Nigeria note 138 at 2. Besides the use of utility bills, this schedule additionally stipulates the use of tax assessment, letter from a person in authority and bank statements but utility bills remain the most requested documentation.
143 What3words Limited, *What is what3words?* available at https://what3words.com/about-us/, accessed on 12 September 2019.
144 Adeyemi Adepetun, What3words will boost Nigeria's addressing system', *Guardian* 16 August 2017, available at https://guardian.ng/technology/what3words-will-boost-nigerias-addressing-system/, accessed on 25 May 2019.
145 Ibid.
146 SnooCODE, *About SnooCODE,* available at https://snoocode.com/about, accessed on 2 September 2019.

5 Rural Digital Financial Exclusion – Community Case Study (Ubulu-Uku, Nigeria)

5.1 Introduction

In the previous chapter, the barriers to accessing financial services were discussed, as well as the regulatory responses to some of these barriers. The delineation of these barriers form the main basis for this chapter, which examines how communities without a banking presence cope with accessing finance. Study themes and user perceptions around the use of digital financial services (DFS) as a solution to greater financial inclusion in Nigeria are also drawn out. Further discussed in the chapter are the study findings and the implications for financial inclusion.

5.1.1 Outline of study

This study was carried out to provide clarity on some issues of financial inclusion. In general, the suitability of laws and institutions responsible for regulating DFS for the excluded class is explored in this book. The empirical study was carried out specifically to garner consumer insights and determine the extent to which the CBN legal and policy initiatives have trickled down to local communities in Nigeria. The study was conducted in Ubulu-Uku (a town in Delta State, Nigeria). The community bank closed shortly before the study was conducted and other banks were located outside the community. Ubulu-Uku is a small town in the Aniocha-South Local Government Area of the state. It is located within a 35-minute drive from the capital city, Asaba, and about 15–30 minutes from neighbouring towns such as Agbor, Isele-Uku and Ogwashi-Uku. Some government ministries are located in Ogwashi-Uku, a neighbouring town where a number of residents work.

There are nine primary and four secondary government schools and a number of private schools. The main occupations of Ubulu-Uku residents include farming (both crop and livestock, particularly poultry), weaving of traditional fabrics, food processing and trading. In addition, there is a significant presence of small and medium-sized enterprises that are increasing the level of economic activities within the community. The formal sector is characterised mainly by teachers, healthcare professionals and lawyers while

DOI: 10.4324/9781003217886-5

the informal sector is made up mainly of farmers, hair stylists, tailors, cloth weavers and traders. Some small-scale industries can also be found here, particularly in the spheres of oil, food and water processing.

The aim of drawing insights from this community was to determine the missing link between regulatory initiatives and legal instruments on digital financial inclusion and widespread financial exclusion, especially in rural settings. The data collected was useful in obtaining user perspectives on financial inclusion barriers and the coping strategies adopted by community members.

5.1.2 Aims and objectives

As noted in Chapter 1, Nigeria has a high financial exclusion rate of 35.9 per cent and an even higher rural exclusion rate as only 81 per cent of the rural population can access finance according to the EFInA survey of 2020.[1] The aim of the study was, therefore, to identify the barriers experienced by excluded communities in accessing formal finance with the purpose of ascertaining the needed policy adjustments for bringing the excluded into formal finance. The specific objectives of the study were to (i) identify the barriers experienced by financially excluded communities in accessing formal finance; (ii) gather information about how communities unserved by financial services providers grapple with the challenges of accessing finance; (iii) ascertain the impact of DFS on rural communities; and (iv) identify policy adjustments needed for bringing the financially excluded into formal finance.

5.1.3 Method of identifying and selecting participants

The empirical method of research was used to gather data on the barriers to accessing finance and the attendant coping strategies employed by study participants. Data collection was done in November 2018 and research analysis from January through March 2019. The purposeful sampling method was used to select the participants to be interviewed to ensure that only participants who met the study criteria were covered. Essentially, participants had to be adults who utilised formal or informal finance services.

It was important to interview people who used these financial services in order to achieve the study objectives. Although insights such as the issue of inability to open an account by reason of landlord's refusal to release electricity bills to tenants were drawn from a participant who had no bank account, it was pertinent to draw insights from actual users of financial services. This improved understanding of the level of engagement with available banking services as well as the coping mechanisms adopted in the absence of these services. To understand the focus on digital financial inclusion, it was appropriate to interview users to ascertain whether or not they were using digital finance channels, the barriers encountered and what policy adjustments were necessary.

A total of 25 adult participants (12 females and 13 males) were interviewed from the formal and informal sectors to draw out representative, rich and divergent views within the community. The formal sector was represented by civil servants from the postal, health, judicial, educational and financial sectors while the informal sector participants included fashion designers, farmers, traders, business owners, a printer and a security guard. Some participants overlapped into both sectors. For example, there was a politician/farmer and a teacher/farmer. Some others were formerly employed in the formal sector but had joined the informal sector upon retirement. These included a retired civil servant-turned-trader and accountant-turned-printer. Participants were aged between 22 and 70 (three were aged between 20 and 35, eleven were in their 40s, four were in their 50 s, six were in their 60s and one was aged 70). In terms of the level of education, seven of the participants had university degrees, eight others had tertiary certificates and diplomas, seven had attained the ordinary school level certificate and the other three had primary six certificates.

Participants were interviewed face-to-face using the in-depth interviews (IdIs) method to draw out profound user insights and compensate for the small sample size. An interview guide comprising 24 open- and closed-ended questions was prepared in English but orally translated to the Igbo language for some participants (See appendix). The open-ended questions were used mainly to elicit detailed answers on interviewees' experiences and perspectives while the close-ended ones covered user demographics and patterns of DFS media usage. The interview guide was designed with the assumption that financial inclusion is comprised of many dimensions that affect the adoption and usage of financial products. The following themes were thus drawn out: knowledge and awareness of financial services; financial services adoption and usage; barriers to accessing finance; coping strategies; consumer perception; and user recommendations.

Questions on user demographics covered preliminary enquiries detailing age, occupation and highest level of education attained. Adoption and usage of financial services were addressed by questions 1, 2, 3, 4, 5, 6, 7, 8 and 9. Issues around barriers to accessing finance were covered by questions 10 and 13 while the knowledge of financial services theme was answered by questions 12, 14, 15, 16, 17, 18 and 19. Consumer perception of digital financial services was laid out in questions 21 and 22 while user recommendations were covered by questions 11, 20, 23 and 24. Finally, the question on coping strategy was asked as a follow-up to question 22.

5.1.4 Key messages

- Low level of consumer trust in DFS and alternative finance providers such as the postal service and mobile network operators results in gravitation towards banks and indigenous savings systems.
- Efficient use of DFS is important to improve financial inclusion for rural consumers but regulators and providers have to imbue trust to ensure consumer patronage.

5.2 Background

The Central Bank of Nigeria (CBN) defines financial inclusion as,

> enhancing access and usage of financial services at affordable costs to the vast majority of disadvantaged and vulnerable low income groups; it is the availability and accessibility of financial products and services to the entire population without discrimination.[2]

According to Enhancing Financial Innovation and Access (EFInA), financial inclusion implies that an individual is served by a formal finance institution such as a bank, a formal other entity such as an insurance company or an informal financial institution such as savings clubs, moneylenders or local remittances using a transport service or recharge cards.[3] The financially excluded in contrast, are persons who do not have or use deposit money banks or other formal or informal financial services; and that save at home and borrow and remit funds through family and friends.[4]

The biennial quantitative study carried out by EFInA in 2018 provided nationally representative data on the state of financial access in Nigeria from 27,470 participants.[5] According to the study, financial exclusion results from barriers such as distance to a bank, financial literacy, irregular income, unemployment, cash preference, the complexity of account opening and a lack of proof of identity documentation.[6] A robust discussion of these barriers was undertaken in Chapter 4. The following section builds on EFInA's quantitative data by providing qualitative details, commentary and insights on the linkages between answers obtained from participants and existing CBN DFS regulatory framework. The discourse on financial inclusion is covered under six themes: knowledge about financial inclusion initiatives, financial services adoption and usage patterns, barriers to accessing finance, coping strategies, consumer perception of DFS and user recommendations.

5.3 Financial inclusion themes

5.3.1 Knowledge about financial inclusion initiatives

Awareness around specific DFS and financial inclusion initiatives of the CBN is low. Even though many users possess digital literacy skills to use some DFS channels such as mobile phones, POS and ATMs, none of the participants could identify a relevant CBN policy or initiative for financial inclusion. It is telling that even participants having jobs relating to finance such as the banker and the school bursar had no idea about these policies. The failure to correctly identify relevant DFS and financial inclusion initiatives of the CBN is evidence of the gap in communicating regulatory instruments to the bottom-of-the-pyramid that are in most need of the information.

To add context to the lack of awareness by the participants working in the finance sector, the school bursar has had no prior experience of working in a bank and the banker had only worked in a community bank. Although under the supervisory purview of the CBN, community banks are not imposed with as many regulations as the deposit money banks. The banker was thus able to name some general CBN policies such as portfolio at risk, liquidity ratio and deposit liability, but none relating to financial inclusion.

Remarkably, participants were highly informed about the required documentation for opening accounts. As provided by the CBN, a bank can request one of four basic documents to open a high-value account including the national identity number card, voter card, driver's licence and international passport. A total of 20 out of the 25 participants answered correctly, identifying at least one identification document requested by the banks to open bank accounts. It is remarkable that the international passport and driver's licence were, however, mentioned by only two participants. Furthermore, utility bills were recurrent answers to the question on identification documentation requested by banks. The electricity bill was particularly cited by 14 participants while waste management bills and house rent were cited by two others. Other requirements mentioned were passport photographs, guarantors, letters of identity and reference forms and letters.

5.3.2 Financial service adoption and usage patterns

The study found that participants utilised bank accounts and additionally used DFS delivery channels such as ATM, POS and Webpay. Fund transfers, airtime top-ups and online shopping were growing financial habits. Almost all participants had bank accounts but two out of the 25 had discontinued account usage. Participants had opened at least one account but some had as many as three. Only two participants had active accounts with the community bank in the town before it was shut down. The others used banks such as Keystone Bank in Ibusa; First Bank and Union Bank in Ogwashi-Uku and United Bank for Africa and Union Bank in Isele-Uku. These were the only banks in these towns while Asaba, the state capital, had branches of all banks. Deposit and withdrawal were the most common activities while paying in cheques and applying for loans were performed to a lesser degree.

The frequency of the usage of bank accounts varied from daily to monthly including branch use, ATM, POS, mobile phone channels and online shopping. Some participants made use of their bank accounts for activities such as transfers and airtime top-up. The highest frequency of bank withdrawals was recorded from a participant who put the number of withdrawals at 10 to 20 times a month due to the nature of her work as a building contractor which required frequent payment of labourers. The least frequent usage was monthly, cited by four participants. Adoption of informal financial services such as rotation savings clubs is also widespread but is discussed as a coping strategy in Section 5.3.4.

In relation to savings and borrowing culture with formal financial service providers, the financial behaviour of participants revealed a penchant for savings and an aversion for credit. Participants indicated having a savings culture while only four participants had obtained a loan from a bank. To the question: 'Have you ever accessed a loan from bank? Participants gave such answers as 'no need', 'I don't have enough funds', 'high interest', 'no project', 'no guarantor/surety' and 'no collateral'. One participant, for instance, mentioned not being confident about getting a loan by reason of not being a civil servant while another indicated the lack of a surety to obtain a loan grant. A participant was also pessimistic about obtaining a bank loan for the reason of being a non-indigene of the community. The issue of land ownership and lack of collateral was also recurrent amongst participants.

Of the four participants who had obtained a bank loan, different reasons were indicated for obtaining the loans namely, salary advance, paying school fees, starting a small business and for an agricultural project. Accordingly, the study recorded a low level of loan default. These financial behaviours aligned with the CBN 2015 baseline survey on financial inclusion which revealed that Nigerians are positively predisposed to savings but disinclined to accessing credit facilities.[7] This is also re-stated in the EFInA survey on financial inclusion in Nigeria which revealed that Nigerians are savings-savvy and credit-averse and that Nigerians favoured borrowing from family and friends over formal financial institutions such as banks.[8]

Only two participants indicated patronising the community bank which was shut down shortly before the study. Since patronage by the selected participants was low, it was not possible to get a lot of answers from the customers about dealings with the bank. However, one recalled being declined a loan of ₦1 million for being beyond the lending capacity of the bank. The bank is currently shutdown and undergoing evaluation by the Nigeria Deposit Insurance Corporation (NDIC) to determine assets and liabilities. As noted by a participant, the bank was unable to meet the Central Bank's mandatory capitalisation requirement. It is noteworthy that the NDIC Act 2007 provides for deposit insurance for all deposit banks' clients in Nigeria to a tune of ₦500,000.

In relation to the adoption of DFS delivery channels, it was found that all participants owned and used a mobile phone. This does not come as a surprise as Nigeria has a significant mobile phone ownership rate of 81 per cent.[9] However, mobile money usage is still limited and mostly comprises electronic transfers. Only one participant indicated using the Webpay channel for online shopping. ATM was a more popular channel as this service was offered by banks while the adoption of point of sale (POS) machines was still growing in acceptance as some participants had trust and safety concerns. One complained about the proximity of a POS provider to a betting facility which he considered unsafe and expressed concerns that bad actors can siphon mobile money simply by getting hold of people's mobile phones.

Significantly, the introduction of POS machines to the community was only recent and thus the question about its popularity was somewhat premature. However, two POS providers were active at the time of the study, one a small-scale finance company and the other a sole proprietor. According to the first, about 20–30 customers came to the facility to withdraw funds daily. Typically, a person wishing to make a POS withdrawal would present a bank card to be debited in exchange for cash of equivalent value. In other words, a cash back-like system is employed and the service is paid for by way of commission. This provider charged ₦200 for every ₦10,000 withdrawn. The second on the other hand utilised a sliding scale starting at ₦200.00 for a withdrawal of ₦10,000, ₦250 for ₦20,000, ₦500 for ₦30,000 and ₦1,000 for all other amounts capped at a daily maximum of ₦60,000. The transaction capacity of this business was, however, set at ₦150,000 in line with the CBN limit on daily transactions. To adhere to this regulatory cap, the second provider explained that an employee had to travel to the bank daily to withdraw ₦100,000 thousand while the other ₦50,000 was transferred from the bank account.

In general, the capacity of the POS providers to improve financial inclusion was at the time of the study still fraught with low levels of trust and acceptance of residents of the community. But this is improving as the community welcomed four new POS providers within one year of the study, bringing the number to six. Information obtained from residents on the present state of affairs shows that there are as many as 45 providers as many shop owners have taken up the provision of the service. It is remarkable that this community, which had few finance access points now has providers at almost every corner. This typifies a successful and niche financial inclusion. Although the transition was slow at first, residents had the opportunity to test out the system until they had grown comfortable. The increase in patronage is being responded to by a corresponding increase in providers, deploying POS machines.

One area where services have been optimised is in the sphere of offering deposit functions thereby harnessing the cash-in-cash-out (CICO) potential. A client can now deposit cash with the POS providers who will in turn transfer the funds to the account of the client. The agent then has funds available to offer withdrawal services without the need to travel to Asaba frequently. The erstwhile model of only offering a withdrawal service was limiting and did not utilise the opportunity to expand the customer base. Currently, POS providers offer payment, withdrawals, deposits and account opening services.

5.3.3 Barriers to accessing finance

Participants had varying answers about the barriers encountered in accessing finance including demand-side, supply-side and regulatory barriers explained below.

5.3.3.1 Demand-side barriers

There were few demand-side barriers, including difficulty in remembering passwords and lack of trust in using digital financial services. More of the barriers faced by participants were related to supply-side and regulatory barriers discussed below.

The paucity of demand-side barriers suggests participants' willingness to use financial services but trust in providers and some provider practices as well as regulatory restrictions create limitations. This is quite telling and implies that if regulators and service providers would fix the other barriers to accessing finance, financial inclusion efforts will likely increase.

5.3.3.2 Supply-side barriers

Participants indicated mostly supply-side barriers related to distance and cost of accessing financial services providers, network system downtimes, low-quality financial products, false debits, unexplained charges, safety, distance and associated transport costs, illiquidity and inconveniences such as delays and long queues.

Opinion was roughly split on whether cost was a barrier to accessing finance. While about half of the participants expressly stated that cost was not at all a barrier, others found cost to constitute a major barrier which 'reduced residents' financial power'. One reason for this discrepancy may be the fact that some residents were already accustomed to making visits to neighbouring communities such as Isele-Uku, Ogwashi-Uku and Asaba (the state capital), where these banks are located for other purposes such as work, school, the market, petrol stations or government offices. Ogwashi-Uku for instance had government ministries where many residents worked. Hence, for such participants, there is no additional cost in utilising banking services. Also, some other participants have learned to just cope with this reality having been repeating the process for many years and had therefore become unperturbed by the transport costs.

From the data gathered, the cost of transport to banks in other communities ranged from ₦300 to ₦1,000 as stated by different participants. This was also dependent on varying fares for different modes of transport such as motorbikes, cars and buses. It is curious, therefore, that participants do not prefer to patronise POS providers. As shown above, in Section 5.3.2, commissions start at ₦200 and peak at ₦1,000. It is also closer to residents and less inconvenient. One participant defended this stance, stating that it costs almost the same amount to patronise the banks or POS providers as a result of comparative commissions and transport costs.

> Their withdrawal charge is so much. It costs N100 to get to the closer one. Also, they charge N300 per transaction. At the end of the day, you spend the same N400 it would cost to go to Asaba. (P11)

The justification for the cost does not, however, explain the time spent in getting to the banks in other communities or the inconvenience or risk of carrying cash in transit, especially on public transport. Sensitisation is still needed to make this medium of financial deployment more efficient, especially with the ongoing plans for the cashless Nigeria project. As noted earlier, trust in these entities is still low and needs proper nurturing as discussed more specifically below in Section 5.3.5 on consumer perception.

5.3.3.3 Regulatory barriers

Regulatory barriers such as cumbersome KYC requirements including requests for utility bills and demand for collateral, sureties and guarantors were on top of the list. Five out of the 25 participants were unable to mention any identification document. In general, participants were dissatisfied by the insistence on utility bills as evidence of address, citing peculiarities in the community that made compliance both harrowing and upsetting. One specifically asserted that the request for utility bills as well as questions around whether houses of clients were painted are 'obsolete' and 'disgusting', particularly as there was no proper addressing system in the community and houses were springing up indiscriminately to further disrupt any existing numbering system.

Another added that street addressing was sometimes done by the residents and utility receipts were usually addressed collectively to a clan and not the individual, making proof of address for individuals in such cases impossible. Yet another cited the issue of landlords withholding utility receipts as of practice, creating a further impediment to proving a person's address. These examples underscore the weight that insistence on presenting utility bills as proof of evidence places on communities. Incidentally, one of the participants who lamented the insistence of banks on the presentation of utility receipts happens to be one of the two participants without a bank account. It is also significant to note that this insistence hardly takes into account the condition of homeless persons who neither have a home address nor proof in the form of utility bills or other documents.

In relation to owning the required identification for opening accounts, the community differed from the EFInA survey finding of 2018 which lists lack of identification documentation as a main barrier to access. One reason for this is that the community benefited from the mobile registration services of the National Identification Management Commission (NIMC) that deployed staff on several occasions to schools to register individuals for the National Identity Number (NIN). Some participants registered in Ogwashi, a neighbouring community while others registered in Asaba, the state capital, Port Harcourt in Rivers State as well as in Ubulu-Uku where mobile registration officers were deployed.

The community recorded an equally high record of those having the permanent voter's card. It was remarked that some politicians, in a bid to win elections, ensured the deployment of registration centres to primary schools in the community to drive registration and voting. The timing according to a participant is also marked in four-year intervals to coincide with the country's election cycle. Two participants remarked that registration centres were opened in primary schools in the community to facilitate registration and possibly win some goodwill for candidates at the election. The fact that residents benefitted from these registration drives therefore impacted positively on the number of persons who opened bank accounts with the voter card.

This widespread ownership of identification documentation does not, however, represent a complete picture of the state of identification documentation ownership around the country. Even in Ubulu-Uku, some participants recounted how they had to surmount long queues, stress and repeat visits ranging from two days to two years to eventually collect the ID documents. Again, as shown by data from the NIMC website, applicants for the national identity card must make three visits before NIN card collection as described above in Chapter 4. So far, about 77 115 343 million Nigerians have been registered by the commission.[10] Although impressive in view of the timelines, more is desired for the adult population of about 106 million. Similarly, data from the Independent Electoral Commission (INEC) also shows that more than 84 million Nigerians have been registered and the issuance of the cards is underway.[11]

5.3.4 Coping strategies

There are two main coping strategies adopted by the community, these being travelling to banks located in other communities and the use of indigenous savings systems. The community bank is no longer an option as it has been shut down and the use of POS providers is still growing.

5.3.4.1 Use of banks in other communities

As stated earlier, most of the participants had at least one bank account in branches located in other communities- First Bank and Union Bank in Ogwashi, Union Bank and Keystone Bank in Ibusa, United Bank of Africa in Isele-Uku and the rest of the banks in Asaba in the state capital. On the average, residents of the community spend about ₦300 to ₦1,000 to reach these banks in a 30-minute to 1-hour journey depending on the availability of public transport, waiting time for taxis to fill up, traffic and weather conditions.

5.3.4.2 The use of indigenous savings systems

A core coping strategy adopted by the community is to resort to local savings clubs, described by participants in related terms such as *Otu, Uta, Nsusu, Ajo, Nkeri* (monthly contribution) and Safe. Contribution cycles vary from daily, weekly to monthly and the duration of the entire scheme is yearly or seasonally depending on the agreement of the members. Weekly savings cycles are counted either in local four-day weeks using traditional market days or the conventional seven-day Sunday to Monday week. A participant recounted that she engaged in this system in the secondary school and funds were distributed in December to coincide with the Christmas festivities. Other seasonal savings mentioned by participants include Easter and New Year contributions. Contributions from these celebrations are sometimes used to buy food items such as rice for members.

These savings clubs could be large or small and membership is defined by close associations. Some are simple savings circles run by an association of friends and associates while others are more formalised groups such as trader and teacher savings groups and those formed by civil servants in ministries. Funds are collected at agreed intervals and distributed in turns to members. A ballot (*Ngbanye*) is sometimes 'used to determine turns'. These funds may be collected during meetings or, in the case of *ajo*, recorded on a card by the fund manager (who is entitled to one-tenth of the contribution as a service charge at the end of the agreed interval). A participant notes that card records are a new invention as no records were used in the past because parties were absolutely trusting of one another.

Local savings clubs serve different financial purposes for residents including providing savings, loan facilities and building a credit history. Many participants were observed to rely on local savings groups for obtaining loans rather than applying to conventional banks. According to one, '*esusu* is better than banks because of the ease of getting a loan'. This preference is attributed to fewer formalities associated with this channel of loan access. For instance, members of savings clubs simply have to apply for loans during periodic meetings without any need to furnish collateral. No documentation is provided by the applicant aside from a recording by the secretary of the loaned amount and interest due. Non-members only have to be introduced by an existing member to guarantee repayment of loaned sum plus interest.

Additionally, these clubs offer a return on investment as interest collected from borrowers throughout the savings period are added to the contribution of each member at the end of the term. Interest ranging from 3, 5 and 10 per cent are charged to borrowers depending on the club. There were comments about the clubs accommodating people who do not already have savings within the funds. Loan requests receive a quick response and enabled members to meet urgent needs without formal applications demanded by banks and cooperative societies.

To secure member funds, local administrators have sought ways to minimise risks. For instance, members can only borrow out of turn or before the agreed date to the tune of the maximum amount to be contributed and non-members must have existing and credible members as sureties. Sums requested by a non-member cannot be higher than that contributed by the club member serving as surety who is also responsible for making good any default by these non-members. Some heads of clubs request two sureties to guarantee repayment. Some others are also departing from the traditional practice of storing funds at home in 'strong boxes' to avoid incidents of theft 'by lending out all funds contributed by members'. While conventional mechanisms of law enforcement such as securing an arrest, instituting a legal action in a court of law or issuing letters of demand are always open to all citizens, these were found to be scarcely utilised in the community.

The study, however, found a few sceptical participants who did not trust the *esusu* system for fear of other members defaulting, as well as concerns around the capacity of these groups to enforce repayment. The fact that these clubs do not lend large sums like the deposit money banks was another source of hesitancy. These participants preferred to only store and borrow funds from deposit money banks in spite of the inconvenience of distance and travel.

5.3.5 Consumer perception of DFS

It was observed from the study that DFS adoption and usage, though growing, is still affected by a lack of trust. Remarkably, even the idea of deploying bank agents to offer DFS was met with dissatisfaction as some participants preferred to travel to physical branches to ensure they were dealing with the designated bank officials. Some participants even preferred to employ the services of friends to complete bank transactions. Participants were divided concerning the capacity of alternative providers such as post office agents and mobile money operators (telecoms providers) to deploy financial services. Some specifically expressed concerns over the fact that these alternative entities were not connected to a bank and thus lacked the competence to offer financial services. Some perceptions about the Mobile Network Operators (MNOs) and the post are detailed below.

5.3.5.1 Perceptions about mobile network operators

Although there was an opportunity for mobile network operators to leverage on brand recognition in telecommunications services to offer financial services, many participants could not fathom how these providers could diversify into finance. In fact, only 4 of the 25 participants indicated that MNOs could be trusted in offering financial services. It was asserted that MNOs are not established for the purpose of offering financial services and therefore can scarcely fit this role.

Some concerns about the capacity of these MNOs to handle customer funds flowed from fear over the risk of liquidation as some participants described mobile network agents to be sole proprietors rather than agents of the telecommunications provider. In fact, some participants viewed these agents as mere 'airtime sellers'. Specifically, one participant described MNO agents as 'human beings' who cannot be individually trusted while another noted that the business of these mobile network agents 'could fold at any time'. Some, while being a bit more accepting opined that these agents could not go beyond small-fund transfers and lack the capacity to offer more sophisticated financial services. On a positive note, however, many participants were open to giving MNOs a chance. One stated she could start out with ₦5,000 to test their competence in offering finance.

The main concerns about MNOs in the community indicate a gap which calls for regulators to engage in financial literacy programmes, particularly with regard to digital financial services. For MNOs to be able to break into many communities including Ubulu-Uku, providers need to be manifestly seen to have regulatory backing to scale up fast.

5.3.5.2 Perceptions about the postal service

Quite like MNOs, the acceptance of the postal service as alternative finance providers was also low. Four participants indicated trust in the capacity of the post, another four were sceptical, many were alarmed and others rejected the idea outright. When asked about the possibility of re-introducing money order services which were popularised by the postal service in the past, some participants described this as an outmoded practise that could not fulfil modern-day financial demands. There were also notions that even though the postal service fulfilled financial needs in the past because residents were able to cash out money orders at the nearest local post offices, this had become too obsolete to play the same role with present modernisation and sophistication of the financial system.

One participant stated that banks and POS machines were sufficient and so there was no use to re-introduce the postal service as the Moneygram financial services, only worked in the past as a result of the lack of alternatives. Similarly, some asserted that even in the glory days of moneygram, efficiency was not optimal as it took about three months to deliver funds to clients. Again, there were concerns around the lack of affiliation with banks and the impossibility of dealing in large amounts of money.

One obvious fact is that the post is currently underutilised and can be expanded to offer more robust financial services. The postal service has been a catalyst for improving financial inclusion in countries such as Brazil, hence, there is a need to convince financially excluded persons of the value in deploying financial services using the extensive network of the post that stretches across the breadth of Nigeria. More insights on the potential for MNOs and the postal service as finance providers are elucidated in the following section.

5.3.5.3 Insights from consumer perceptions

The lack of confidence in alternative providers could be a result of the fact that the capacity of these providers is yet to be effectively tested in Nigeria. Although money orders were introduced by the postal service in the past, digital finance sophistication at the time was low and could not optimise the service. Also, the postal service in some rural communities serves the function of letter and parcel delivery without more. The study found that the post office in the community had only two staff members and large unused office space, some of which was occupied by a primary school. Although the interviewed staff indicated that the office had the capacity to deliver letters around the world, many participants expressed doubts. Similarly, MNOs are still perceived as mere airtime and Internet data delivery agents and have never had the opportunity to demonstrate their capacity to offer mobile money except when working in conjunction with banks, serving as a network for banks to offer digital money or serving their function as super-agents.

There is, however, every indication that with the recent inclusion of MNOs as alternative finance providers by the CBN, patronage may increase backed by dedicated sensitisation and consumer awareness. Significantly, Mpesa, the main mobile payment system in Kenya, was tested in rural communities unserved by banks and contributed to the extension of financial services to about 83 per cent of the population.[12]

There were, however, some positive responses for the operation of alternative providers. One of the participants, a telecommunications agent, is confident that alternative providers could efficiently offer financial services using her business as an example. There were also views that financial services such as savings and deposits could be offered by both MNOs and the postal service while post offices could additionally offer credit. Likewise, it was asserted that the postal service could work because phones have reduced the burden of sending letters and so posts could diversify into this new space. It was also mentioned that money order worked in the past and could thus be re-engineered to meet present-day demands.

5.3.6 User recommendations

The response to the suggestion to bring a bank to the community was resoundingly positive and participants mostly suggested that this had the potential to ease the process of accessing finance. One participant stressed the need for investors to build a bank closer to residents. When asked what type of bank was fitting, many suggested a 'better bank' or 'standard bank' which was described to include banks such as First Bank, Access Bank and Guaranty Trust Bank.

This does not come as a surprise as a result of the massive industry recapitalisation exercise embarked upon in 2004 by the CBN to strengthen the financial standing of all banks in Nigeria. Since the introduction of this recapitalisation policy, no bank has experienced bankruptcy and the CBN had been quick to mandate banks with signs of weakness to merge with stronger banks or be taken over. Some examples include the United Bank of Africa (UBA) and Standard Bank merger in 2005.[13] Polaris Bank was also birthed in 2018 after purchasing the assets, and assuming liabilities, of the now-defunct Skye Bank.[14] More recently in 2019, Diamond Bank has had to merge with Access Bank.[15]

The suggestion by some participants that ATMs be installed in the community was telling as the distance was a major barrier cited by participants and had to be addressed. According to one, investors could make closer financial services a reality by building out bank branches in the community as participants recounted enduring standing in long bank queues and safety concerns around travelling to withdraw funds. There were also suggestions for a reduction of interest rates and scaling back on the emphasis on collateral. A seemingly trivial issue such as the employment of friendlier staff was suggested by one participant, indicating the value that clients attach to face-to-face and cordial services of bank officials.

Regarding DFS use, participants recommended improved trust and the introduction of enabling regulation. There was a call for insurance to secure customer funds and the introduction of door-to-door banking to help disabled or disadvantaged persons. It was suggested that banks should not expect so much profit from rural communities but rather a leverage on profits from bigger branches in urban areas. This could also help to scale urban/rural remittances as Nigerians hold a store for sending money to dependent relatives.

Further, participants recommended addressing stringent bank requests such as not insisting on land titles as collateral for loan requests as many rural landowners have no titles or official certificates of occupancy. Notably, rural lands in Nigeria mainly have the rural rights of occupancy and not the certificates of occupancy issued by the government in urban areas. In noting that other neighbouring communities such as Agbor and Ogwashi-Uku had banks as a result of the presence of government agencies/ministries and a polytechnic (benefitting from a wide customer base of civil servants and students), one participant suggested that establishing such entities in Ubulu-Uku could increase economic activity and in turn attract banks. Finally, it was suggested that banks should seek collaborations with entities such as the post to deepen client reach and mitigate financial risks.

5.4 Lessons for financial inclusion

From the foregoing, it is observed that in this community, as in many others, three key elements are evident. First, that conventional banks remain the most trusted financial services providers in rural communities, even though they are not easily accessible. This underscores the store which excluded populations place on safeguarding funds. Second, cash is still king in many transactional settings while digital financial services are still playing catch-up. This can only be addressed when the customer experience of value from DFS offerings equals or exceeds what cash currently offers in terms of convenience, trust and safety. Third, DFS offerings must be tailored to mirror the actual needs of the excluded. The importance of this last point lies in the fact that DFS policies which portray regulatory preferences rather than mirroring the needs of the excluded, even if adopted in early phases, may suffer lack of continued patronage, as is the case with account dormancy. These three elements are discussed below.

5.4.1 Conventional banks are trusted but not easily accessible

Banks have generally demonstrated disinterest in building branches in rural communities leading to a low rural financial inclusion rate of 19 per cent.[16]

According to EFInA, informal finance is more dominant in urban centres while rural areas are still largely bereft of banking services.[17] Without a natural incentive to invest in rural communities, there is a need for regulations to foster this. These regulations have to target the peculiarities of the society and incentivise providers to expand branches to rural areas. Participants, for instance, suggested the need to make policies and design banking products that accommodate the needs of a predominantly agrarian society such as Ubulu-Uku. As noted by one participant, the community relies on seasonal products which require 'entirely different financial policies and products'.

A participant noted that the community has grown from a village to a town and has the clout of businesses to support the commercial viability of a bank. Similarly, another noted that Ubulu-Uku had the advantage of a 'booming environment that will patronise the banks'. Presumably, bringing a bank to this community would not only serve residents but would also serve surrounding communities.

If alternative providers are to become relevant in rural communities, the issue of trust must be addressed. Consumer protection mechanisms have to be adopted and relayed to residents. Awareness about channels of redress should also be a priority and speedy redress channels including for small claims need to be made available to address issues such as wrong debits and data privacy breaches. These channels should be available at multiple levels starting from channels put in place by specific providers to industry and regulatory level channels to assure fairness, accountability and transparency. Users should also be able to access these services with the usual medium of communication employed by providers and toll-free lines should be made available to report fraud or follow up on reports. Overall, awareness is needed to foster financial consumer rights and duties.

5.4.2 Cash is still king

Cash is still observed to be a key factor among participants and this is evident in the reluctance of some participants to go digital, especially where the channels of digitalisation are offered by non-banks whose success in core areas is less than perfect. Digital transactions are still perceived to be associated with fraud, as mentioned by one participant who preferred physical transactions at banks. Likewise, another expressed dissatisfaction with DFS channels including POS and mobile phone transfers. This aversion for DFS by the participant stems from an unpleasant encounter his wife had had with petty thieves who stole her phone and succeeded in transferring some of her money. The matter had been reported and was under investigation but, according to him, the experience had deterred the couple and both want nothing to do with digital finance channels in future.

Again, POS agents in the community, still grapple with residents' acceptance. Improving trust around the safety of DFS is therefore crucial and has the potential to improve adoption of financial services and reduce the number of trips residents make to neighbouring communities to access these services.

Notably, some participants argued that the acceptance of DFS is dependent on the sort of service offered. For example, handiworks that attract small pay are viewed by some to be incompatible with DFS. Even where participants agree to the use of digital services, there is an observed insistence about getting a credit notification from the bank as a precondition to confirming the authenticity of a transaction. Some participants stated that cash is important and it will take good practice and patience for digital to ever replace cash.

Significantly, acceptance of DFS can be aided by ensuring that service providers are willing to accept DFS. For instance, one participant, a dealer in chicken eggs, though prepared to use DFS for her business must comply with the payment mode prescribed by her egg supplier who insists on payment at a bank in another community and the presentation of bank deposit slips before orders are fulfilled.

5.4.3 Tailored regulatory policies are essential

There is still a mismatch between the financial inclusion policies of the Central Bank and the financial behaviour of rural residents. One area of concern is the issue of informal financial services. As revealed by this study, indigenous savings groups are quite popular even though these products are regarded by the CBN as unsafe and unregulated. This misses out on the opportunity to mirror the preferences of local populations rather than imposing conventional banking services that are foreign, inconvenient or unacceptable to users. In rural areas, informal services have been observed to be more 'convenient, flexible, simple, easier to engage with and better able to meet specific needs'.[18] Informal finance makes up 85 per cent of rural savings systems including moneylenders, daily collectors, traders and indigenous credit institutions (*esusu*) with a high rate of loan repayment and low default.[19] Additionally, informal systems such as *esusu* and *ajo* have stood the test of time and provided an age-old source of capital, loan, savings facility and credit history building for countless persons, particularly in the rural areas.

Though not considered illegal, the CBN still characterises informal savings systems as 'unregulated, unsecured, unorganised, small, short term and mostly for activities in the rural areas, households or small entrepreneurial ventures without the capacity to take commercial scale'.[20] The CBN also maintains that large informal markets could create incomplete markets, undermine monetary policy transmission and miss the anticipated objectives of the regulators.[21] However, the CBN needs to go beyond these classifications to bring some structure and clarity to these savings systems and improve the safety of funds by outlawing unconscionable commissions, registering savings collectors and bringing to justice, persons who embezzle local funds. This is currently the case in Ghana where the Bank of Ghana now registers *susu* collectors to make funds safer and minimise the incidence of collectors absconding with members' funds.[22]

Furthermore, ATMs are not deployed in the community. Evidently, the 2020 Guidelines on Operations of Electronic Payment Channels in Nigeria prohibit banks from installing standalone ATMs.[23] However, this misses the opportunity to make use of existing structures such as the post offices to increase the reach of financial access points. This could also address issues related to distance, cost of banking services and transportation as well as the inconveniences of travelling to other communities to access finance.

CBN has the responsibility of addressing the policies according to the specific needs of the excluded. Authors have noted that financial education could be easily included in school curricular for school-age users and provided on mainstream media and technology for more educated persons.[24] Again, it has been recommended that face-to-face interventions such as simple classroom-based group training could be used to reach less literate persons and the use of radio programmes in local languages focused on basic financial terms such as budgeting, planning, savings and credit could also be explored.[25] Most importantly, the CBN needs to ensure that financial products deployed by providers adequately mirror the financial access needs of the users and reflect the socio-economic context of communities where these services are deployed.

5.5 Summary of findings

The study found varying levels of adoption of digital financial services among participants. Usage patterns were also found to be different. All participants had mobile phones but only a few used these to access finance. The use of POS and ATM was quite popular, unlike Internet banking which was reported to be used by one participant. It was also observed that there was a low level of awareness about CBN financial inclusion policies as no participant could name or describe any regulatory policy on financial inclusion. Also, only one participant had heard of a low-value account. Cost, distance and network failure were among the major barriers cited by participants to accessing finance from conventional banks.

Accordingly, residents coped with the dearth of banks in the community by travelling an average of 15–35 minutes to an hour to access banking services in neighbouring communities and the State Capital in Asaba. But this journey can take as much as an hour depending on traffic, waiting time and the elements. Another predominant coping strategy adopted by the community was the use of indigenous savings clubs that offer savings and loan facilities to members. Fund holders ensured the safety of funds by lending the savings to borrowers in need of a loan. Of all the participants interviewed, two had had the unpleasant personal experience of being defrauded by the executives of these clubs but some of the funds had been recovered. Safety is now being improved in these clubs by lending out all available funds and insisting on credible sureties.

The consumer perception of alternative providers and bank agents is low as many preferred to deal with banks at a branch office notwithstanding the inconvenience. Significantly, patronage of alternative providers is growing. Participants were beginning to accept finance deployed with the use of POS devices around the community. Though scepticism was expressed with regard to financial services offered by MNOs and the postal service, some participants were willing to try out these entities, starting with small funds transfers. Users had proffered a number of recommendations to aid access to finance including building out rural bank branches, investing in infrastructure and initiating policies that ensure the safety of funds.

The issue of trust cannot be over emphasised as users have been shown to ground the decision to use particular service providers or products on the trust reposed. It is therefore important to address the issue of trust profoundly. Two related concerns are privacy and surveillance, particularly with digital financial services where access to data of subjects is vital to the proper rendition of the services. For instance, mobile money services require information such as name, card details, pins or passwords. Without the necessary safeguards in relation to privacy, users could become victims of privacy intrusions. The same relates to surveillance as clients can unfairly come under surveillance without adherence to the necessary data protection standards. These two issues need therefore to be addressed to advance trust.

From the foregoing, it is observed that excluded communities would only adopt financial access channels that are trusted and suited to their specific needs. Thus the introduction of some DFS channels, though demonstrated to be successful in some jurisdictions, can result in low adoption and usage rates when the financially excluded are not convinced of their appropriateness. For example, the introduction of digital financial services, though shown to bring tremendous success in some jurisdictions, is still struggling to gain acceptance in a community such as *Ubulu-Uku* where residents need time to become confident and trusting in using services offered by alternative providers.

Again, the ardent resolve to use banking services in neighbouring communities, in spite of the challenges of distance, cost, time, safety concerns and other inconveniences, demonstrates that when money is concerned, even financially excluded communities rather seek out trusted parties than yet-to-be trusted alternative providers. Furthermore, the fact that some participants in the study insisted on taking long journeys to the banks to make withdrawals or deposit funds is a testament to the fact that the excluded are more interested in the safety of funds than convenience. DFS providers can therefore successfully reach these populations by assuring both. Similarly, the persistence in the use of *esusu*, even without any regulatory protection as described in Section 5.3.4.2, signals the need to tailor financial services for the excluded to local contexts.

5.6 Conclusion

This chapter provided an outline of the Ubulu-Uku empirical study and detailed the aim, objectives and purpose of this study. The method employed in identifying participants was described. The study analysis considered six themes around knowledge about financial inclusion initiatives; financial services adoption and usage patterns; barriers to accessing finance; coping strategies; consumer perception of DFS; and user recommendations. Lessons for financial inclusion were discussed in relation to the need for improved trust in DFS, cash as king and the value of tailored regulatory initiatives. This chapter was concluded with a summary of the study findings.

Notes

1 EFInA, Access to Financial Services in Nigeria 2020 Survey, June 3, 2021, at 62, available at https://a2f.ng/wp-content/uploads/2021/06/A2F-2020-Final-Report.pdf, accessed on 19 September 2021.
2 Central Bank of Nigeria, *CPD FAQs* at 3, available at https://www.cbn.gov.ng/Devfin/CPD_FAQs.pdf, accessed on 12 May 2019.
3 Enhancing Financial Innovation and Access (EFInA), *Key Findings: EFInA Access to Financial Services in Nigeria (A2F) 2016 Survey* (2017) at 12, available at https://www.efina.org.ng/wp-content/uploads/2019/03/Key-Findings-A2F-2016.pdf, accessed on 21 July 2020.
4 Ibid.
5 Enhancing Financial Innovation and Access in Nigeria (EFInA), *Key Findings: EFInA Access to Financial Services in Nigeria Survey* (2018) at 6 and 62, available at https://www.efina.org.ng/wp-content/uploads/2019/01/A2F-2018-Key-Findings-11_01_19.pdf, accessed on 20 June 2019.
6 Ibid.
7 Central Bank of Nigeria, *Nigeria Financial Literacy Baseline Survey Report* (2015) at 6.
8 EFInA 2018 note 5 at 27–8.
9 EFInA note 2020 1 at 2020 7, 28 and 64.
10 NIMC, Enrolment Dashboard 2022, available at https://nimc.gov.ng/enrolment-dashboard-february-2022/#:~:text=NIMC's%20enrolment%20figures%20as%20at,across%20the%20North%20and%20South, accessed on 28 February 2022. See also NIMC, *NIMC Enrols over 28m Nigerians and Legal Residents* (2019), available at https://www.nimc.gov.ng/nimc-enrols-over-28m-nigerians-and-legal-residents/, accessed on 25 August 2019. National Identification Management Commission, Enrollment Dashboard 2022, available at https://nimc.gov.ng/enrolment-dashboard-march-2022/, accessed on 6 July 2022.
11 Eniola Akinkuotu, '84.2 million registered to vote in 2019, says INEC', *The Punch* September 7, 2018, available at https://punchng.com/84-2-million-registered-to-vote-in-2019-says-inec/, accessed on 25 August 2019.
12 Reuters 'M-Pesa helps drive up Kenyans' access to financial services – study', available at https://www.reuters.com/article/kenya-banking/m-pesa-helps-drive-up-kenyans-access-to-financial-services-study-idUSL8N21L2HK, accessed on 25 August 2019.
13 UBA Group, History, available at https://www.ubagroup.com/about-uba/history/, accessed on 28 February 2022.
14 Polaris Bank, *Our History,* available at https://www.polarisbanklimited.com/about-us/our-history/, accessed on 26 July 2019.
15 Access Bank, Our History, available at https://www.accessbankplc.com/pages/About-Us/Our-History.aspx, accessed on 28 February 2022.
16 EFInA 2020 note 1 at 62.
17 EFInA 2016 note 3 at 23.
18 Hennie Bester, Christine Hougaard, Jeremy Gray et al, *Homefield Advantage: Learning from the Popularity of Local Financial Services Providers* (2016) at 10–11, available at https://cenfri.org/wp-content/uploads/2017/02/MAP-global-insight-note-3_Homefield-advantage_Cenfri-FinMark-Trust-UNCDF_2016.pdf, accessed on 14 November 2018 9–12.

19 Adekoge Adeleke, *The Informal Financial Markets in Nigeria*, (2014) at 2 and 9, available at https://www.cbn.gov.ng/Out/2016/MPD/UNDERSTANDING%20MONETARY%20POLICY%20SERIES%20NO%2043.pdf, accessed on 13 December 2018.
20 Ibid at 2.
21 Ibid at 17.
22 Financial Inclusion Insights, *Ghana,* available at http://finclusion.org/country/africa/ghana.html#overview, accessed on 10 July 2019.
23 Central Bank of Nigeria, Guidelines on Operations of Electronic Payment Channels in Nigeria 1.2 of 2020.
24 Adekoge Adeleke note 19 at 13 and 14.
25 Ibid.

6 Emerging Technology and Implications for Financial Inclusion

6.1 Introduction

This chapter examines some emerging technologies including distributed ledger technology, cryptocurrency, central bank digital currencies (CBDCs), data analytics, robo-advising, application programme interface, peer-to-peer lending, artificial intelligence and digital identity. The chapter opens with a description of the background of the state of the financial technology (fintech) industry in Nigeria. Thereafter, the selected technology is discussed with a focus on the Nigerian context. The aim is to establish whether these technologies offer solutions that ease the burden of financial exclusion. In reviewing each of these trends, the description, benefits, potential for financial inclusion as well as any likely detriment to consumers is highlighted.

6.2 The financial technology sector in Nigeria: A brief overview

Financial technology (fintech) is 'the application of technology to financial services in a manner that drives the transformation or disruption of the traditional processes in the financial system'.[1] Emerging financial technology is helping financial institutions address the gaps in the financial market, particularly in obtaining rich insights from client data and offering suitable products to different customer segments. Artificial intelligence, distributed ledgers, application programming interface (API) and digital identification are some fintech solutions currently being deployed in financial markets around the world. Big data analytics is helping companies to compute client scores from credit history for loan applications, while peer-to-peer lending provided by social media platforms enables simplified consumer co-lending and gifting.

In general, the fintech industry in Nigeria is accelerating. Yaba in Lagos is emerging as a community for tech start-ups, including Paga, Konga, Jumia and Andela.[2] CcHUB, for example, runs 'a lab and pre-incubation space for technologists, social entrepreneurs, government, technology companies, impact investors and hackers to catalyse creative social technology ventures and co-create new solutions to social problems in Nigeria'.[3] The government of

DOI: 10.4324/9781003217886-6

Lagos State through the ministries of education and science and technology has also launched a computer programming initiative called Code, to develop a coding curriculum for primary, secondary and tertiary institutions.[4] Nigerian start-ups boast of impressive net worth and investments with flutterwave being valued at $3 billion and attracting $250 million in recent investment.[5]

More specifically, financial technology solutions are increasingly evident in the Nigerian financial sector with increased collaborations observed between banks and technology companies. Access Bank and PayWithCapture, a fintech company launched a mobile payment app that facilitates payment transfers across all banks while Zenith Bank is partnering with Reach fintech to develop a group savings tool.[6]

Emerging technologies such as artificial intelligence are also increasingly being applied to financial services. Credpal, Direct Pay Online, OneFi and Specta social lender by Sterling Bank utilise artificial intelligence to personalise services, assess risk and determine credit score.[7] Branch, a mobile financial services provider, offers lending, services using machine learning algorithms to analyse smartphone data (call logs and SMS history), verify customer identity and determine loan eligibility and credit score without requiring paperwork or guarantors from clients without credit history.[8] Likewise, PiggyVest, an investment Fintech uses data from an expense tracker to offer advisory investment services to users.[9]

Some platforms even accept payment in bitcoin including Gsm2me which enables mobile purchases, Minku, an online boutique and accessories company and Shopnow, an e-commerce platform that facilitates importation.[10] There are also cryptocurrency exchanges such as BitPesa, Binance and NairaEx and blockchain-based companies such as Stella and Oradian that seek to offer instant payment services to the financially excluded.[11] Chat boxes such as Leo adopted by the United Bank of Africa Group, enable account opening, funds transfer and utilities settlement.[12]

The Central Bank of Nigeria (CBN) financial inclusion drive, the increasing rate of smartphone penetration and e-commerce transactions, government intervention in establishing innovation hubs and the regulatory efforts in the payment services are projected to be fintech growth and investment drivers.[13] Also promising is Nigeria's mobile phone ownership rate of 81 per cent.[14] Total inflow from Nigerians living abroad is $34 billion.[15] This equally could have positive impacts on financial activity and money circulation within the financial sector.

The following section explores some of the outlined emerging technology as well as possible implications for financial inclusion in Nigeria. A discussion on this topic is important as these technologies are growing in prominence without the needed regulatory rules to provide clarity to providers and users. Detailing the potential detriments will therefore serve as a pointer for future regulatory endeavours.

6.3 Emerging trends in technology and potential for improving financial inclusion

In this section, emerging trends that are predicted to impact the finance sector are explored. Distributed ledger technology, cryptocurrency, central bank digital currencies (CBDCs), data analytics, robo-advising, application programme interface, peer-to-peer lending, artificial intelligence and digital identity are selected. Although the benefits of these technologies are increasingly being promoted by technology companies and are also already in use around the world including in Nigeria, research on the specific benefits for financial inclusion is still sparse. Unlike the preceding section where the digital financial services clime in Nigeria is discussed, a more general overview is given in this present section. Where relevant, the situation in Nigeria is detailed. Potential spaces for deployment as well as likely detriments are specified.

Notably, some of these technologies bear some similarities. For example, even though distributed ledger technology (DLT) and cryptocurrencies are discussed separately, it is notable that many cryptocurrencies are built on blockchain, which is a type of DLT. Likewise, artificial intelligence, although discussed separately in relation to loan grants, is an underlying technology for robo-advisors, data analytics, big data and peer-to-peer lending. Where necessary, these similarities are pointed out below in the course of the discussion.

6.3.1 Distributed ledger technology

DLT is defined as 'synchronised digital databases that are replicated across a network of computers'.[16] The DLT manages data securely on a peer-to-peer (P2P) network of computers applying synchronised data sharing, consensus-based governance and cryptography and could be open or closed, permissionless or permissioned.[17] Using a decentralised ledger, DLT is able to continuously keep details of data at multiple locations.[18] DLT also keeps these data permanently in connected blocks that are safe from tampering using sophisticated cryptographic signatures.[19] Together, these connected blocks of information are called a blockchain. The blockchain includes subsets of a ledger replicated for access by all persons concerned, who are able to see all alterations made.[20]

Blockchain could be public, private or hybrid. Public blockchain is open, decentralised, publicly visible and consensus-led with no single owner while private or permissioned ones have a single authority that controls access to read from and write to the blockchain.[21] The hybrid or consortium model is partly decentralised, open to a privileged group and controlled by a consensus process using a set of rules agreed upon by all parties.[22]

Blockchain operates decentralised P2P networks meaning that connected computers are deemed equal and work concurrently as client and server to each other in contrast to most central computing networks that store and distribute information to other client networks.[23] Blockchain is referred to as a single point of truth as every node on a blockchain network stores real-time updates of the ledger and participates in the consensus process.[24] Each blockchain records data modifications in time-stamped blocks connected to a previous block to form a chain which can be updated only cryptographically by the agreement of a majority of the network users (nodes), thereby retaining all the data modification history.[25] In other words, changes can only be made by a requesting and broadcasting amendments to all parties to the transaction for validation.[26]

Therefore, to tamper with this system or cover any changes, an invader has to prevail over numerous proof-of-work contests to publish a particular block and other succeeding blocks.[27] Further, as the blockchain is represented in a freely distributable file without a master copy, any attempt to alter the file is detected by users as each new block represents a cryptographic pool of transactions, linked to a parent block using a hash digest.[28] Therefore, it is both computationally difficult and expensive to change the chain without changing all blocks that follow and so this instils trust without relying on a central authority.[29]

On the regulatory level, blockchain can reduce KYC compliance costs and increase the transparency of transactions as timestamps on each block reveal the transaction history and references to previous blocks.[30] Banks and regulators can gain access to transactional and cross-institutional data to investigate financial networks and identify bad actors in real time as it is more difficult for criminals to falsify transaction tracks because of the distributed nature of blockchain.[31] Blockchain holds the potential to reduce the time and cost spent by banks on account reconciliation as all transactions are confirmed by parties and are secure from revision and tampering once recorded.[32] Blockchain could become a tool of self-regulation for activities of business and industry groups to coordinate with the potential for supplementing, complementing or substituting laws, tackling anti-money laundering (AML).[33] Blockchain additionally helps to verify user identity which eases customer onboarding, improves accountability and transparency and reduces costs as well as incidents of error, fraud, data duplication and processing delays.[34] Blockchain can also generate databases that are decentralised and enable user data control as well as identities that are borderless and irreversible with impact on financial inclusion.[35] Again, decentralisation discards the need for middlemen and improves and integrity of transactions by permitting public viewing of ledgers.[36] Immutability and incorruptibility of data are also guaranteed by a complicated string of mathematical numbers, impossible to be altered without notice.[37] Blockchain additionally benefits from tamper-resistance, data integrity and fast information sharing.[38] These equally discard the need for trusted central authorities such as clearing houses in financial transactions by disseminating copies of the records to all parties.[39]

On the flipside, blockchain operates anonymous systems in order to protect confidential information of users but also poses the risk of concealing the identity of users and making it difficult to track individual payments.[40] Again non-proof-of-work chains though not being susceptible to adverse disruption on the recent state of the chain, could be vulnerable to long-range attacks which enable a sufficient number of bad actors to efficiently rewrite an entire ledger almost immediately.[41] Furthermore, the immutability of blockchain means that smart contracts can self-execute transactions without giving banks the chance to resolve problems and misunderstandings such as funds transfer to the wrong recipients.[42]

Blockchain is equally expensive to deploy and may not be cost-effective for some financial services providers. Authors have also argued that although blockchain has proved useful in enabling secure virtual currencies, the prediction for economic development is difficult and necessitates deliberation that prevents the flooding of the industry with incompatible standards.[43] It has also been noted that though showing potential promise in the future, this technology may not impact budding clients in the short or medium term'.[44]

From the foregoing, it is shown that blockchain is useful in delivering secure network transactions. However, cost-effectiveness, appropriate standards and security measures are needed. In Nigeria, some fintechs such as Stella and Oradian are already deploying blockchain to offer instant payment services to benefit the financially excluded.[45] It is expected that more companies will adopt this trend and improve transparency, security and trust for clients and regulators.

6.3.2 Cryptocurrencies

In the introduction to this section, the relationship between cryptocurrency and DLT discussed in Section 6.3.1 was shown. Many cryptocurrencies are built on blockchain, which is a type of DLT. Cryptocurrencies are, however, discussed in this section as a medium of exchange in financial transactions. Blockchain was discussed in general in Section 6.3.1 as an underlying technology for assuring secure and immutable digital audit trails in financial transactions. Bitcoins and quorum are used as examples in the succeeding discourse cryptocurrency are 'a digital or virtual currency that is secured by cryptography, which makes it nearly impossible to counterfeit or double-spend.[46] Cryptocurrencies are decentralised networks based on blockchain technology that facilitate funds transfer between parties without being offered or managed by central authorities or third parties such as banks and therefore immune from interference or manipulation.[47]

Bitcoin is the first blockchain-based cryptocurrency to be created.[48] Bitcoin is a consensus-led and decentralised peer-to-peer payment network that discards the need for central authorities or middlemen, developed in 2009 by Satoshi Nakamoto (supposedly a pseudonym) to pay for goods or services, purchase, exchange and earn more bitcoins.[49] Bitcoin can only work correctly with a complete consensus among all users, recorded on a public blockchain ledger that contains every transaction ever processed and thus enables users to compute and verify the validity of each transaction.[50] The price of bitcoin is determined by the law of supply and demand while lost bitcoin wallets though remaining on the blockchain remain dormant and have the effect of removing money out of circulation as the private keys remain lost and invariably impossible to spend.[51]

Bitcoins have also aided law enforcement in the arrest of criminals involved in illegal online business.[52]

However, concerns about the lack of underlying assets, susceptibility to fluctuation and hacks and use in surreptitious criminal activities are decreasing regulatory acceptance of the coins. This is increased by the semi-anonymous nature of cryptocurrency transactions which has historically concealed illegal activities, such as evasion of taxes and money laundering and has led to unsuspecting consumers losing funds which are difficult to recover by national law enforcement agencies.[53] Furthermore, the irreversibility of Bitcoin transactions after execution leaves users without the opportunity to correct even simple mistakes such as a wrong address once entered in the bitcoin public ledger.[54] There are also issues around low scalability and the amount of transaction time, fees and the energy needed to mine new bitcoins.[55]

Authors have argued that bitcoins are still not set to fulfil the role of money in relation to serving as a store of value, medium of exchange and unit of account as a result of volatility and the paucity of acceptance by retailers and consumers.[56] However, bitcoin proponents are hopeful that as more users apply bitcoins to spending rather than to speculative investing, volatility will diminish and concerns around scalability and transaction time will wane especially following the recent expansion of the block and the introduction of lightning network solutions.[57]

In the meantime, companies are already looking into more stable coins that are backed by underlying assets and are potentially less prone to volatility. Two of these are discussed below, namely the Diem by Meta, (formerly, Facebook) and Quorum by JP Morgan. Although these have now been cancelled, the discourse on privacy, enterprise acceptance and regulatory challenges that confronted the successful launch of these coins is illustrative.

Meta announced the intended launch of the Diem cryptocurrency (first named Libra which was said to be designed on a safe and stable open-source blockchain, secured by real assets reserved and managed by an independent association made up of diverse entities that have the sole power to create (mint) and destroy (burn) Diem.[58] According to Meta, this was to ensure that persons or businesses globally could access money quickly, fairly and affordably, transfer funds abroad and make diverse payments ranging from tuitions, rentals and even buying coffee.[59] This announcement was, however, met with criticisms and the early exit of seven partners including PayPal, eBay, Visa and MasterCard.[60] World leaders and central banks also expressed concerns around the propensity to put the global financial system at risk and increase data threats, consumer detriments and the privatisation of money supply.[61]

Notably, Meta is one of the largest social media platforms in the world and could have easily leveraged this dominance to the provision of financial services which could disrupt the industry and lead to a loss of financial system control by national finance regulators. Against the backdrop of the grave Cambridge Analytica incident in 2016 when the data of millions of consumers were leaked, Meta has yet to demonstrate how future security intrusions will be averted. Regulators were not convinced that the company could improve financial inclusion without a clear guarantee of accompanying safeguards as to the safety of funds, protection of user data and integrity of the financial system. Without these safeguards, it is unclear how consumers could seek redress, particularly for small claims or cross-border transactions.

Furthermore, the Diem could have potentially ushered in an entire network of providers and authorised dealers including brokers, asset managers, custodians, exchanges, digital identity providers and verifiers whose identities and qualifications are yet to be defined.[62] It was also argued that Meta could have invariably played the role of a financial services regulator without a legal public mandate to adhere to.[63] Again, response to salient questions around which entities determine the weighting of sovereign currencies, reserve governance, maintenance of value and liquidity, resolution of conflicts of interest and exclusive rights to and cost of purchasing new coins were unanswered.[64] It was also pertinent for regulators to ponder on the question as to why the provision of digital currency and invariably, monetary policy decisions should be outsourced to a private company with the potential to control the entire economy without the guarantee of users' privacy.[65]

Again, although Meta asserted that customer verification requirements applicable to other finance providers would be complied with, there was still the potential to compete with the national legal tender and weaken the capacity of the national regulators to manage the monetary policy.[66] More so, Meta's promise of speedy payments could compromise KYC, money laundering laws and banks' mandate to monitor accounts for suspicious dealings, restrict money transfer and open up systemic risks without liquidity/deposit insurance safeguards.[67] Therefore, the launch of the Diem was trailed by sustained opposition amid concerns about risks to the global financial system, AML and monetary sovereignty.[68] Consequently, the planned launch has now been cancelled by the Diem Association and assets sold to Silvergate Capital Corporation for $182 million.[69]

Likewise, the JP Morgan Bank sought to launch a different type of stable currency named Quorum, based on the Ethereum blockchain technology. Quorum was described by the bank as an open-source blockchain platform with added privacy, strong permissions and one versatile, scalable platform to solve business needs.[70] The Quorum digital coin was to represent a fiat currency with a value, equivalent to one US dollar and to enable instantaneous funds transfer.[71] JP Morgan asserted that, if properly controlled, cryptocurrencies could hold advantages for blockchain by decreasing risks, reducing capital requirements and facilitating real-time fund transfers.[72]

Quorum only made it to the prototype stage intended for a small number of institutional clients before expansion to other entities but has had to be sold to ConsenSys, a software development company amid claims of the lack of profitability and enterprise acceptance.[73] Other stable cryptocurrencies backed by fiat, commodities and cryptocurrency such as Tether, USD Coin and Dai exist. However, a discussion on their individual features and potential are beyond the scope of this work.

In general, concerns around cryptocurrency are leading central banks and national governments to restrict or totally ban these currencies. In Nigeria, the authorities had earlier warned that investments are unregulated and investors could be at risk of loss. The CBN published a circular to stress that 'cryptocurrencies such as Bitcoin, Ripples, Monero, Litecoin, Dogecoin, Onecoin are not legal tender in Nigeria and that exchanges such as NairaEx are not licensed or regulated by the CBN'.[74] The bank cautioned that dealers and investors dealing in cryptocurrencies in Nigeria are not protected by law or regulated around the world; hence, loss of client funds without redress could ensue if these entities shut down.[75] Similarly, the Securities and Exchange Commission advised Nigerians to exercise extreme caution when investing in cryptocurrencies as the promoters are not recognised or authorised to receive deposits or provide any investment or other financial services due to the high risk of loss and the possibility of being fraudulent pyramid schemes.[76]

However, the CBN had previously release a press statement addressed to all banks, non-banks and other financial institutions banning cryptocurrencies and ordering banks to report anyone found to be dealing in currency and subsequently fined three banks to the tune of ₦800 million for defaulting.[77] But, in the presence of alternatives for exchanging cryptocurrencies, a ban enforced through banks' monitoring of accounts is counterproductive as users can utilise alternatives by virtue of their availability and tradability across borders. Exchanges can be completed on computer applications in Nigeria and abroad or held in foreign bank accounts and cryptocurrency wallets. It is no wonder therefore that in spite of these warnings and subsequent ban, cryptocurrency exchanges are still operating in Nigeria and platforms. CBN has now introduced the eNaira, a central bank digital currency discussed in Section 6.3.3. It will be interesting to see if Nigerians migrate to this digital currency or continue to gravitate towards cryptocurrencies.

Importantly, cryptocurrencies are complex to use compared to simply accessible mobile payment options used by Mpesa. Blockchain and cryptocurrencies are not built for scaling up, and although a private blockchain is being deployed by organisations such as the World Food Programme to help about 100 000 Syrian refugees, the same cannot be replicated to reach large unbanked populations.[78] The speed of completing transactions on blockchain is also slow compared to state-of-the-art financial systems. For instance, while the processing speed for Bitcoins is three to seven for each second, Visa boasts about 24,000 transactions per second.[79] It will, therefore, take some time for cryptocurrencies to advance financial inclusion.[80] To achieve this, cryptocurrencies need to be deployed or at least backed by payment system regulators to enable usage in varied transactions. This will also increase the chances that people will adopt this service.

6.3.3 Central bank digital currencies

Central Bank Digital Currencies (CBDCs) is a virtual money backed and issued by a central bank.[81] Essentially, these are alternatives to the cash held in digital forms on a wallet or as a token on a blockchain or other system. The

Bank of International Settlement (BIS) reports that CBDCs are being explored by 87 countries, seven of which have launched a digital currency, several such as the Project Dunbar comprising South Africa, Singapore, Malaysia and Australia are conducting cross-border tests and 17 countries including China and South Korea are in pilot stages.[82]

Seven (7) countries have launched a digital currency the first being Barbados and the latest, Nigeria. The BIS is to test the CBDC roll-out in Australia, Malaysia, Singapore and South Africa.[83] The BIS is also developing six CBDC-related proofs of concept with the aim of preserving some features of the present financial system model while enabling innovation.[84] China has been testing in different cities since and authorities have handed tens of millions of renminbi to citizens for the New Year to trial CBDCs in some Chinese cities.[85] Experts project that the failure to innovate a CBDC could divest central banks of monetary control and work hardship on the economy.[86]

Significantly, central banks have historically optimised technology for innovation, cost reduction wider customer reach to make the most of network effects and the preference for public money.[87] The fact that private money has arrived the scene means that the Central banks must act timely to evolve the digital future of money.[88] CBDCs usher in programmable money which opens the door for self-executing smart contracts.[89] This is of great appeal to individuals and businesses in an increasingly digital environment. Whether out of the fear of being left out or a conscious regulatory effort to continue to take centre stage in the issuance and regulation of money, the launch of CBDCs is becoming a trend.

The launch of the CBDCs, it is hoped, would garner a share of the market, and avoid the toppling of the central bank as apex authority over the issuance of money and control of the monetary policy. This could also prevent the elimination of banks and other financial institutions as intermediaries. CBDCs could facilitate international trade, aid financial inclusion, provide a low cost and quicker means of making remittance, and help social interventions, monetary policy effectiveness, payment systems efficiency and tax collection.[90]

But CBDCs could also impact the monetary policy by reducing the reserve balance held as deposits in commercial banks which could present a destabilising effect on the payment system.[91] Multiple demands on CBDCs could usher in a bank run and cybersecurity risks.[92]

Another risk is from the geo-political angle as CBDCs could topple dominant currencies such as the dollar from international trade.[93] Again the portability of the CBDCs according to some experts could lead to the substitution of some country currencies for stronger currencies.[94] Again, CBDCs could like the digital currencies before it, open the door to financial crimes through hacks, system circumvention and data compromise. CBDCs could equally affect credit intermediaries if no minimum is placed on what individuals can hold.[95] There is also the potential that government control of individuals, abuse of freedoms, data privacy concerns and security at an individual, domestic and international level could emanate.[96]

Therefore, policymakers must strive to ensure that CBDCs offer a better value proposition in terms of lower cost and promotion of financial inclusion, drive transparency, reduce crimes and aid monetary policy efficiency.[97] It is argued that a model CBDC should not be an alternative to national monetary systems, but rather mirror each country's fiat currency, and apply blockchain for better regulation.[98] This, like fiat is to be 'fixed in nominal terms, universally accessible and valid as legal tender for all public and private transactions'.[99]

In terms of design, research shows that financial consumers want CBDCs to embody 'privacy, security, broad usability, convenience, programmability, usability for micro-payments, as well as safeguard monetary and financial stability, enhance neutrality in digital payments, promote financial inclusion, access, innovation and openness.[100] A properly designed CBDC should embody low cost, convertibility, instant settlement, continuous availability and a high degree of security, resilience, flexibility and safety as important features and offer a safe, neutral, integrated and interoperable payment system, open to competition and innovation.[101] CBDCs should also meet standards of consumer use cases, public policy objectives and technology.[102]

CBDCs could be issued directly by the Central Bank without the involvement of the commercial banks or indirectly through the banks as intermediary which caters for client interface and there is no claim on the central bank.[103] Direct transmission of CBDCs to users could usher concerns around the disintermediation and reduce the balance sheet of commercial banks.[104]

Clients can access CBDCs via an account or with the use of tokens. The account-based model requires client identification while the token-based model uses cryptography and private keys and offers anonymity and greater access to users.[105] For the account-based model, the central bank could either open accounts for consumers and be responsible for onboarding at the danger of reputational risk, or enable banks and other financial institutions to deploy their payment platforms in a competitive environment.[106] Here, central banks do not have balance sheets or backup systems in case the private sector runs into technical outages.[107]

The second model, the token-based CBDC is similar to cash and is held on digital wallets and the balance reduces in tandem with payments.[108] These function like a digital bank account, where the central bank holds the account rather than a commercial bank.[109] While the key concern in an account-based system is client identification that of the token-based system is to ensure the validity of each token.[110] The verification for the token-based model is based on a computational procedure that is highly complex, energy-intensive and expensive as the entire chain of ownership of the tokens must be stored both on a blockchain ledger as well as on the individual nodes on the payment network.[111] The token-based model also predisposes the financial system to financial crimes and heralds concerns around money laundering, the financing of terrorism and tax evasion.

Ultimately, it has been proposed that an ideal CBDC should be an account-based, costless medium of exchange held directly at the central bank or made available through public–private partnerships with commercial banks.[112] Central Banks must, however, continue to work on issues around whether

CBDCs would be affected by inflation or should earn interest like other government zero-risk, short-term securities to fulfil the store of value element of money. The choice of the non-interest-bearing model may not incentivize deposits and could in turn miss out on the benefits of mass adoption.[113] The role of the central bank as a banker of last resort needs to be preserved, particularly, since during a financial crisis the bank can provide emergency liquidity to financial institutions or deposit insurance funds.[114]

In Nigeria, eNaira was launched in October 2020 by the CBN as a digital equivalent of the cash Naira, as a liability of the CBN and exchanged on par with the Naira.[115] The CBN maintains that the eNaira adheres to the BIS Hippocratic Oath for CBDC design. According to the bank, the first principle to 'do no harm' to the existing payment system is respected as the eNaira does not interfere with the use of money alternatives such as the physical naira, reserves and settlement accounts.[116] According to the bank, the eNaira also lends itself to the second principle concerning innovation and efficiency due to its openness to innovation and competition.[117] To meet unique payment needs, CBN expands on the three general principles from the BIS to introduce five Nigeria-specific principles to guide the eNaira design, namely, inclusivity and access, innovation and collaboration, efficiency, resilience and proudly Nigerian.[118]

The eNaira is designed as a hybrid CBDC or a two-tiered CBDC architecture wherein the CBN remains responsible for issuing the eNaira, managing the wallet, maintaining the central ledger and devising rules for implementation, monitoring and innovation while leveraging on distribution, payment and dispute resolution efficiencies of FSPs.[119] The infrastructure is built upon the open-source-permissioned hyperledger fabric variant of the distributed ledger technology (DLT) that is configurable, versatile, optimisable, scalable, and open to innovation.[120] This enables the core requirements of financial systems which include underlying identity frameworks, permissioned payment networks, high performance, low latency of transaction confirmation, privacy and confidentiality of transactions and data pertaining to business transactions.[121]

The CBN manages the wallets while FSPs act as nodes on the network to provide transaction processing, confirmation, record immutability and distribution to users.[122] The account-based model according to the bank, ensures inclusive access and financial system integrity and leverages on existing identity infrastructure, namely the Bank Verification Number, national identity number, and tax identification number that offers robust KYC and extends finance to the financially excluded.[123] To reduce the impact of pervasive industry disruption, the CBN has chosen to restrict the eNaira to micro-payments with limits on wallets.[124]

Expected benefits include driving the availability and usability of central bank money, strengthening the payment system, improving financial inclusion, lowering costs of cash processing, aiding revenue and tax collection, facilitating Diaspora remittances, improving efficiency of cross-border payments and enabling direct welfare disbursements to citizens.[125] The Central Bank maintains that the eNaira will conform to the data privacy provisions in the NITDA Data Protection Regulations 2019 and the AML/CFT checks championed by FSPs.[126]

There are still concerns around the eNaira. For instance, the complexity and Internet dependency of some usage platforms means that the eNaira could exclude uneducated populations including less literate persons and those who do not have access to Internet services or digital devices.[127] Again, the effect of the eNaira on disintermediation and the impact on bank funding and credit availability is a matter of some concern as users will need to convert some of their existing bank deposits into eNaira and hold the eNaira in wallets outside of banks.[128] This could reduce deposit liabilities, decrease funds for bank lending, affect liquidity management and shrink bank balance sheets.[129] Even a shift from retail to wholesale provision to stave off the negative effects of disintermediation could still affect costs, interest on credit assets and profit and additionally disrupt existing retail market strategies.[130]

6.3.4 Data analytics and big data

Data has been described as 'the new oil of the digital era'.[131] Data prove proving useful in financial transactions for many use cases as troves of datasets now characterised as big data flood the financial market. Big data systems can hold much larger datasets compared to traditional databases, ingest incoming high volume data in real-time and gather and store data in different formats.[132] Hence, Volume, velocity and variety are the chief characteristics of big data. Big data have been defined as diverse data having huge volume and speed of accumulation such as client information, social network profiles, e-mails, logs from call centres, tweets and sensor data from mobile phones and smart meters and cars'.[133]

To analyse these large data sets, big data analytics are invaluable. Big data analytics employ advanced analytic techniques in testing out a broad range of data that transcend the present capacity of traditional databases to process large datasets.[134] Here, client data obtained from phone usage, profiles or social graphs that represent social network relationships, online shopping habits and remittances can be used to determine credit creditworthiness.[135] Specifically, digital financial service (DFS) providers obtain data from 'transactional data, mobile call records, call centre recordings, customer and agent registrations, airtime purchase patterns, credit bureau information, social media posts, geospatial data and more'.[136]

With these rapid advances in data capture, transmission and storage, including advanced analytics and machine learning, big data can reduce the time and cost spent on searching, aggregating information and identifying patterns and relationships for KYC and other suspicious investigations.[137] Insights from data analytics are useful for revealing trends and metrics to optimise business efficiency.[138] Big data analysis is also valuable for the real-time identification and recalculation of risk portfolios and for the detection of fraudulent behaviour.[139] Artificial intelligence (AI) obtained in real-time from mobile, social, video and audio networks, the Internet of Things (IoT), big data and transactional applications are useful for improving insights.[140] AI, for instance, has the potential to advance data analytics and deepen financial inclusion in the longer term by effectively providing banks with insightful data for enhanced automation, cost savings and scalability for serving low-income clients.[141]

Big data acquired by financial services providers can additionally help in 'strategic business decisions, designing of customised products for clients, client acquisition and cross-selling'.[142] This can promote customer loyalty, automated processing, decision-making, performance monitoring and accurate risk assessment of persons without credit histories in loan applications.[143] Big data enables companies to speedily compile large datasets, identify clients, save costs and assess risk for faster loan consideration and designing specific financial products.[144]

Customer understanding also increases with the use of 'alternative data, including social media activity, email usage, utility payments history, mobile phone records, and psychometric testing optimised by advanced data analytics tools'.[145] Policymakers can additionally obtain detailed insights using access and usage trends to develop outlook and strategies that drive inclusion.[146]

In spite of the benefits, big data presents privacy risks for clients as personal and sensitive information such as interest and activities collected may be at risk of exposure or lead to denial of a client loan for previous late repayments without further information on the circumstances that led to the default.[147] Clients with similar characteristics can also be profiled and denied access to financial products and services.[148] Additionally, big data aggregation could lead to social exclusion where algorithms are used to determine creditworthiness based on skin colour or place of residence, and price discrimination can be applied to customers considered too risky or unprofitable.[149]

Big data also helps banks with risk management and avoids de-risking.[150] De-risking is embarked upon by banks to comply with the Anti-Money Laundering and Counterfeiting of Terrorism (AML/CFT) recommendations of the Financial Action Task Force (FATF). Although the AML/CFT requirements were meant to simplify due diligence by transferring high-risk compliance resources and taking out financial inclusion barriers of lower-risk customers, this, unfortunately, excludes the poor, perceived to generate too small an income to justify compliance costs.[151]

Big data also ushers information asymmetry as providers acquire huge amounts of data without the knowledge of clients, hence drawing profound conclusions without adhering to data protection standards including client consent.[152] This is imperative to address as a result of the ease of identifying clients in digital transactions. Research has shown that as little as four data points (such as approximate locations and times) are enough to identify about 95 per cent of users in a database of 1.5 million people which is enough to track clients' daily lifestyles and locations with little consumer safeguards.[153]

Again, there is a lack of market supervision and regulation in addition to unclear legal frameworks on big data, especially with regard to data protection.[154]

Though banks in many cases are bound by data protection laws, entities such as MNOs and fintech companies are scarcely bound by these rules and could pose a problem for responsible client data use.[155] Data generated by this process also creates black boxes that are complex for both financial institutions and regulators to understand; opening the opportunity for manipulation.[156]

Another difficulty arises from establishing who collects, stores or uses data and who should be responsible for data misuse in the chain of actors, especially on a cross-sectional and international level. Without this information, it becomes increasingly difficult to pursue consumer safeguards such as data access, the right to object to and correct information use and abuse. There is also some difficulty in finding collaboration in data acquisition by entities such as utility companies, MNOs, social media platforms and data vendors.[157] Significantly, there is evidence of the fact that as much as 82 per cent of users do not read privacy policies before accepting them because they are lengthy and written in unfamiliar jargon.[158]

Authors have therefore suggested that countries need to ensure that data collection is transparent, addresses the 'why' about consumer behaviour and the power imbalance around data use by providers, including enabling objection to inaccuracies.[159] Rules for ownership of data also need to be spelt out and ethical use of data, ingrained in the policies of actors in the chain of finance provision.

Big data analytics can help financial inclusion by fact-checking potential customer identity. This is also useful in determining suitability for loans for clients without credit histories. In Nigeria, fintech companies such as Branch and PiggyVest rely on data gathered from transaction logs and related sources to offer lending and financial advisory services.[160] Data protection and privacy standards must, however, be respected when dealing with personal and sensitive financial consumer data.

6.3.5 Artificial intelligence

As noted in the introduction, artificial intelligence is a versatile technology that aids many digital financial services trends. Robo-advising, peer-to-peer lending, data analytics and big data, for instance, employ this technology to understand and analyse client data as well as to offer advice. In this section, however, artificial intelligence is discussed specifically in relation to the consideration of loan applications by financial services providers.

AI is 'a suite of technologies, enabled by adaptive predictive power and exhibition of some degree of autonomous learning, that dramatically advances the ability to recognise patterns, anticipate future events, create good rules, make good decisions and communicate with others'.[161] AI is praised for possessing the potential to bring value to business by using intelligent automation to replace repetitive manual tasks, increase workers' judgement, improve interactions with customers and develop intelligent products.[162] 'A digital financial ecosystem needs regulatory mechanisms to provide feedback and proactive guidance that encourage prioritising consumer financial welfare rather than using supervisory models that overemphasise punitive and reactionary enforcement'.[163] AI can serve this function.

In spite of the benefits, AI is argued to potentially usher 'legacy problems such as product steering, discriminatory pricing, unfair credit rationing, exclusionary filtering, and digital redlining as human input is absent to deal with unintended or nuanced marginal problems'.[164] There are also issues around algorithmic bias, especially with the concerns around blanket exclusion of specific classes of consumers by a system that is still under consideration by regulators.[165] Further, it has been argued that AI algorithms, though proficient at complex computational tasks, are lacking in the capacity to mimic true human intelligence beyond pattern recognition unlike human intelligence.[166]

There are several examples of the use of AI in the financial services sector in Nigeria. The Stanbic IBTC Bank PLC's bluebots are used to perform anti-money laundering checks, credit risk assessment, confirm cheques, populate Microsoft Excel templates, launch web browsers, log into secure web pages, scrap the Web and extract data.[167] Similarly, Diamond Bank's Ada provides personalised services to customers using lessons from past interactions and can open accounts, transfer funds, buy airtime, pay utility bills and check stock prices.[168] Leo, the United Bank for Africa personal assistant, additionally helps in social media banking and can open a new account, transfer funds and initiate loan applications for users.[169]

Although AI is useful to design personalised products suitable for specific consumer segments, efforts must, however, be made by the regulators to prevent companies from using this advancement in technology to unfairly exclude classes of consumers from accessing finance.

6.3.6 Robo-advisors

Robo-advisors are defined as 'digital platforms that use automated algorithm to offer financial advice and automatically invest assets based on the financial situation and future goals of clients with no human supervision'.[170] Robo-advisors also refer to low-cost online platforms which serve as alternatives to traditional financial human advisors and manage clients' portfolios using automated algorithm.[171] Some models are strictly machine-automated and do not require any human input or interference. But there are some hybrid models that combine algorithms with human guidance to serve clients that require more complex financial portfolios.[172]

Robo-advising is growing out of an increasing need for scalability, cognitive advice and next-generation user experience.[173] These platforms, unlike traditional human advisors, are always available to clients.[174] Investment decisions are based on client's investment purpose, timeframes, strategies, goals, risk appetite and risk metrics as well as client's income and years to retirement.[175]

In terms of potential, robo-advisors could increase investment habits in citizens. These robots can add transparency to decision-making and investment, improve customer experience using web and mobile applications, provide low-cost products and encourage passive investing.[176] This service also promises low-cost services in financial transactions.[177]

Robo-advisors are further praised for their capacity to make investment decisions that are not based on human emotions. Thus no panic sales or over-excited purchases are made as specified and pre-set algorithms and client goals are the basis for investment decisions. Again, these require no investment knowledge on the part of the users, employ simple strategies and are not time-consuming.[178] Hence, incidents of behavioural biases, human and machine design subjectivity and bias for products that pay commissions are reduced.[179] Robo-advisors unlike their human counterparts are also able to monitor several assets simultaneously.[180]

Robo-advisors, however, usher new regulatory challenges for regulators that are more attuned to dealing with humans rather than machines.[181] Robo-advisors are criticised for lacking empathy and sophistication as a result of minimal human presence and operate on the assumption that clients are financially sophisticated with defined goals and understanding of financial circumstances.[182] These advisors also entail costs associated with simplistic and not tailored questions like human assistants and so do not give a comprehensive view of client's financial situation.[183] Robo-advising can lead to consumer disengagement as a result of automation and jettison of consumer rights in the early stages of the robo-advisory trend.[184] There are also concerns around the limited investor options, difficulty in getting human-to-human interaction, and the fact that users may have to open multiple brokerage accounts to invest in new stocks.[185]

From a financial inclusion perspective, the introduction of robo-advising seems too early for the excluded class. Robo-advising requires some level of financial capability and digital sophistication on the part of the individual users to set the necessary financial needs parameters. Hence, financial capability is needed to decipher financial products and set investment goals that suit individual circumstances as well as the digital sophistication to adequately input relevant information and communicate with the machines.

These robots may therefore be ahead of the curve for the financially excluded that might not own smartphones, afford Internet services to monitor financial trends or possess the digital and financial sophistication to understand complex investment portfolios. It has been suggested that simpler financial services be deployed until financial capability is attained to aid informed financial decision-making by the financially excluded classes.

6.3.7 Application programming interface

An API is 'a simple and standardised means by which technology platforms from different vendors or locations communicate with one another, allowing for the controlled yet seamless flow of data between systems'.[186] APIs are also defined as 'mechanisms that enable software programs to "talk" to one another by selling access to data and systems to third parties'.[187] APIs can be classified according to functions. Payment APIs, for example, enable payment and receipt of funds; data APIs share and aggregate data, ecosystem expansion APIs facilitate loan consideration and opening of accounts, while consent and identity APIs aid KYC, data sharing and funds circulation.[188] MTN Uganda, Finserve (a subsidiary of Equity Bank) and Paystack have all opened a set of payment APIs to drive customer growth and activity.[189]

APIs could be open, private or market places. Open APIs are designed for general, repeatable use, are openly accessible to third parties and are presently deployed by MTN Uganda, Nedbank in South Africa and Equity Bank, Kenya.[190] Private APIs, on the other hand, are designed to grant specific internal or external, pre-authorised parties access to certain functionalities, based on predetermined requirements but lack the feature of repeatability.[191] Lastly, the API marketplace is offered by third parties on behalf of any number of financial institutions and offers services such as document aggregation, KYC, onboarding and the linking of fintech innovators with financial institutions.[192]

APIs connect innovative app developers and startups with DFS providers looking to reach customers.[193] These partnerships could for instance ensure that financial institutions' regulatory approvals and core banking capabilities are effectively combined with fintech innovators' ability to iterate rapidly and develop new products for underserved or unproven customer segments.[194] APIs also ensure lower costs for marketplace participants by spreading the costs of constructing APIs among a larger number of participating financial institutions.[195] It has been estimated that adopting API standards will provide more seamless integration and cost savings for better customer experience.[196]

APIs are largely enabled by open banking which is 'the use of open technologies by third-party providers to build services and applications around financial institutions so that customers can view and manage multiple accounts from a centralised location'.[197] Open banking holds promise for advancing diverse business offerings such as sites for comparing the rates of loans, fixed deposits and returns on current accounts as well as centralised KYC management.[198] Open banking also enables direct, easier and seamless client access to accredited financial institution data to drive better price comparison, improved services and enhancing competition and innovation.[199] Fintechs additionally have the opportunity to access and share the needed data to understand customer financial behaviour, create new solutions, widen customer base and adequately assess borrowers' financial position, goals, purchasing preferences and likelihood to repay loans.[200]

There is potential for this to scale up as the Nigerian fintech space presents several examples of successful collaborations. CBN, for instance, has been able to encourage collaboration in some banking components such as the Bank Verification Number (BVN), Nigeria Uniform Bank Account Number (NUBAN) and the NIBSS Instant Payment (NIP).[201] Incidentally, Interswitch and Paga have adopted open banking since partnering with Open Technology Foundation (OTF), a non-profit championing the deployment of this trend in the country.[202] CBN has also introduced the Regulatory Framework for Open Banking in Nigeria 2021.

Like all technological trends, however, it is pertinent to consider and address risks that can create consumer detriment, especially in Nigeria's quest for financial inclusion. For instance, there are concerns that open banking can weaken bank/customer relationships and expose customers to fintech competitors.[203] Open banking is also prone to reputational risk in cases of data breaches, even if the breach occurred on the platform of a collaborator.[204] There are also concerns that issues surrounding capital and funding could emanate from easy circulation of client deposits among the participating banks.[205] API can usher significant upfront investment of time and resources in addition to risks of converting from complex legacy IT and core banking systems which were not initially designed to be accessed via API.[206]

To address these concerns, there is the need to adopt APIs with caution. Certifications are needed to ensure that APIs adopted by parties are built according to specifications.[207] Data protection laws also require strengthening to ensure that consumer consent is granted before personal or sensitive information is shared with partner institutions. This should be augmented by personal information management tools to enable consumers to amend incorrect information and delete changed life and financial circumstances. Also, regulators must mandate responsible data processing to ensure client safety and privacy.

6.3.8 Peer-to-peer lending

Peer-to-peer (P2P) lending has been defined as 'a form of direct money lending to individuals or businesses through an online platform that matches lenders with the potential borrowers without an official financial institution participating as an intermediary'.[208] P2P loans are usually unsecured but some secured loans backed by luxury goods also exist.[209]

There are various models deployed by P2P platforms. The information intermediation model is a platform that matches lenders and borrowers, allows parties to trade directly using agreed terms and incurs any credit risks that arise; while the guarantee model goes further than merely matching the parties to providing guarantees for principal and interest borrowed.[210] A third model is the asset securitisation model which repackages standard form securities from partitioned cash-generating assets for sale to investors.[211] Lastly, the debt assignment model helps lenders and P2P platforms to deliver loans to clients and subsequently sell the claims from the loans to platform investors.[212] P2P lending is driven by advanced credit analytics which lowers default risk and by extension, the interest rate and cost of extending credit, compared to brick-and-mortar establishments.[213]

In terms of the benefit to businesses, cost savings arise also from lower operating costs and the lower cost of regulatory compliance.[214] For users, P2P provides low-cost lender and borrower acquisition and accessibility to cheaper funds.[215] Again, P2P enables lenders and borrowers to identify one another and to agree to personalised terms thereby doing away with intermediary intrusions.[216] P2P lending is said to humanise the lending process by drawing on a public sense of community and transparency and further encourages repayment as a result of the consciousness that individuals, and not banks will suffer for defaults.[217]

However, with P2P lending platforms, credit-worthiness and other client information are more difficult to ascertain, which could result in a higher risk of default and foist a strain on lenders seeking compensation.[218] The insufficiency of information on borrowers can also result in the misallocation of credit where viable consumers are excluded and over-indebtedness by reckless lending to clients without ascertaining repayment capacity.[219] Again, access to credit without proper risk evaluation and high-interest rates could lead to over-indebtedness for borrowers.[220]

Consequently, P2P has been shown to fail in many economies as fast as it has grown due to reasons such as information asymmetry between parties, insufficient capital, unsanctioned guaranties, inefficient players (mainly drawn by the opportunity for high returns) and improper conduct of due diligence.[221] Even in China where P2P has taken scale, there are still stories of lost funds, especially with regard to Ponzi schemes disguised as lending platforms. The loosely regulated *Ezubo*, hailed by the media and government officials as an award-winning online credit financial brand is one example that resulted in massive financial losses when it was later discovered to be a Ponzi scheme.[222]

In Nigeria, companies such as SureCredit, Aella Credit and Social Lender developed by Sterling Bank are in operation.[223] KiaKia is a licensed lender that uses machine learning, big data and artificial intelligence to facilitate peer-to-peer lending and Flint facilitates borrowing for rent, medical expenses, school fees, etc.[224]

P2P holds some potential in the Nigerian financial market by creating the opportunity for people to lend outside of social circles. As discussed in Chapter 4, Nigerians prefer to borrow from family and friends. Funds are thus limited to the capacity of these small social circles. P2P, therefore, has the potential to expand this network and also helps secure the privacy of financial transactions, especially for women. Women are among the main financially excluded consumer segments in need of financial inclusion initiatives given the bias in the exclusion rate between the sexes as shown in Chapter 1. Women can also escape cultural norms and save for future needs, family emergencies or economic shocks. Critical challenges such as lack of trust, inadequate understanding of the relatively new concept, nascent national ID scheme, old laws and lengthy court processes could, however, manifest.[225] Nigeria has also had its fair share of Ponzi schemes which have made the public weary.

In Indonesia, the regulators are curbing funds mismanagement as well as high return and interest rates by adopting tighter lending measures such as requiring that borrowers have bank accounts and also encouraging lending platforms to collaborate with banks.[226] With increased financial literacy and sensitisation, this trend can potentially develop in aid of better access to finance in Nigeria.

6.3.9 Digital identification

Ensuring a legal identity for everyone including registration of birth by the year 2030 is provided as goal 16.9 of the sustainable development goals of the United Nations. Identity is said to be a public good and a requisite for modern life since proof of identity is crucial for a person's engagement in socio-economic and political life existence.[227] Identification (ID) extends far beyond registration to enable participation in civic duties and legal rights as well as financial inclusion.[228] Official identity also transcends policy and convenience and is a fundamental human right that facilitates voting, education, banking, welfare, health and economic advancement.[229]

Identity can be functional or foundational. Functional identification supports a specific service or population group without linking to schemes set up for other purposes while foundational systems are mainly deployed by the government to cater to the entire country.[230] Identity can also be physical such as an identity card or a digital identification.

Digital identity (ID) can be defined as

> the digital representation of the information known about a specific individual or organisation encompassing a claim (assertion of the truth of something, typically one which is disputed or in doubt), an identifier, knowledge of a secret personally-identifying information and membership of a given group (e.g. people under 16).[231]

A digital identity also refers to 'a collection of electronically captured and stored identity attributes that uniquely describes a person within a given context and is used for electronic transactions'.[232] Digital identity is characterised by various features ranging from 'biographic data (e.g. name, age, gender, address) and biometric data (fingerprints, iris scans, handprints) as well as other attributes that are more broadly related to what the person does or something someone else knows about the individual'.[233]

Digital ID 'provides remote assurance that a person is who they purport to be'.[234] This also provides the opportunity to boost efficiency and innovation by enabling government and business to deliver services electronically, particularly in reaching disadvantaged groups.[235] Digital ID has the potential to help countries with weak or non-existent national identification systems and additionally help to create and automate such systems through biometrics, digital databases, digital credentials and mobile, online and offline applications.[236]

Significantly, increased digitisation is leading to new ways of identifying people using machine learning and algorithm analysis to gather data from mobile phones, social media participation and e-commerce.[237] Data from connected devices, e-commerce and social and professional platforms can generate detailed data about location, reputation, professional connections and social lives of people even without knowing the name, age or date of birth of persons.[238]

Advances in digital technology are also facilitating digital identification verification. Mobile authentication aids MNOs to authenticate client identity digitally rather than with an ID card, while algorithmic ID authenticates identity using patterns and unique features garnered from the digital trails of clients.[239] Blockchain-backed ID can be used to permanently record and access transactions, eliminate false asset claims and resolve land titling issues.[240]

Digital identity also helps individuals to prove and assert identity in an instantaneous, paperless manner, access benefits and services, claim entitlements and equally helps the government in fiscal management, revenue generation, accountability, transparency and the removal of fake and duplicate entries.[241] Identity further facilitates better communication between people and citizens.[242] Additionally, digital identity can help in the distribution of public goods, the reduction of corruption and the incidents of ghost or duplicate beneficiaries.[243] Digital ID can decrease the risks of human error or abuse by integrating data and assuring quality control.[244] Digital ID additionally helps persons to access 'education, healthcare and labour markets and fosters safe migration'.[245]

However, digital ID without the proper design or controls can make specific populations of persons susceptible to unfair targeting for financial profit as well as political manipulation and social control by limiting access to services such as travel, payments and social media sites.[246] Additionally, without mandating data standards such as data minimisation, consent and related standards of protection, data breaches can occur without redress for users. Again, people without the required sophistication or trust to access these systems may be excluded without alternative manual options.[247] Identity theft which is 'the use of personally identifying information belonging to one individual by another for financial or personal gain' is a further concern exacerbated by the emergence of synthetic identity which enables fraudsters to falsely get included in a digital database.[248]

One common form of digital identification is biometrics. Biometrics is defined as 'metrics related to human characteristics including, fingerprint, face recognition, palm veins, etc.'[249] Biometrics is also 'the use of electronically captured facial features, iris patterns or fingerprints to authenticate a person's identity'.[250] This is the 'biological and behavioural characteristic of an individual from which distinguishing, repeatable biometric features can be extracted for the purpose of biometric recognition'.[251] Biometrics is growing in popularity due to decreasing cost of using technology to capture and authenticate biometric features.[252]

Biometrics include fingerprints, iris scans and palm prints. DNA matching, iris, retina face and hand geometry, fingerprint recognition, gait and voice have also been included.[253] Biometrics use distinctive physiological or behavioural characteristics to authenticate a person's identity and can monitor system access and aid customer identification, verification and due diligence.[254] This is comparably more secure and easier to use than other authentication factors such as passwords and tokens and unlike knowledge- or token-based authenticators, biometrics cannot be lost or forgotten.[255] Furthermore, biometrics are for the most part inclusive even for disabled persons. For instance, research shows that iris scans are not sight-dependent and so are usable even for the blind except in the case of diseases such as cataract.[256] In Nigeria, biometric audits have been used to decrease government pension payouts by about 40 per cent.[257]

But biometrics could usher privacy and data protection issues. It is expected that DFS providers in deploying biometric systems would adhere to the provisions of the NITDA Data Protection Act 2019, which provides for the responsibility of data controllers and processors as well as consumer data rights. Technological infallibility is equally a concern. For instance, fingerprint scanners have been tricked to accept reactivated latent prints and artificial fingers made with forged fingerprints, candle wax or gelatine.[258] Research by Indian experts, however, demonstrates that the chances of infallibility are low as there is only a 0.057 per cent probability of erroneous duplicates entered against a gallery of 84 million people.[259]

Similarly, fingerprints can be affected by cuts or burns, significant weight gain or loss, age and medical conditions such as arthritis.[260] Loss of fingers and skin pigmentation could also affect fingerprinting and can in rare cases be mistaken.[261] Privacy cannot also be guaranteed in terms of passive capture where for instance, 'fingerprints can be retrieved from smooth surfaces, iris templates can be extracted from high-quality facial photographs and simple voice recognition systems might be fooled by a covertly obtained recording'.[262] Again, without independent evaluations, sellers of the devices may not freely provide information on failure rates and anti-spoofing technologies are not always efficient.[263]

The efficiency of biometrics can, however, be improved by requiring more than one metric of identification to increase the chances of authenticity and also guarantee that even disabled persons such as paraplegic persons and persons with some eye deformities are included. It has also been suggested that eliminating ambient conditions, such as humidity for fingerprinting, reducing excess light for facial capture and controlling bandwidth, connection quality and language for voice recognition can aid effective capture.[264]

Notably, the BVN of the CBN as well as the national identity card, voter's card, driver's licence and international passport are also built on clients' biometrics. The BVN is a mandatory requirement in Nigeria for operating a bank account. The national identity management commission (NIMC) in Nigeria has embarked on a data harmonisation project to converge these datasets into one large national database.[265]

Beyond the effort of the NIMC, it is important to note that the identity ecosystem in Nigeria is fragmented with 13 government agencies offering ID services at the federal level and four at the state level at an estimated total cost of USD 4.3 billion and ongoing efforts to harmonise records.[266] Although the cost of conducting national registration can prove expensive establishing a public–private partnership between government and companies to take care of initial financial burden, ensuring revenue flows and sustainability could be helpful.[267] It is hoped that as harmonisation improves more people will sign up for financial services resulting in greater financial inclusion in Nigeria.

6.4 Summary of legal issues raised by foregoing financial service technologies

Although some legal issues raised by the foregoing technologies are embedded within the discussion on the emerging issues in the above section, a brief commentary is necessary. It is important to acknowledge that even though, these technologies bring some benefits to the finance industry, certain risks are also evident. For instance, as outlined above, it is notable that blockchain, although praised for improving the security of financial transactions by maintaining an immutable audit trail, is still laden with high costs, slow processing rates and complexity of deployment. Again, the anonymity offered by blockchain can conceal surreptitious activities such as terrorism financing and money laundering.

Similarly, data analytics and big data raise privacy risks when personal and sensitive data are divulged to third parties without the consent of the data subject. There are also risks from social exclusions of consumer groups including the poor or rural dwellers that may not be perceived as creditworthy by algorithms. Similarly, artificial intelligence can bring about discriminatory pricing and algorithm bias that exclude the poor. There is also the potential that the merely reaching decisions with the use of pattern recognition can prove detrimental to consumers.

With regard to robo-advisors, the need for improved financial capability and digital channels sophistication means that it may still take some years before this technology is utilised by the excluded. Furthermore, API is vital to interoperability between providers and enables consumers to access financial services more conveniently. However, the open banking component could weaken banker-customer relationships and introduce reputational and systemic risks from data breaches on an individual provider's platform, with implications for other providers within the group.

Cryptocurrency and stable currency are gaining prominence around the world, but the potential to rival national currencies is being met with resistance. Digital coins such as the Diem and Quorum are criticised for being deployed by private organisations without the public responsibility to protect the financial system. The coins are also fraught with high transaction costs, slow processing times and irreversibility of transactions which makes amendments difficult. The potential to replace national regulators is also being resisted. The central bank digital currency, though backed by national government, programmable and able to promote financial system efficiency and transparency could also usher in social control, disintermediation and affect financial integrity through hacks.

Concerning peer-to-peer lending, trust and ascertaining the identity of consumers are still major concerns because the national identification management system in Nigeria is still a work in progress. This issue also pertains to the use of digital identification in Nigeria, particularly when only one metric of identification is allowed. People have been able to circumvent the functionality of iris and fingerprint scanners and extreme weight loss or gain, loss of fingers and skin pigmentation could make the fingerprints ineffective when used in identification verification systems.[268] Also, unfair targeting, blanket exclusions and data breaches present further detriments to the consumer.

Overall, it is important to ensure that the risks posed by these technological exploits do not hide under the wings of financial service innovation to expose consumers and the financial system to avoidable risks.

Concluding remarks

About 1.4 billion people globally and 35.9 per cent of Nigerians have no access to financial services due to reasons such as distance, financial illiteracy, irregular income, unemployment and account ineligibility. The foregoing research was important due to the scale of financial exclusion, the proven capacity of financial inclusion to lift people out of poverty, the need for tailored regulatory policies and the opportunity to harness the value and ubiquity of DFS for the financially excluded.

This research analysed the suitability of the enabling laws and institutions for digital financial services in Nigeria for addressing the needs of the financially excluded. In considering this, the reasons why a significant number of Nigerians remain financially excluded, in spite of the abundance of regulatory initiatives, were addressed. Using a combination of doctrinal and empirical methods, the burden of accessing financial services was highlighted, strategies for financial inclusion were considered and options for suitable legal and institutional frameworks were explored.

The analysis indicates that the path to financial inclusion in Nigeria is characterised by a myriad of laws, gradual DFS adoption rates, a mainly bank-centred regulatory model and a wide disparity in the pattern of inclusion across gender and geographical strands. Transaction costs remain significant and cash is still king. There is a need to therefore adopt a more consumer-centred approach to regulation, permit more alternative providers for onboarding of diverse segments of consumers and adapt laws and regulatory policies that are tailored to the needs of the excluded. Additionally, increased financial literacy and transactional capacity are needed to harness digital financial services. It is expected that this book will inform regulatory changes that will enable a methodical migration of more of the financially excluded class into the formal finance sector both in Nigeria and other climes.

Notes

1 Bangko Sentral ng Philipinas, *Financial Inclusion in the Philippines* (2018) at 5, available at http://www.bsp.gov.ph/downloads/Publications/2018/FIP_1Sem2018.pdf, accessed on 15 July 2020.

2 KPMG, *FinTech in Nigeria: Understanding the Value Proposition* (2016) at 7, available at https://assets.kpmg/content/dam/kpmg/ke/pdf/idas/thought-leaderships/ng-fintech-in-nigeria-understanding-the-value-proposition.pdf, accessed on 15 July 2020.

3 Co-creation Hub, *About Us,* available at https://cchubnigeria.com/about/, accessed on 27 September 2019.

4 KPMG note 2 at 7. See also Moses Adeniyi, 'Education: LASG executes 1,097 projects, introduces 25,000 pupils to coding, other computer training in 2-yrs', *NewsDirect,* May 21, 2021, available at https://nigeriannewsdirect.com/education-lasg-executes-1097-projects-introduces-25000-pupils-to-coding-other-computer-training-in-2-yrs/, accessed on 28 February 2022.
5 MacDonald Dzirutwe, *Fintech Startup Flutterwave Raises $250 Million at over $3 Billion Valuation* February 16, 2022, available at https://finance.yahoo.com/news/fintech-startup-flutterwave-raises-250–080714915.html, accessed on 7 March 2022.
6 KPMG note 2 at 12.
7 EFInA, 'Overview and lessons learnt from global fintech landscape and Nigerian fintech landscape', *EFInA FinTech Report,* December 2018 at 18, available at https://www.efina.org.ng/wp-content/uploads/2019/04/EFInA-FinTech-Report-Global-and-Nigeria-Landscape.pdf, accessed on 19 December 2019.
8 Deloitte, *Fintech in Nigeria and the Women who Lead'* (2019) at 9, available at https://www2.deloitte.com/content/dam/Deloitte/ng/Documents/financial-services/ng-fintech-in-Nigeria-and-the-women-who-lead-29032019.pdf, accessed on 19 December 2019.
9 Ibid at 11.
10 Buy Bitcoin Worldwide, *Popular Exchanges to Buy Bitcoin in Nigeria,* available at https://www.buybitcoinworldwide.com/nigeria/, accessed on 15 July 2020.
11 KPMG note 2 at 29.
12 United Bank of Africa, *Hi I Am Leo,* available at https://www.ubagroup.com/nigeria/personal-banking/digital-banking/chat-with-leo/, accessed on 2 December 2019.
13 Enhancing Financial Innovation and Access in Nigeria (EFInA), *Key Findings: EFInA Access to Financial Services in Nigeria* Survey (2020) at 14, available at https://a2f.ng/wp-content/uploads/2021/06/A2F-2020-Final-Report.pdf, accessed on 14 January 2021.
14 Ibid at 7.
15 Kunle Aderinokun, Diaspora Remittances Hit $34bn as Nigerian Migrant Workers Top List, August 29, 2021, available at https://www.thisdaylive.com/index.php/2021/08/29/diaspora-remittances-hit-34bn-as-nigerian-migrant-workers-top-list/, accessed on 28 February 2022.
16 Jim Woodsome & Vijaya Ramachandran, *Fixing AML: Can New Technology Help Address the De-risking Dilemma?* (2018) at 46.
17 Ibid at 46–8.
18 Bangko Sentral ng Ibid at 15.
19 Makada Henry-Nickie, *How Artificial Intelligence Affects Financial Consumers* (2019), available at https://www.brookings.edu/research/how-artificial-intelligence-affects-financial-consumers/, accessed on 26 October 2019.
20 Ibid.
21 Karim Sultan, Umar Ruhi & Rubina Lakhani, *Conceptualizing Blockchains: Characteristics and Applications* (2018) at 53, available at https://arxiv.org/ftp/arxiv/papers/1806/1806.03693.pdf, accessed on 15 October 2019.
22 Ibid.
23 Michael Pisa & Matt Juden, *Blockchain and Economic Development: Hype vs. Reality* (2017) 7, available at https://emsdialogues.org/wp-content/uploads/2020/02/blockchain-and-economic-development-hype-vs-reality.pdf, accessed on 15 October 2019.
24 Ibid at 8.
25 Jim Woodsome & Vijaya Ramachandran note 16 at 48.
26 Karim Sultan, Umar Ruhi & Rubina Lakhani note 21 at 52.
27 Michael Pisa & Matt Juden note 22 at 9.
28 Karim Sultan, Umar Ruhi & Rubina Lakhani note 21 at 51.
29 Ibid at 52.
30 International Finance Corporation, *Can Blockchain Technology Address De-Risking in Emerging Markets*? (2017) at 2, available at https://www.ifc.org/wps/wcm/connect/

f0defcac-ebac-487e-912a-8d8a7a8b07ff/EMCompass+Note+38+Derisking+and+Blockchain+5–24+FINAL.pdf?MOD=AJPERES&CVID=lMWVNUO, accessed on 15 July 2020.

31 Ibid.

32 Ibid at 1.

33 Alfio A. Puglisi, *Evolving Regulatory Frameworks: Blockchain as a Form of Trust — Comparative Evidence,* 212, in Doron Goldbarsht & Louis de Koker, Financial Technology and the Law Combating Financial Crime, edited by Law, Governance and Technology Series 47, Springer 2022.

34 Ethan Loufield, Dennis Ferenzy &Tess Johnson, *Accelerating Financial Inclusion with New Data: Joint Report from the Centre for Financial Inclusion at Accion and Institute of International Finance* (2018) at 24, available at https://content.centerforfinancialinclusion.org/wp-content/uploads/sites/2/2018/08/AcceleratingFINewData_Final_2018.06.26.pdf, accessed on 15 July 2020.

35 Ibid.

36 Ilker Koksal, *The Benefits of Applying Blockchain Technology in Any Industry* (2019), available at https://www.forbes.com/sites/ilkerkoksal/2019/10/23/the-benefits-of-applying-blockchain-technology-in-any-industry/#547e32c549a5, accessed on 23 November 2019.

37 Ibid.

38 Jim Woodsome & Vijaya Ramachandran note 16 at 50.

39 Karim Sultan, Umar Ruhi & Rubina Lakhani note 21 at 52.

40 International Finance Corporation note 30 at 2.

41 Esteban Landerreche & Marc Stevens, 'On immutability of blockchains' in W Prinz & P Hoschka (eds) *Proceedings of the 1st ERCIM Blockchain Workshop 2018* (2018).

42 Alice Merry, 'Women worldwide struggle to access banking services: Bitcoin is only making that worse, October 29, 2018, *Time,* available at https://time.com/5431809/blockchain-financial-inclusion-gender-gap/, accessed on 15 October 2019.

43 Michael Pisa & Matt Juden note 22 at 34-5.

44 Ethan Loufield, Dennis Ferenzy & Tess Johnson, note 34 at 24.

45 KPMG note 2 at 29.

46 Jake Frankenfield, *Cryptocurrency* (2019), available at https://www.investopedia.com/terms/c/cryptocurrency.asp, accessed on 3 December 2019.

47 Ibid.

48 Ibid.

49 Bitcoin, *FAQ*, available at https://bitcoin.org/en/faq#what-about-bitcoin-and-consumer-protection, accessed on 3 December 2019.

50 Ibid.

51 Ibid.

52 Ibid.

53 See Alana Maurushat and Dan Halpin, *Investigation of Cryptocurrency Enabled and Dependent Crimes,* in Law, Governance and Technology Series 47 Financial Technology and the Law Combating Financial Crime, Edited by Doron Goldbarsht & Louis de Koker, Springer 2022, 248-9. See also Jake Frankenfield note 46.

54 Adriana Magdas, *Cryptocurrencies and Financial Inclusion – Why I Am a Skeptic ... For Now at Least* (2014), available at https://www.centerforfinancialinclusion.org/cryptocurrencies-and-financial-inclusion-why-i-am-a-skeptic-for-now-at-least, accessed on 15 September 2019.

55 Michael Pisa, *Questioning the Role of Bitcoin for Financial Inclusion* (2017), available at https://www.cgdev.org/blog/questioning-role-bitcoin-financial-inclusion, accessed on 14 November 2019.

56 Michael Pisa & Matt Juden note 22 at 10.

57 Michael Pisa note 55.

58 Libra, *Libra White Paper*, available at https://libra.org/en-US/white-paper/, accessed on 21 December 2019.
59 Ibid.
60 Richard Partington, 'How the wheels came off Facebook's Libra project', *Guardian,* 18 Oct 2019, available at https://www.theguardian.com/technology/2019/oct/18/how-the-wheels-came-off-facebook-libra-project, accessed on 4 December 2019.
61 Ibid.
62 Saule Omarova & Graham Steele, 'There's a lot we still don't know about Libra', *New York Times,* Nov 4, 2019, available at https://www.nytimes.com/2019/11/04/opinion/facebook-libra-cryptocurrency.html, accessed on 14 December 2019.
63 Ibid.
64 Ibid.
65 Mehrsa Baradaran, 'Facebook's cryptocurrency won't help the poor access banks. Here's what would', *Washington Post,* October 29, 2019, available at https://www.washingtonpost.com/outlook/2019/10/29/facebooks-cryptocurrency-wont-help-poor-access-banks-heres-what-would/, accessed on 15 November 2019.
66 Michael Pisa, *Facebook's Big Bet on Digital Currency: What Libra Could Mean for Global Payments and Remittances* (2019), available at https://www.cgdev.org/blog/facebooks-big-bet-digital-currency-what-libra-could-mean-global-payments-and-remittances, accessed on 2 December 2019.
67 Mehrsa Baradaran note 65.
68 BBC, 'Facebook 'rethinks' plans for Libra cryptocurrency', 4 March 2020, available at https://www.bbc.com/news/business-51730772, accessed on 14 March 2022.
69 BBC, 'Facebook-funded cryptocurrency Diem winds down', 1 February 2022, available at https://www.bbc.com/news/technology-60156682, accessed on 14 March 2022.
70 Quorum, *Evolve with Quorum: The Proven Blockchain Solution for Business*, available at https://www.goquorum.com/, accessed on 23 September 2019.
71 JP Morgan Chase & Co., *J.P.Morgan Creates Digital Coin for Payments* (2019), available at https://www.jpmorgan.com/global/news/digital-coin-payments, accessed on 23 September 2019.
72 Ibid.
73 Ibid. See also Patrick Thompson, 'JP Morgan offloads unprofitable Quorum network', 31 August 2020, https://coingeek.com/jpmorgan-offloads-unprofitable-quorom-network/#:~:text=JPMorgan%20sold%20Quorum%20because%20they,to%20adopt%20and%20implement%20Quorum, accessed on 22 March 2022. See also Michael Kapilkov, *JPM Blockchain Creator Says the Project Was Going Nowhere, JPMorgan Wanted Rid of It,* available at https://cointelegraph.com/news/quorum-s-creator-says-the-project-was-going-nowhere-jpmorgan-wanted-rid-of-it, accessed on 22 March 2022.
74 Central Bank of Nigeria, 'Virtual currencies not legal tender in Nigeria, *CBN Press Release,* February 28, 2018, available at https://www.cbn.gov.ng/Out/2018/CCD/Press%20Release%20on%20Virtual%20Currencies.pdf, accessed on 24 November 2019.
75 Ibid.
76 SEC Nigeria, *Public Notice on Investments in Cryptocurrencies and Other Virtual or Digital, Currencies,* 12 January 2017, available at http://sec.gov.ng/public-notice-on-investments-in-cryptocurrencies-and-other-virtual-or-digital-currencies/, accessed on 20 November 2019.
77 Central Bank of Nigeria, BSDDIR/GEN/LAB/14/001, 5 February 2021. See also Dennis Erezi, 'CBN slams ₦800 million fines on banks for flouting cryptocurrency order', 06 April 2022, available at https://guardian.ng/news/cbn-slams-%E2%82%A6800-million-fines-on-banks-for-flouting-cryptocurrency-order/, accessed on 8 April 2022.
78 Alice Merry note 42.
79 Ibid.

80 Adriana Magdas note 54.
81 Atlantic Council, *Central Bank Digital Currency Tracker*, available at https://www.atlanticcouncil.org/cbdctracker/, accessed on 3 December 2021.
82 Ibid.
83 Amalia Estenssoro, *Central Bank Digital Currencies: Back to the Future,* April 30, 2021, available at https://www.stlouisfed.org/publications/regional-economist/second-quarter-2021/central-bank-digital-currencies-back-future, accessed on 3 December 2021.
84 Benoît Cœuré, *Central Bank Digital Currency: The Future Starts Today* (2021), available at https://www.bis.org/speeches/sp210910.htm, accessed on 3 December 2021.
85 James Kynge & Sun Yu *Virtual Control: The Agenda Behind China's New Digital Currency,* February 17 2021, available at https://www.ft.com/content/7511809e-827e-4526-81ad-ae83f405f623, accessed on 3 December 2021.
86 Michael D Bordo & Andrew T Levin, NBER Working Paper Series Central Bank Digital Currency and the Future of Monetary Policy, 23711, 5 August 2017, available at http://www.nber.org/papers/w23711, accessed on 4 December 2021.
87 Amalia Estenssoro note 83.
88 Benoît Cœuré note 84.
89 Roberto Lorini & Marco Monaco, *Central Bank Digital Currency PwC Overview,* 2020, 6, available at https://www.pwc.com/it/it/publications/assets/docs/central-bank-digital-currency.pdf, accessed on 5 December 2021.
90 Central Bank of Nigeria, *CBN Selects Technical Partner for Digital Currency Project,* Press Release, August 30 2021, available at https://www.cbn.gov.ng/Out/2021/CCD/CBN%20Press%20Release%20(CBDC)%2030082021.pdf, accessed on 4 December 2021.
91 Bill Nelson, *The Benefits and Costs of a Central Bank Digital Currency for Monetary Policy,* April 15, 2021, available at https://bpi.com/the-benefits-and-costs-of-a-central-bank-digital-currency-for-monetary-policy/, accessed on 4 December 2021.
92 Atlantic Council note 81.
93 Jonathan Thun & Espen Marinius Hansen, *Are Central Bank Digital Currencies the Future of Money?* Available at https://www.paconsulting.com/insights/are-central-bank-digital-currencies-the-future-of-money/, accessed on 4 December 2021.
94 Shobhit Seth, *Central Bank Digital Currency (CBDC),* August 25, 2021, available at https://www.investopedia.com/terms/c/central-bank-digital-currency-cbdc.asp, accessed on 4 December 2021.
95 Amalia Estenssoro note 83.
96 Jonathan Thun & Espen Marinius Hansen note 93.
97 Atlantic council note 81.
98 Alberto Gallo, *Central Bank Digital Currencies Will Fix Bad Policy,* May 25, 2021, available at https://www.bloomberg.com/opinion/articles/2021-05-25/central-bank-digital-currencies-will-fix-bad-monetary-policy#:~:text=Central%20bank%20digital%20currencies%2C%20or,to%20strengthen%20central%20bank%20oversight, accessed on 5 December 2021.
99 Michael D Bordo & Andrew T Levin Working Paper note 86.
100 Benoît Cœuré note 84.
101 Ibid.
102 Ibid.
103 Roberto Lorini note 89 at 12 and 13.
104 Ibid at 10.
105 Ibid at 15. See also Louis de Koker & Doron Goldbarsht, *Financial Technologies and Financial Crime: Key Developments and Areas for Future Research* 304-5 and 307, in Doron Goldbarsht & Louis de Koker, Financial Technology and the Law Combating Financial Crime edited by Law, Governance and Technology Series 47, Springer 2022.
106 Adrià Morron Salmeron & Ricard Murillo Gili, *The e-Monetary Policy of the New Digital Economy,* 2019, available at https://www.caixabankresearch.com/en/economics-

markets/monetary-policy/e-monetary-policy-new-digital-economy, accessed on 5 December 2021.

107 Agustín Carstens, *Digital Currencies and the Future of the Monetary System,* Bank of International Settlements, Hoover Institution Policy Seminar, Basel, 27 January 2021, 10, available at https://www.bis.org/speeches/sp210127.pdf, accessed on 3 December 2021.

108 Jonathan Thun et al note 93.

109 Ibid.

110 Ibid.

111 Michael D Bordo & Andrew T Levin note 86.

112 Ibid.

113 Roberto Lorini & Marco Monaco note 89 at 11.

114 Michael Bordo and Andrew Levin note 86.

115 Central Bank of Nigeria, *Regulatory Guidelines on the eNAIRA,* iv, available at https://www.cbn.gov.ng/Out/2021/FPRD/eNairaCircularAndGuidelines%20FINAL.pdf, accessed on 6 December 2021.

116 Ibid at 9.

117 Ibid.

118 Ibid.

119 Ibid at 10.

120 Ibid at 11.

121 Ibid.

122 Ibid.

123 Ibid.

124 Ibid at 17.

125 Ibid at iv.

126 Ibid at 15.

127 Ibid at 17.

128 Ibid at 16.

129 Ibid.

130 Ibid at 17.

131 *Economist,* 'The world's most valuable resource is no longer oil, but data', May 6 2017, available at https://www.economist.com/leaders/2017/05/06/the-worlds-most-valuable-resource-is-no-longer-oil-but-data, accessed on 12 November 2019.

132 Jim Woodsome & Vijaya Ramachandran note 16 at 25.

133 Nicola Jentzsch, *Data Protection in the Context of Digital Financial Services and Big Data* (2016) at 5, available at http://www2.giz.de/wbf/4tDx9kw63gma/Datenschutz-Diskussionspapier_E_140416_Internet.pdf?cv=1.

134 IBM, *What Is Big Data Analytics*? available at https://www.ibm.com/analytics/hadoop/big-data-analytics, accessed on 12 November 2019.

135 Nicola Jentzsch note 133 at 4.

136 International Financial Corporation & the MasterCard Foundation, *Data Analytics and Digital Financial Services* at 11, available at https://www.ifc.org/wps/wcm/connect/369c10de-1703-4497-876f-9cdf0367a4d4/IFC+Data+Analytics+and+Digital+Financial+Services+Handbook.pdf?MOD=AJPERES&CVID=lRrkzEd, accessed on 12 November 2019.

137 Jim Woodsome & Vijaya Ramachandran note 16 at 25.

138 Jake Frankenfield, 'Data analytics', *Investopaedia* (2019), https://www.investopedia.com/terms/d/data-analytics.asp, accessed on 12 November 2019.

139 Philippe Breul, 'Leveraging Big Data for Financial Inclusion: Opportunities and Risks Interview with Digital Finance FinDev Gateway (2016), available at https://www.findevgateway.org/interview/2016/nov/leveraging-big-data-financial-inclusion-opportunities-and-risks, accessed on 13 November 2019.

140 IBM note 134.

141 Ethan Loufield, Dennis Ferenzy & Tess Johnson note 34 at 23-4.
142 Philippe Breul note 139.
143 International Financial Corporation & the MasterCard Foundation note 136 at 12.
144 Nicola Jentzsch note 133 at 6.
145 Ethan Loufield, Dennis Ferenzy & Tess Johnson note 34 at 7.
146 International Financial Corporation & the MasterCard Foundation note 136 at 11.
147 Philippe Breul note 139.
148 Ibid.
149 Nicola Jentzsch note 133 at 7 and 9.
150 Karen Gifford, *Enhancing Anti-money laundering and Financial Access: Can New Technology Achieve Both*? (2018) at 4, available at https://www.brookings.edu/wp-content/uploads/2018/04/es_20180413_fintech_access.pdf, accessed on 16 July 2020.
151 Ibid.
152 Nicola Jentzsch note 133 at 7 and 9.
153 Ibid at 8.
154 Ibid at 7.
155 Ibid at 7 and 10.
156 Ibid at 7.
157 Ethan Loufield, Dennis Ferenzy & Tess Johnson note 34 at 8.
158 International Financial Corporation & the MasterCard Foundation note 136 at 23.
159 Philippe Breul note 139.
160 Deloitte note 8 at 9 and 10.
161 Deloitte, *The New Physics of Financial Services: How Artificial Intelligence Is Transforming the Financial Ecosystem* at 5, available at https://www2.deloitte.com/content/dam/Deloitte/uk/Documents/financial-services/deloitte-uk-world-economic-forum-artificial-intelligence-summary-report.pdf, accessed on 14 November 2019.
162 Roy Jubraj, Tom Graham & Eve Ryan, *Redefine Banking with Artificial Intelligence* (2018) at 2, available at https://www.accenture.com/_acnmedia/pdf-68/accenture-redefine-banking.pdf, accessed on 17 July 2020.
163 Makada Henry-Nickie note 19.
164 Ibid.
165 Ibid.
166 Ibid.
167 Ademola Adeyoju, *Financial Technology and Artificial Intelligence: A Disruptive Union Vol 2* (2019) at 3, available at https://www.aelex.com/wp-content/uploads/2019/03/FINANCIAL-TECHNOLOGY-ARTIFICIAL-INTELLIGENCE_-A-DISRUPTIVE-UNION-_compressed-1.pdf, accessed on 3 December 2019.
168 Ibid.
169 Ibid.
170 Jake Frankenfield, 'What is a robo-advisor?' *Investopaedia,* Oct 1, 2019, available at https://www.investopedia.com/terms/r/roboadvisor-roboadviser.asp, accessed on 27 November 2019.
171 Facundo Abraham, Sergio L Smuckler & José Tessada, 'Robo-advisors: Investing through machines' (2019), *World Bank Research and Policy Brief* 134881 at 1, available at http://documents1.worldbank.org/curated/en/275041551196836758/pdf/Robo-Advisors-Investing-through-Machines.pdf, accessed on 16 July 2020.
172 KPMG, 'Striking a balance in robo-advisory' (2018), available at https://home.kpmg/xx/en/home/insights/2018/02/striking-a-balance-in-robo-advisory-fs.html, accessed on 12 November 2019.
173 KPMG note 2 at 36.
174 Jake Frankenfield, 'What is a robo-advisor?' *Investopaedia,* Oct 1, 2019, available at https://www.investopedia.com/terms/r/roboadvisor-roboadviser.asp, accessed on 27 November 2019.

175 Facundo Abraham, Sergio L Smuckler & José Tessada note 171 at 1.
176 Daniel O'Keefe, Jonathan Warmund & Ben, 'Robo advising: Catching up and getting ahead' (2016) at 5, available at https://home.kpmg/content/dam/kpmg/pdf/2016/07/Robo-Advising-Catching-Up-And-Getting-Ahead.pdf, accessed on 25 November 2019 at 5.
177 KPMG note 2 at 36.
178 Dana Anspach, *What Is a Robo Advisor and How Do They Work*? (2019), available at https://www.thebalance.com/what-is-a-robo-advisor-and-how-do-they-work-4097134, accessed on 1 December 2019.
179 Facundo Abraham, Sergio L Smuckler & José Tessada note 171 at 3.
180 Ibid.
181 Tom Baker & Benedict G. C. Dellaert, 'Regulating robo advice across the financial services industry (2018), *Iowa Law Review* at 713.
182 Jake Frankenfield note 174.
183 Facundo Abraham, Sergio L Smuckler & José Tessada note 171 at 3.
184 Ibid at 3 and 4.
185 Dana Anspach, *What Is a Robo Advisor and How Do They Work*? (2019), available at https://www.thebalance.com/what-is-a-robo-advisor-and-how-do-they-work-4097134, accessed on 1 December 2019.
186 Price Waterhouse Cooper (PWC), *The Case for Open Banking in Nigeria* at 6, available at https://www.pwc.com/ng/en/assets/pdf/case-open-banking-nigeria.pdf, accessed on 24 October 2019.
187 Consultative Group to Assist the Poor (CGAP), 'Partnerships explore impact of open APIs on financial inclusion' (2018), *CGAP News*, available at https://www.cgap.org/news/cgap-partnerships-explore-impact-open-apis-financial-inclusion, accessed on 25 November 2019.
188 International Monetary Fund, 'Policy paper fintech: The experience so far' *Press Release* No. 19/255, 2019 at 41, available at https://www.imf.org/~/media/Files/Publications/PP/2019/PPEA2019024.ashx, accessed on 19 April 2020.
189 Ibid.
190 Dan Kleinbaum, *Building Innovation: APIs, Fintechs and Financial Institutions* (2019), available at https://www.centerforfinancialinclusion.org/building-innovation-apis-fintechs-financial-institutions, accessed on 23 November 2019.
191 Ibid.
192 Ibid.
193 Consultative Group to Assist the Poor (CGAP) note 187.
194 Dan Kleinbaum note 190.
195 Ibid.
196 Price Waterhouse Cooper note 186 at 12.
197 Price Waterhouse Cooper (PWC) note 5.
198 Damola Yusuf, '*The Case for Open Banking in Nigeria* (2019) at 25 available at https://www.pwc.com/ng/en/assets/pdf/financial-focus-2019.pdf, accessed on 24 November 2019.
199 Suman Podder, *Leveraging the Provisions of Open Banking to Fight Financial Crimes* at 30 in Doron Goldbarsht & Louis de Koker, *Financial Technology and the Law Combating Financial Crime,* Law, Governance and Technology Series 47, Springer 2022.
200 Price Waterhouse Cooper (PWC) note 186 at 10 and 11.
201 Ibid at 12.
202 Oluchi Chibuzor, *Interswitch, Paga Adopt Open Banking to Champion Advocacy in Nigeria* (August 21, 2019), available at https://openbanking.ng/interswitch-paga-adopt-open-banking-to-champion-advocacy-in-nigeria/, accessed on 1 October 2019.
203 Price Waterhouse Cooper (PWC) note 186 at 13.
204 Ibid.

205 Ibid 11.
206 Dan Kleinbaum note 190.
207 Price Waterhouse Cooper note 186 at 14.
208 Corporate Finance Institute, *Peer-to-Peer Lending,* available at https://corporatefinanceinstitute.com/resources/knowledge/finance/peer-to-peer-lending/, accessed on 17 September 2019.
209 Ibid.
210 Chang-Hsien Tsai, 'To regulate or not to regulate? A comparison of government responses to Peer-to-Peer Lending among the United States, China, and Taiwan' (2018), *U. Cin. L. Rev.* 87 (1077), available at https://scholarship.law.uc.edu/uclr/vol87/iss4/5 14, accessed on 20 November 2019.
211 Ibid at 15.
212 Ibid at 16.
213 Tyler Aveni, *The Role of Peer-to-Peer Lending in Financial Inclusion* (2014), available at https://www.centerforfinancialinclusion.org/the-role-of-peer-to-peer-lending-in-financial-inclusion, accessed on 14 December 2019.
214 Kern Alexander, *Financial Inclusion: The Role of Fintech and Digital Financial Services* (2017) at 4, available at https://unctad.org/meetings/en/Presentation/c1mem5_2017_115_S3_Alexander_2.pdf 4, accessed on 19 November 2019.
215 Corporate Finance Institute note 208.
216 Kern Alexander note 214 at 4.
217 Tyler Aveni note 213.
218 Kern Alexander note 213 at 4.
219 Liliana Rojas-Suarez & Lucía Pacheco, *An Index of Regulatory Practices for Financial Inclusion in Latin America: Enablers, Promoters, and Preventers* (2017) at 44, available at https://www.cgdev.org/sites/default/files/index-regulatory-practices-financial-inclusion-latin-america_0.pdf, accessed on 1 October 2019.
220 Corporate Finance Institute note 208.
221 KPMG Siddharta Advisory, *The Fintech Edge First Edition: Peer-to-Peer Lending* (2018) at 4, available at https://assets.kpmg/content/dam/kpmg/id/pdf/2018/11/id-the-fintech-edge-p2p-lending.pdf, accessed on 23 November 2019.
222 Susy Cheston, *Why We Aren't Surprised That Ezubo, the P2P Lender in China, Is a Ponzi Scheme* (2016), available https://www.centerforfinancialinclusion.org/why-we-arent-surprised-that-ezubo-the-p2p-lender-in-china-is-a-ponzi-scheme, accessed on 20 September 2019.
223 KPMG note 2 at 26.
224 'Firm to assist MSMEs', *Guardian,* 19 June 2019, Available at https://guardian.ng/business-services/firm-to-assist-msmes/, accessed on 20 November 2020. See also Chiwete, *Welcome to the NewFint,* available at https://blog.fint.ng/2019/10/18/welcome-to-the-new-fint/, accessed on 10 November 2019.
225 KPMG note 2 at 26.
226 KPMG Siddharta Advisory note 221 at 4.
227 National Identification Management Commission (NIMC), *A Strategic Roadmap for Developing Digital Identification in Nigeria: Approved Report* (2017) at 9, available at https://www.nimc.gov.ng/docs/reports/strategicRoadmapDigitalID_Nigeria_May2018.pdf, accessed on 2 November 2019.
228 United States Agency for International Development (USAID), *Identity in a Digital Age: Infrastructure for Inclusive Development* at 3, available at https://www.usaid.gov/sites/default/files/documents/15396/IDENTITY_IN_A_DIGITAL_AGE.pdf, accessed on 12 on September 2019.
229 World Bank Group, *World Bank Group Brief on Digital Identity* at 1, available at http://pubdocs.worldbank.org/en/413731434485267151/BriefonDigitalIdentity.pdf, accessed on 2 September 2019.

230 United States Agency for International Development (USAID) note 228 at 12.
231 E. Bertino, *Digital Identity Management Techniques and Policies* at 2, available at https://www.itu.int/dms_pub/itu-t/oth/06/04/T06040040040001PDFE.pdf, accessed on 2 November 2019.
232 World Bank Group, *G20 Digital Identity Onboarding* at 3, available at https://www.gpfi.org/sites/gpfi/files/documents/G20_Digital_Identity_Onboarding.pdf, accessed on 23 September 2019.
233 Ibid.
234 Ibid.
235 Ibid.
236 Ibid.
237 United States Agency for International Development (USAID) note 228 at 42.
238 World Bank Group note 232 at 14.
239 United States Agency for International Development (USAID) note 228 at 43.
240 Ibid at 57.
241 National Identification Management Commission (NIMC) note 227 at 9.
242 World Bank Group note 232 at 1.
243 Alan Gelb & Anit Mukherjee, *The Aadhaar Debate: Where Do We Go from Here?* (2018), available at https://www.cgdev.org/blog/aadhaar-debate-where-do-we-go-here, accessed on 24 September 2019.
244 Olivia White, Anu Madgavkar, James Manyika et al, *Digital Identification: A Key to Inclusive Growth*, available at https://www.mckinsey.com/business-functions/mckinsey-digital/our-insights/digital-identification-a-key-to-inclusive-growth, accessed on 13 September 2019.
245 Ibid.
246 Ibid.
247 Ibid.
248 See Louis de Koker & Doron Goldbarsht, *Financial Technologies and Financial Crime: Key Developments and Areas for Future Research* at 307 in Doron Goldbarsht & Louis de Koker, Financial Technology and the Law, Combating Financial Crime, edited by Law, Governance and Technology Series 47, Springer 2022. See also E. Bertino note 231 at 6.
249 Chenshan & Rob Reeve, *DFS Vendor Platform Features* (2017) at 6, available at https://www.itu.int/en/ITU-T/focusgroups/dfs/Documents/201702/ITU_FGDFS_Report-DFSVendorPlatform.pdf, accessed on 16 November 2019.
250 World Bank Group note 232 at 2.
251 Biometrics Institute, *What Is Biometrics,* available at https://www.biometricsinstitute.org/what-is-biometrics/, accessed on 18 July 2020.
252 Jim Woodsome & Vijaya Ramachandran note 16 at 74.
253 Biometrics Institute, *Types of Biometrics,* available at https://www.biometricsinstitute.org/what-is-biometrics/types-of-biometrics/, accessed on 18 July 2020.
254 Jim Woodsome & Vijaya Ramachandran note 16 at 71.
255 Ibid at 71 and 77.
256 Frances Zelazny, *The Evolution of India's UID Program: Lessons Learned and Implications for other Developing Countries* (August 2012) at 15, available at https://www.cgdev.org/sites/default/files/1426371_file_Zelazny_India_Case_Study_FINAL.pdf, accessed on 7 September 2019.
257 World Bank Group note 232 at 2.
258 Xavier Giné, Jessica Goldberg, Shalini Sankaranarayanan et al, *Use of Biometric Technology in Developing Countries* at 10 and 11, available at http://siteresources.worldbank.org/DEC/Resources/Policy_paper-biometrics.pdf, accessed on 9 September 2019.
259 Alan Gelb & Julia Clark, *Identification for Development: The Biometrics Revolution,* Centre for Global Development (2013) at 10.
260 Xavier Giné, Jessica Goldberg, Shalini Sankaranarayanan et al note 258 at 10.

261 Ibid.
262 United States Agency for International Development (USAID) note 228 at 46.
263 Ibid at 47.
264 Alan Gelb & Anna Diofasi, *The Future of Identification and Development: Centre for Global Development Preliminary Discussion Paper* (2015) at 48, available at https://www.cgdev.org/sites/default/files/identification-development-what-have-we-learnt-and-where-are-we-going.pdf, accessed on 14 May 2019.
265 Central Bank of Nigeria, *National Financial Inclusion Strategy* (Revised 2018) at 10, available at https://www.cbn.gov.ng/out/2019/ccd/national%20financial%20inclusion%20strategy.pdf, accessed on 8 July 2020.
266 National Identification Management Commission (NIMC) note 227 at 86.
267 World Bank Group note 232 at 2.
268 Xavier Giné, Jessica Goldberg, Shalini Sankaranarayanan et al note 258 at 10 and 12.

Appendix

Rural participants interview sheet

Personal Information

Participant's Code No____________________________________
Contact address ____
Phone number ____
Occupation____
Level of education ______________________________________

Types of digital devices used (level of technological and DFS sophistication) (Mobile Phone, ATM, POS, Webpay)

Others____

Information on formal finance participation

1 Do you have a bank account?

   a Yes
   b No

2 If yes, how often do you use your bank account?
   ____
   ____

3 What are the services you access from your bank?
   ____
   ____

4 Have you ever accessed a loan or other services from your bank?

   a Yes
   b No

5 Indicate the type of loan or service
   ____
   ____

6 Was there any default on your part in the terms of the service offered (e.g. loan repayment default?)

a Yes
b No

7 If yes, what was the reason for the default?

____

____

8 Do you know of relatives or friends who have defaulted in the past?

a Yes
b No

9 If yes, what were the reasons?

10 What difficulties do you face in accessing formal financial services from the banks? (Remittances, transaction queries, accessing loans, etc.)

____

____

11 What do you think can be done to make it easier for rural dwellers to get better access to formal financial services from the banks?

____

____

12 What identification requirements for account opening do you know?

____

____

13 What identification requirements for account opening do you have?

____

____

14 Are you aware of the CBN policy on low-value accounts?

a Yes
b No

15 Please mention and describe the policy

____

____

16 Do you know of any other CBN initiatives (policies, regulations and guidelines) that aid excluded persons in accessing finance?

____

____

17 If your answer to Q14 is yes, do you have a low-value account?

a Yes
b No

18 What services are available to you on this account?

____

____

19 Do you think this account serves your purpose? Please give reasons

____

____

20 What other services would you like to access from the banks that are presently not offered to you?

21 Would you be open to dealing with an agent working on behalf of a bank? Please give reasons

a Yes
b No

22 Do you think that other entities such as post offices and telecommunications companies can offer financial services?

a Yes
b No

23 If yes, what services do you think can be offered by these entities?

____

____

24 Other comments

____

____

Note: Follow-up questions may be asked depending on the answers obtained from the interviewee.

Bibliography

Books

Alana, Maurushat and Dan Halpin *Investigation of Cryptocurrency Enabled and Dependent Crimes* In Law, Governance and Technology Series 47 Financial Technology and the Law Combating Financial Crime Edited by Doron Goldbarsht & Louis de Koker Springer 2022 248–249.

Alfio A. Puglisi *Evolving Regulatory Frameworks: Blockchain as a Form of Trust—Comparative Evidence* In Law, Governance and Technology Series 47 Financial Technology and the Law Combating Financial Crime Edited by Doron Goldbarsht & Louis de Koker Springer 2022 212.

Bambale, Yahaye *Islamic Law of Commercial and Industrial Transactions* (2007), Malthouse Law Books, Lagos.

de Koker, Louis & Doron Goldbarsht *Financial Technologies and Financial Crime: Key Developments and Areas for Future Research* In Law, Governance and Technology Series 47 Financial Technology and the Law Combating Financial Crime Edited by Doron Goldbarsht & Louis de Koker Springer 2022 304–305 and 307.

Mannan, MA *Islamic Economic Theory and Practice* (1980), Idarah-i Adabiyat-I, Delhi, India.

Lenton, Pamela and Mosley, Paul *Financial Exclusion and the Poverty Trap* (2012) Routledge, Abingdon.

Suman Podder *Leveraging the Provisions of Open Banking to Fight Financial Crimes* In Law, Governance and Technology Series 47 Financial Technology and the Law Combating Financial Crime Edited by Doron Goldbarsht & Louis de Koker Springer 2022 at 30.

Yong-Shik, Lee *Law and Development: Theory and Practice* (2019), Routledge.

Trubek, David & Santos, Alvaro *The New Law and Economic Development: A Critical Appraisal* (2006), Cambridge University Press, New York, 1–18, chapter 1.

Trubek, David *The New Law and Economic Development: A Critical Appraisal* (2006), Cambridge University Press, New York, 74–94, chapter 3.

Journal articles

Agarwal, Khushboo, 'Playing in the regulatory' (2018) *New York University Journal of Law & Business*, available at https://www.nyujlb.org/single-post/2018/01/08/Playing-in-the-Regulatory-Sandbox, accessed on 21 June 2019.

Arner, DW, Buckley, RP, Zetzsche, DA, Veidt, R, 'Sustainability, FinTech and financial inclusion' (2020) 21 *European Business Organization Law Review* at 7–35, 10.1007/s40804-020-00183-y

Ayua, I, 'Law and development in Africa' (1986) 3 (1) *International Journal on World Peace* at 71–81.

Baderin, Mashood, 'Law and development in Africa: Towards a new approach' (2011) 1 (1) *NIALS Journal of Law and Development* at 1–48, available at https://www.researchgate.net/publication/256086798_Law_and_Development_in_Africa_Towards_a_New_Approach, accessed on 12 May 2019.

Baker, Tom & Benedict, G C Dellaert, 'Regulating robo advice across the financial services industry' (2018) 103 *Iowa Law Review* at 713–750.

Bara, A, 'Mobile money for financial inclusion: Policy and regulatory perspective in Zimbabwe' (2013) 5 *African Journal of Science, Technology, Innovation and Development* at 345–354, available at 10.1080/20421338.2013.829287, accessed on 1 June 2018.

Boateng, Kwadwo, 'Ghana's progress on reaching out to the unbanked through financial inclusion' (2018) V (Special Issue 2) *International Journal of Management Studies.*

Buckley, Ross et al, 'Building FinTech ecosystems: Regulatory sandboxes, innovation hubs and beyond' (2020) 61 *Washington University Journal of Law & Policy* at 55–98, available at https://openscholarship.wustl.edu/law_journal_law_policy/vol61/iss1/10/

Cairns, John, 'Watson, Walton, and the history of legal transplants' (2013) 41 *Ga J Int'l & Comp L* at 637–696.

Chang-Hsien, Tsai & Peng, Kuan-Jung, 'The fintech revolution and financial regulation: The case of online supply chain financing' (2017) 4 (1) *Asian Journal of Law and Society* at 109–132.

Kevin, Davis & Trebilcock, Michael, 'Legal reforms and development' (2001) 22 (1) *Third World Quarterly* at 21–36, available at https://www.jstor.org/stable/3993343, accessed on 10 June 2019.

Louis, Del Duca & Levasseur, Alain, 'Impact of legal culture and legal transplants on the evolution of the U.S. legal system' (2010) *American Journal of Comparative Law* at 1–29, available at https://www.jstor.org/stable/20744530, accessed on 14 May 2019.

Garoupa, Nuno & Ogus, Anthony, 'A strategic interpretation of legal transplants' (2006) 35 (2) *Journal of Legal Studies* at 339–363.

Garth, BG, 'Law and society as law and development' (2003) 37 *Law and Society Review* at 305–314.

Grajzl, Peter & Dimitrova-Grajzl, Valentina, 'The choice in the lawmaking process: Legal transplants vs. indigenous law' (2009) 5 *Rev L & Econ* at 615–660.

Lee, Yong-Shik, 'General theory of law and development' (2017) 50 (3) *Cornell International Law Journal* at 416–471.

Legrand, Pierre, 'The impossibility of legal transplants' (1997) 4 *Maastricht J Eur & Comp L* at 111–124.

Lizarazo-Rodriguez, Liliana 'Mapping law and development' (2017) 4 (4) *Indon J Int'l & Comp L* at 761–898.

Louis, de Koker & Jentzsch, Nicola, 'Financial inclusion and financial integrity: Aligned incentives?' (2013) 44 *World Development* at 268.

Louis, Lydie & Chartier, Frederic, 'Financial inclusion in South Africa: An integrated framework for financial inclusion of vulnerable communities in South Africa's regulatory system reform' (2017) 1 (1) *Journal of Comparative Urban Law and Policy* at 170–196.

Malady, L, Buckley, RP, Didenko, A, Tsang, C-Y, 'A regulatory diagnostic toolkit for digital financial services in emerging markets' (2018) 34 *Banking and Finance Law Review* at 1–30, available at https://www.researchgate.net/publication/328118839_A_Regulatory_Diagnostic_Toolkit_for_Digital_Financial_Services_in_Emerging_Markets

Mousourakis, George, 'Legal transplants and legal development: A jurisprudential and comparative law approach' (2013) 54 *Acta Jur Hng* at 219–236.

Niglia, Leone, 'Of harmonization and fragmentation: The problem of legal transplants in the Europeanization of private law' (2010) 17 *Maastricht J Eur & Comp L* at 116–136.

Nyaga, Joseph Kariuki, 'Mobile banking services in the East African Community (EAC): Challenges to the existing legislative and regulatory frameworks' (2014) 4 *Journal of Information Policy* at 270–295, available at http://www.jstor.org/stable/10.5325/jinfopoli.4.2014.0270275, accessed on 1 June 2018.

Ohnesorge, John, 'Developing development theory: Law and development orthodoxies and the northeast Asian experience' (2007) 28 (2) *U Pa J Int'l Econ L* at 219–308.

Ordor, Ada, 'Tracking the law and development continuum through multiple intersections' (2015) 8 (2) *Law and Development Review* at 333–360.

Peerenboom, Randall, 'Toward a methodology for successful legal transplants' (2013) 1 (1) *Chinese Journal of Comparative Law* at 4–20.

Penca, Jemeja, 'Transnational legal transplants and legitimacy: The example of clean and green development mechanisms' (2016) 36 *Legal Stud* at 706–724.

Tamanaha, Brian, 'The lessons of law and development studies' (1995) 89 (2), *American Journal of International Law* at 470–486.

Trubek, David, 'Law and development 50 years on' (2001) In *International Encyclopedia of Social and Behavioural Sciences*, University of Winsconsin, 1–11, available at https://edisciplinas.usp.br/pluginfile.php/5549221/mod_resource/content/1/Trubek%20%282012%29.pdf

Tsai, Chang-Hsien, 'To regulate or not to regulate? A comparison of government responses to peer-to-peer lending among the United States, China, and Taiwan' (2018) 87 (4) *U Cin L Rev* at 1077–1122, available at: https://scholarship.law.uc.edu/uclr/vol87/iss4/5, accessed on 22 February 2019.

Watson, Alan, 'The birth of legal transplants' (2013) 41 *Ga. J. Int'l & Comp. L.* at 605–608.

Zetzsche, DA, Buckley, RP, Arner, DW, 'Blockchain distributed ledgers and liability' (2018) 2 *Journal of Digital Banking* at 296–308.

Zetzsche, DA, Buckley, RP, Arner, DW, 'The distributed liability of distributed ledgers: Legal risks of blockchain' (2018) 2018 *University of Illinois Law Review* at 1361–1406, available at 10.2139/ssrn.3018214

Zetzsche, DA, Buckley, RP, Arner, DW, Barberis, JN, 'From FinTech to TechFin: The regulatory challenges of data-driven finance' (2018) 14 *New York University Journal of Law and Business* at 393–446, available at 10.2139/ssrn.2959925

Institutional Publications

Abraham, Facundo, Schmukler, Sergio L & Tessada, José 'Robo-Advisors: Investing through machines' (2019), available at https://www.iif.com/portals/0/Files/private/finewdata_cfi.pdf, accessed on 30 November 2019.

Accion Smart Campaign (2014), available at http://www.smartcampaign.org/storage/documents/Tools_and_Resources/20140821_EoS_DfS_MFIs.pdf, accessed on 3 June 2018.

Agcaoili, Lawrence *Big Banks Establish More Branch-Lite Units* (2018), available at https://www.philstar.com/business/banking/2018/10/09/1858385/big-banks-establish-more-branch-lite-units, accessed on 1 July 2019.

Alliance for Financial Inclusion, *Maya Declaration: Commitments You Can Bank On*, available at https://www.afi-global.org/maya-declaration, accessed on 11 April 2019.

Alliance for Financial Inclusion, Agent Banking in Latin America (2012), available at https://www.afi-global.org/sites/default/files/discussion_paper_-_agent_banking_latin_america.pdf, accessed on 22 July 2019.

Alliance for Financial Inclusion, Mobile Financial Services Regulatory Approaches to Enable Access (2010), available at https://www.findevgateway.org/sites/default/files/mfg-en-paper-mobile-financial-services-regulatory-approaches-to-enable-access-nov-2010.pdf, accessed on 23 July 2019.

Alliance for Financial Inclusion, National Financial Inclusion Strategies: Current State of Practice (2015), available at https://www.afi-global.org/sites/default/files/publications/fisplg-state_of_practice.pdf, accessed on 28 March 2019.

Asli Demirgüç-Kunt, Leora Klapper, Singer, Dorothe et al, *The Global Findex Database 2021: Financial Inclusion, Digital Payments, and Resilience in the Age of COVID-19* (2022), available at https://openknowledge.worldbank.org/bitstream/handle/10986/37578/9781464818974.pdf, accessed on 6 July 2022.

Australian Securities and Investment Commission, Regulatory Sandbox, available at https://asic.gov.au/for-business/your-business/innovation-hub/regulatory-sandbox/, accessed on 27 February 2019.

Aveni, Tyler *The Role of Peer-to-Peer Lending in Financial Inclusion December* (2014), available at https://www.centerforfinancialinclusion.org/the-role-of-peer-to-peer-lending-in-financial-inclusion, accessed on 14 December 2019.

Bangko Sentral ng Philipinas, National Strategy for Financial Inclusion (2015), available at http://www.bsp.gov.ph/downloads/publications/2015/PhilippinesNSFIBooklet.pdf, accessed on 8 July 2019.

Bangko Sentral ng Philipinas, *Financial Inclusion in the Philippines,* Issue No. 8 Series of 2018, available at http://www.bsp.gov.ph/downloads/Publications/2018/FIP_1Sem2018.pdf, accessed on 17 February 2019.

Bankgo Sentral ng Philipinas, *BSP Adopts Enhanced Oversight Framework for Money Service Businesses* (2017), available at http://www.bsp.gov.ph/publications/media.asp?id=4276&yr=2017, accessed on 20 July 2019.

Benson, Carol & Clotteau, Nils *Digital Financial Services (DFS) Glossary* ITU-T Focus Group Digital Financial Services (2017) at 6.

Benson, Carol Coye, Niehaus, Charles & Mashayekhi, Mina et al *The Digital Financial Services Ecosystem*, ITU-T Focus Group on Digital Financial Services (2016).

Bertino, E *Digital Identity Management Techniques and Policies*, available at https://www.itu.int/dms_pub/itu-t/oth/06/04/T06040040040001PDFE.pdf, accessed on 2 November 2019.

Bester, Hennie, Gray, Jeremy, Hougaard, Christine et al, *Mapping the DNA: Using Consumer Insights to Unlock the Potential of Financial Inclusion* (2016), available at https://www.uncdf.org/map/article/2036/mapping-the-dna-using-consumer-insights-to-.unlock-the-potential-of-financial-inclusion, accessed on 12 November 2018.

Bester, Hennie, Hougaard, Christine, Gray, Jeremy et al, *Homefield Advantage: Learning from the Popularity of Local Financial Services Providers* (2016), available at https://cenfri.org/wp-content/uploads/2017/02/MAP-global-insight-note-3_Homefield-advantage_Cenfri-FinMark-Trust-UNCDF_2016.pdf, accessed on 14 November 2018.

Bester, Hennie, Gray, Jeremy, Hougaard, Christine et al, *The King Is (Not) Dead: Why Digital Payments Are Not Replacing Cash* (2016), available at http://www.uncdf.org/download/file/127/4223/note05pdf, accessed on 16 July 2019.

Bill and Melinda Gates Foundation, *Financial Services for the Poor*, available at https://www.gatesfoundation.org/What-We-Do/Global-Growth-and-Opportunity/Financial-Services-for-the-Poor, accessed on 14 April 2019.

Boulanger, Christian, *Law and Development as Practice and as Theory: From Self-estrangement to Alienation?* (2015), available at https://barblog.hypotheses.org/832, accessed on 14 June 2019.

Breul, Philippe, *Leveraging Big Data for Financial Inclusion: Opportunities and Risks*, available at https://www.findevgateway.org/interview/2016/nov/leveraging-big-data-financial-inclusion-opportunities-and-risks, accessed on 13 November 2019.

Biometrics Institute, *What Is Biometrics?* available at https://www.biometricsinstitute.org/what-is-biometrics/, accessed on 18 July 2020.

Chenshan & Rob Reeve, *DFS Vendor Platform Feature* (2017), available at, https://www.itu.int/en/ITU-T/focusgroups/dfs/Documents/201702/ITU_FGDFS_Report-DFSVendorPlatform.pdf, accessed on 27 May 2018.

Cheston, Susy, *Why We Aren't Surprised that Ezubo, the P2P Lender in China Is a Ponzi Scheme* (2016), available at https://www.centerforfinancialinclusion.org/why-we-arent-surprised-that-ezubo-the-p2p-lender-in-china-is-a-ponzi-scheme, accessed on 20 September 2019.

Columbia University, *The DFS Observatory at Columbia University* ([N.d.]), available at https://dfsobservatory.com/, accessed on April 2019.

Consultative Group to Assist the Poor (CGAP), *About CGAP*, available at https://www.cgap.org/about, accessed on 30 April 2019.

Consultative Group to Assist the Poor (CGAP), *Branchless Banking Agents in Brazil: Building Viable Networks*, available at www.cgap.org/technology 16 Feb. 2010 26; https://www.gsma.com/mobilefordevelopment/wp-content/uploads/2012/06/agentnetworksinbrazilcgapfgv1_7.pdf, accessed on 16 July 2019.

Consultative Group to Assist the Poor (CGAP), Partnerships Explore Impact of Open APIs on Financial Inclusion (2018), available at https://www.cgap.org/news/cgap-partnerships-explore-impact-open-apis-financial-inclusion, accessed on 25 November 2019.

Corporate Finance Institutes, *Peer-to-Peer Lending* ([N.d.)]), available at https://corporatefinanceinstitute.com/resources/knowledge/finance/peer-to-peer-lending/, accessed on 17 September 2019.

Doyle, Chris, *Market Definition and Dominance: ITU Competition Policy Workshop*, Geneva, 20-22 November 2002, available at https://www.itu.int/osg/spu/ni/competition/Presentations/Market%20Definition%20-CDoyle.pdf, accessed on 23 June 2018.

Dunham, Brian, *Striking a Balance in Robo-Advisory*, available at https://home.kpmg/xx/en/home/insights/2018/02/striking-a-balance-in-robo-advisory-fs.html, accessed on 12 November 2019.

European Commission, *Definition of Relevant Market: Summary of Legislation*, available at https://eur-lex.europa.eu/legal-content/EN/TXT/?uri=LEGISSUM%3Al26073, accessed on 28 February 2019.

Financial Action Task Force FATF, Guidance: Anti-Money Laundering and Terrorist Financing Measures and Financial Inclusion (2013), available at http://www.fatf-gafi.org/media/fatf/content/images/Updated-2017-FATF-2013-Guidance.pdf, accessed on 18 May 2018.

Financial Inclusion Insights, Bangladesh, available at http://finclusion.org/country/asia/bangladesh.html#dataAtAGlance, accessed on 13 July 2019.

Financial Inclusion Insights, Ghana, available at http://finclusion.org/country/africa/ghana.html#overview, accessed 10 July 2019.

Gelb, Alan & Diofasi, Anna, *The Future of Identification and Development Centre for Global Development* 74 (2015), available at https://www.cgdev.org/sites/default/files/identification-development-what-have-we-learnt-and-where-are-we-going.pdf, accessed on 14 May 2019.

Gelb, Alan & Clark, Julia, *Identification for Development: The Biometrics Revolution* (2013), Centre for Global Development, Washington DC.

Gelb, Alan & Mukherjee, Anit, *The Aadhaar Debate: Where Do We Go from Here*? (2018), available at https://www.cgdev.org/blog/aadhaar-debate-where-do-we-go-here, accessed on 24 September 2019.

Gifford, Karen, *Enhancing Anti-money Laundering and Financial Access: Can New Technology Achieve Both*? (2018), Brookings Institution Press, Washington DC.

Giné, Xavier Jessica Goldberg, Sankaranarayanan, Shalini et al *Use of Biometric Technology in Developing Countries,* at available at https://pdfs.semanticscholar.org/f170/2284eaf9adb4baf998e35915fdd479890d4b.pdf?_ga=2.144424309.1377114917.1587533580-1841856800.1587533580, accessed on 22 April 2020.

Grameen Foundation, By the Number, available at https://grameenfoundation.org/our-impact/numbers, accessed on 21 May 2012.

GSMA, Success Factors for Mobile Money Services: A Quantitative Assessment of Success Factors (2016) 1, available at https://www.gsmaintelligence.com/research/?file=923539C02F5D39174BA09C6851EFC25A&download, accessed on 2 June 2018.

Herbert Smith Freehills *Hong Kong Launches Regulatory Sandbox in Wake of Developments in Australia, Malaysia, Singapore, and the UK* (2016), available at https://sites-herbertsmithfreehills.vuturevx.com/103/12430/landing-pages/2016.09.30-apac-fintech-briefing.pdf, accessed on 13 July 2018.

How Regulators Can Foster Innovation without Destabilising the Entire Financial Services Ecosystem (2017), available at https://medium.com/@SustainableDFS/innovation-sandboxes-as-a-tool-for-driving-financial-inclusion-in-nigeria-bdb26761944e, accessed on 20 June 2018.

International Business Machine (IBM), *What Is Big Data Analytics?* available at https://www.ibm.com/analytics/hadoop/big-data-analytics, accessed on 12 November 2019.

International Telecommunications Union (ITU), *Focus Group on Digital Financial Services,* available at https://www.itu.int/en/ITU-T/focusgroups/dfs/Pages/default.aspx, accessed on 12 April 2019.

Iyer, Ramesh, *Financial Inclusion in India Is Soaring: Here's What Must Happen Next,* available at https://www.weforum.org/agenda/2019/01/financial-inclusion-in-india-is-soaring-heres-what-must-happen-next/, accessed on 2 May 2019.

Jenik, Ivo, *Regulatory Sandboxes: Potential for Financial Inclusion?* (2017), available at http://www.cgap.org/blog/regulatory-sandboxes-potential-financial-inclusion, accessed on 23 June 2018.

Jentzsch, Nicola, *Data Protection in the Context of Digital Financial Services and Big Data* (2016), available at https://kipdf.com/data-protection-in-the-context-of-digital-financial-services-and-big-data-discus_5af9f4497f8b9acf418b45cf.html, accessed on 3 June 2022.

Woodsome, Jim & Ramachandran, Vijaya, *Fixing AML: Can New Technology Help Address the De-risking Dilemma?* (2018), Centre for Global Development, available at https://www.cgdev.org/sites/default/files/fixing-aml-can-new-technology-help-address-de-risking-dilemma.pdf, accessed on 12 March 2019.

JP Morgan Chase & Co., *J.P. Morgan Creates Digital Coin for Payments* (2019), available at https://www.jpmorgan.com/global/news/digital-coin-payments, accessed on 23 September 2019.

Roy, Jubraj, Graham, Tom & Ryan, Eve, *Redefine Banking with Artificial Intelligence* (2018), available at https://www.accenture.com/_acnmedia/pdf-68/accenture-redefine-banking.pdf, accessed on 25 September 2019.

Kleinbaum, Dan, *Building Innovation: APIs, Fintechs and Financial Institutions* (2019), available at https://www.centerforfinancialinclusion.org/building-innovation-apis-fintechs-financial-institutions, accessed on 23 November 2019.

Koksal, Ilker, *The Benefits of Applying Blockchain Technology in Any Industry* (2019), available at https://www.forbes.com/sites/ilkerkoksal/2019/10/23/the-benefits-of-applying-blockchain-technology-in-any-industry/#547e32c549a5, accessed on 23 November 2019.

KPMG Siddharta Advisory, *The Fintech Edge First Edition: Peer-to-Peer Lending*, (2018), available at https://assets.kpmg/content/dam/kpmg/id/pdf/2018/11/id-the-fintech-edge-p2p-lending.pdf 4, accessed on 23 November 2019.

Lamido, Sanusi, 'Banking reform and its impact on the Nigerian economy' (lecture, University of Warwick's Economic Summit, UK) 17th February (2012), available at https://www.cbn.gov.ng/OUT/SPEECHES/2012/GOV_WARWICK_150211.PDF, accessed on 15 November 2017.

Landerreche, Esteban & Stevens, Marc, 'On immutability of blockchains' In *Proceedings of the 1st ERCIM Blockchain Workshop 2018, Reports of the European Society for Socially Embedded Technologies,* ERCIM-Blockchain Edited by W Prinz & P Hoschka ERCIM-Blockchain, Amsterdam, Netherlands 2018.

Libra, *Libra White Paper*, available at https://libra.org/en-US/white-paper/, accessed on 21 December 2019.

Loufield, Ethan, Ferenzy, Dennis & Johnson, Tess *Accelerating Financial Inclusion with New Data; Joint Report Four: Mainstreaming Financial Inclusion* Part Four (2018), available at https://www.iif.com/portals/0/Files/private/finewdata_cfi.pdf, accessed on 9 June 2019.

Macharia, Ken 'CBA, Safaricom mark 5 |years of M-Shwari with customer savings of Sh12.6Bn' (2017) *Capital Business* December 6, available at https://www.capitalfm.co.ke/business/2017/12/cba-safaricom-mark-5-years-m-shwari-customer-savings-sh12-6bn/, accessed on 27 February 2019.

Macmillan, Rory, *Digital Financial Services: Regulating for Financial Inclusion: An ICT Perspective* GDDFI Discussion Paper 57 ([N.d.]), available at https://www.itu.int/en/ITU-D/Conferences/GSR/Documents/GSR2016/Digital_financial_inclusion_GDDFI.pdf, accessed on 1 July 2018.

Mas, Ignacio, *What Is the Telecom Regulator's Role in Fostering Mobile Money*? (2012), available at http://www.cgap.org/blog/what-telecom-regulator%E2%80%99s-role-fostering-mobile-money#comments, accessed on 16 June 2018.

MasterCard Building Electronic Payment Acceptance at the Base of the Pyramid to Advance Financial Inclusion (2017), available at https://newsroom.mastercard.com/wp-content/uploads/2017/09/Mastercard_Financial-Inclusion_Merchant-Acceptance_FINAL.pdf, accessed on 29 May 2018.

Mattern, Max, *How Ghana Became One of Africa's Top Mobile Money Markets* (2018), available at https://www.cgap.org/blog/how-ghana-became-one-africas-top-mobile-money-markets, accessed on 10 July 2019.

Mazer, Rafe & Rowan, Philip, *Competition in Mobile Financial Services: Lessons from Kenya and Tanzania,* CGAP Working Paper (2016), available at http://www.cgap.org/sites/default/files/Working-Paper-Competition-in-MFS-Kenya-Tanzania-Jan-2016.pdf, accessed on 16 May 2018.

McKinsey Global Institute, Digital Finance for All: Powering Inclusive Growth in Emerging Economies (2016), available at https://www.mckinsey.com/~/media/McKinsey/Global%20Themes/Employment%20and%20Growth/How%20digital%20finance%20could%20boost%20growth%20in%20emerging%20economies/MGI-Digital-Finance-For-All-Executive-summary-September-2016.ashx, accessed on 13 March 2018.

McLean, Sue, *UK: FCA's Regulatory Sandbox – Lessons Learnt* (2017), available at http://www.mondaq.com/uk/x/643458/fin+tech/FCAs+Regulatory+Sandbox+Lessons+Learnt, accessed on 17 June 2018.

Miriri, Duncan, 'Kenya's Equity Bank, Safaricom team up to expand digital banking' (2019) *Reuters* April 29, available at https://www.reuters.com/article/us-kenya-equity-group-hol-safaricom/kenyas-equity-bank-safaricom-team-up-to-expand-digital-banking-idUSKCN1S51IC, accessed on 16 August 2019.

Monetary Authority of Singapore, FinTech Regulatory Sandbox, available at http://www.mas.gov.sg/Singapore-Financial-Centre/Smart-Financial-Centre/FinTech-Regulatory-Sandbox.aspx, accessed on 21 April 2019.

Nobelprize.org, *The Nobel Peace Prize for 2006* (2006), available at https://www.nobelprize.org/nobel_prizes/peace/laureates/2006/press.html, accessed on 6 May 2018.

O'Keefe, Daniel Jonathan Warmund & Lewis, Ben, *Robo Advising: Catching Up and Getting Ahead* ([N.d.)]), available at https://home.kpmg/content/dam/kpmg/pdf/2016/07/Robo-Advising-Catching-Up-And-Getting-Ahead.pdf, accessed on 25 November 2019.

Chibuzor, Oluchi, *Interswitch, Paga Adopt Open Banking, to Champion Advocacy in Nigeria* (2019), available at https://openbanking.ng/interswitch-paga-adopt-open-banking-to-champion-advocacy-in-nigeria/, accessed on 1 October 2019.

Oxford Business Group, Increased Use of Mobile Money Boosts Financial Inclusion in Ghana (2018), available at https://oxfordbusinessgroup.com/analysis/moveable-feast-expansion-mobile-money-boosting-financial-inclusion, accessed on 12 July 2019.

Pazarbasioglu, Ceyla et al, *Digital Financil Services* (2020), available at http://pubdocs.worldbank.org/en/230281588169110691/Digital-Financial-Services.pdf, accessed on 30 January 2021.

Pisa, Michael & Juden, Matt,*Blockchain and Economic Development: Hype vs. Reality* (2017), Centre for Global Development, Washington, DC, available at https://www.cgdev.org/publication/ blockchain-and-economic-development-hype-vs-reality, accessed on 15 October 2019.

Pisa, Michael, *Facebook's Big Bet on Digital Currency: What Libra Could Mean for Global Payments and Remittances* (2019), available https://www.cgdev.org/blog/facebooks-big-bet-digital-currency-what-libra-could-mean-global-payments-and-remittances, accessed on 2 December 2019.

Pisa, Michael, *Questioning the Role of Bitcoin for Financial Inclusion* (2017), available at https://www.cgdev.org/blog/questioning-role-bitcoin-financial-inclusion, accessed on 14 November 2019.

Pollari, Ian, *The Rise of Digital Platforms in Financial Services* (January 2018) 2, available at https://assets.kpmg.com/content/dam/kpmg/xx/pdf/2018/02/kpmg-rise-of-digital-platforms.pdf, accessed on 13 November 2018.

Price Waterhouse Cooper (PWC), *The Case for Open Banking in Nigeria* ([N,d.]), available at https://www.pwc.com/ng/en/assets/pdf/case-open-banking-nigeria.pdf, accessed on 24 October 2019.

Ravikumar, T, *Accessing the Role of Banking in Financial Inclusion Process in India*, available at http://www.microfinancegateway.org/sites/default/files/mfg-en-paper-assessing-role-of-banking-sector-in-financial-inclusion-process-in-india-may-2013.pdf, accessed on 30 May 2018.

Regulatory Compliance: An Assessment of the Development of Anti-Money Laundering Reporting Compliance of the Pawnshop and Money Service Business Industry: Strategic Analysis Report, available at http://www.amlc.gov.ph/images/PDFs/2018%20Strategic%20Analysis%20Report%20on%20Pawnshop%20and%20MSB.pdf, accessed on 13 July 2019.

Rudman, Desmond & Ostrovsky, Siam, *Dominance Test: A Superfluous Jurisdictional Hurdle?* Document 12 (2010), available at http://www.compcom.co.za/wp-content/uploads/2014/09/article-dominance-test.pdf, accessed on 9 June 2018.

Sanni, Serah, *Nigeria: Crypto Currency in Nigeria: Regulatory Framework & Related Issues* (2019), available at http://www.mondaq.com/Nigeria/x/855410/fin+tech/Crypto+Currency+In+Nigeria+Regulatory+Framework+Related+Issues, accessed on 18 November 2019.

Suárez, Sandra, *Poor People's Money: The Politics of Money in Mexico* (2016), available at https://ac-els-cdn-com.ezproxy.uct.ac.za/S0308596116300027/1-s2.0-S0308596116300027-main.pdf?_tid=19f52bdc-de6d-4664-b420-133ea6c3422b&acdnat=1528174867_101c04ef5f82d09d39da45de9838f02, accessed on 12 May 2018.

Sultan, Karim, Ruhi, Umar & Lakhani, Rubina, *Conceptualizing Blockchains: Characteristics and Applications* (2018), available at https://arxiv.org/ftp/arxiv/papers/1806/1806.03693.pdf, accessed on 15 October 2019.

Sustainable and Inclusive DFS, *Innovation Sandboxes as a Tool for Driving Financial Inclusion in Nigeria*, available at https://medium.com/@sustainabledfs/innovation-sandboxes-as-a-tool-for-driving-financial-inclusion-in-nigeria-bdb26761944e, accessed on 17 June 2019.

UN Declaration on the Right to Development Resolution 41/128 of 4 December (1986), available at https://www.ohchr.org/en/professionalinterest/pages/righttodevelopment.aspx, accessed on 12 August 2018.

United States Agency for International Development (USAID), *Identity in a Digital Age: Infrastructure for Inclusive Development*, available https://www.usaid.gov/sites/default/files/documents/15396/IDENTITY_IN_A_DIGITAL_AGE.pdf, accessed on 12 September 2019.

United States Agency for International Development, *Digital Finance for Development: A Handbook for USAID Staff* (2014), available at https://www.fhi360.org/resource/digital-finance-development-handbook-usaid-staff, accessed on 20 September 2018.

White, Olivia, Sperling, Owen, Madgavkaret, Anu et al, *Digital Identification: A Key to Inclusive Growth*, available at https://www.mckinsey.com/business-functions/mckinsey-digital/our-insights/digital-identification-a-key-to-inclusive-growth, accessed on 13 September 2019.

Woodsome, Jim & Ramachandran, Vijaya, *Fixing AML: Can New Technology Help Address.*

World Bank,*Deepening Financial Inclusion in Mexico's Rural Area* (2018), available at https://www.worldbank.org/en/results/2018/07/02/profundizar-la-inclusion-financiera-en-areas-rurales-de-mexico, accessed on 21 July 2019; available at https://www.cgdev.org/sites/default/files/fixing-aml-can-new-technology-help-address-de-risking-dilemma.pdf, accessed on 3 June 2022.

World Bank Group, *Achieving Effective Financial Inclusion In South Africa: A Payments Perspective*, available at http://www.treasury.gov.za/publications/other/Achieving%20Effective%20Financial%20Inclusion%20in%20South%20Africa.pdf, accessed on 22 June 2019.

World Bank Group, *World Bank Group Brief on Digital Identity*, available at http://pubdocs.worldbank.org/en/413731434485267151/BriefonDigitalIdentity.pdf, accessed on 2 September 2019.

World Bank Group, *Financial Inclusion: Overview*, available at http://www.worldbank.org/en/topic/financialinclusion/overview, accessed on 30 April 2019.

World Bank Group, *G20 Digital Identity Onboarding*, available at https://www.gpfi.org/sites/gpfi/files/documents/G20_Digital_Identity_Onboarding.pdf, accessed on 23 September 2019.

World Bank, *UFA2020 Overview: Universal Financial Access by 2020* (2018), available at http://www.worldbank.org/en/topic/financialinclusion/brief/achieving-universal-financial-access-by-2020, accessed on April 2019.

World Bank, *UFA2020 Overview: Universal Financial Access by 2020,* available at https://www.worldbank.org/en/topic/financialinclusion/brief/achieving-universal-financial-access-by-2020, accessed on 28 December 2018.

World of Bank, *Pakistan: Building Equality for Women on a Foundation of Identity,* available at https://id4d.worldbank.org/country-action/pakistan-building-equality-women-foundation-identity, accessed on 9 July 2019.

Yusuf, Damola, *The Case for Open Banking in Nigeria*, available at https://www.pwc.com/ng/en/assets/pdf/financial-focus-2019.pdf 25, accessed on 24 November 2019.

Zamir, Zahid, *Prohibition of Interest (Riba) in Islam: The Social, Moral and Economic Rationale (Part I),* available at http://www.nzibo.com/riba/WHY%20DOES%20ISLAM%20PROHIBIT%20INTEREST%20%28RIBA%29.pdf, accessed on April 2018.

Zelazny, Frances, *The Evolution of India's UID Program; Lessons Learned and Implications for other Developing Countries*, available at https://www.cgdev.org/files/1426371_file_Zelazny_India_Case_Study_FINAL.pdf, accessed on 7 September 2019.

Zhou, Mimi *Law and Autonomous Systems Series: Innovation without Authorisation? The Regulatory Black Box of Cryptocurrencies in China* (2018), available at https://www.law.ox.ac.uk/business-law-blog/blog/2018/04/law-and-autonomous-systems-series-innovation-without-authorisation, accessed on 28 July 2019.

Nigerian policy documents/publications

Adeleke, Adegoke *The Informal Financial Markets in Nigeria* (2014), Central Bank of Nigeria (CBN Understanding Monetary Policies Series no 43) available at https://www.cbn.gov.ng/Out/2016/MPD/UNDERSTANDING%20MONETARY%20POLICY%20SERIES%20NO%2043.pdf, accessed on 13 December 2018.

Aziz, Aliyu *A Digital Identity: The Cornerstone to Effective Service Delivery*, available at http://www.id4africa.com/2019_event/presentations/PS1/3-Aliyu-Aziz-NIMC-Nigeria.pdf, accessed on 28 July 2019.

Central Bank of Nigeria (CBN), *Financial Inclusion Newsletter*, March 2018.

Central Bank of Nigeria (CBN), 'Virtual currencies not legal tender in Nigeria' (2018) CBN Press Release, February 28, available at https://www.cbn.gov.ng/Out/2018/CCD/Press%20Release%20on%20Virtual%20Currencies.pdf, accessed on 24 November 2019.

Central Bank of Nigeria (CBN), Directive BPSD/DIR/GEN/CIR/0122014, Abuja, accessed on 17 May 2019.

Central Bank of Nigeria (CBN), *Financial Inclusion Newsletter* (2016) 1 (1), available at https://www.cbn.gov.ng/Out/2016/CCD/JANUARY%202016%20Volume%201,%20Issue%201%20Web.pdf, accessed on 21 April 2017.

Central Bank of Nigeria (CBN), *Financial Inclusion Secretariat: The 2017 Annual Report on the National Financial Inclusion Strategy Implementation* (2018), Abuja.

Central Bank of Nigeria (CBN), *Financial Inclusion Secretariat:The 2018 Annual Report on the National Financial Inclusion Strategy Implementation* (2019), Abuja, available at https://www.cbn.gov.ng/Out/2019/CCD/Annual%20Report%202018%20Financial%20Inclusion.pdf, accessed on 24 May 2020.

Central Bank of Nigeria (CBN), *National Financial Inclusion Strategy* (2012), available at https://www.cbn.gov.ng/Out/2012/publications/reports/dfd/CBN-Summary%20Report%20of-Financial%20Inclusion%20in%20Nigeria-final.pdf, accessed on 15 March 2019.

Central Bank of Nigeria (CBN), *National Financial Inclusion Strategy* 2018 (2019), available at https://www.cbn.gov.ng/Out/2018/CCD/Exposure%20Draft%20of%20the%20National%20Financial%20Inclusion%20Strategy%20Refresh_July%206%202018.pdf, accessed on 3 March 2020.

Central Bank of Nigeria (CBN), *Nigeria Financial Literacy Baseline Survey Report* (2015), Abuja, Nigeria.

Central Bank of Nigeria (CBN), *Payment Modes in Nigeria*, available at https://www.cbn.gov.ng/Paymentsystem/Modes.asp, accessed on 16 September 2019.

Central Bank of Nigeria (CBN), *Payments System Vision 2020*, available at https://www.cbn.gov.ng/icps2013/papers/Agric%20Payments%20Initiative%20Breakout%20Session%20v1.pdf, accessed on 25 March 2019.

Central Bank of Nigeria (CBN), *Review of Restrictions and Limits on Levels I and II of the Tiered Know Your Customer ("KYC") Accounts* (2018), available at https://www.proshareng.com/news/REGULATORS/Review-of-Restrictions—Limits-on-Levels-I—II-of-the-Tiered-KYC-Accounts/31637, accessed on 15 August 2018.

Central Bank of Nigeria, *Financial Literacy: Overview*, available at https://www.cbn.gov.ng/Devfin/finliteracy.asp, accessed on 28 February 2017.

Enhancing Financial Innovation and Access in Nigeria (EFInA), *Access to Financial Services in Nigeria 2010 Survey: Key Findings* (2010), available at https://www.efina.org.ng/wp-content/uploads/2018/12/EFInAAccess-to-Financial-Services-in-Nigeria-2010-surveyKey-Findings.pdf, accessed on 23 March 2019.

Enhancing Financial Innovation and Access in Nigeria (EFInA), *Key Findings: EFInA Access to Financial Services in Nigeria (A2F) 2016 Survey* (2017), available at http://www.efina.org.ng/assets/A2F/2016/Key-Findings-A2F-2016.pdf, accessed on 26 June 2019.

Enhancing Financial Innovation and Access in Nigeria (EFInA), *Scoping Study on Super Agents* (2016), available at https://www.efina.org.ng/wp-content/uploads/2018/12/EFInA-Super-Agents-Scoping-Study.pdf, accessed on 5 October 2018.

Enhancing Financial Innovation and Access in Nigeria (EFInA), *Access to Financial Services in Nigeria 2012 Survey Key Findings* (2012 updated May 2013), available at https://www.efina.org.ng/wp-content/uploads/2018/12/EFInA-Access-to-Financial-Services-in-Nigeria-2012-surveyKey-Findings.pdf, accessed on 18 May 2019.

Enhancing Financial Innovation and Access in Nigeria (EFInA), *Key Findings: EFInA Access to Financial Services in Nigeria Survey* (2018) at 6 and 62, available at https://www.efina.org.ng/wp-content/uploads/2019/01/A2F-2018-Key-Findings-11_01_19.pdf, accessed on 20 June 2019.

Enhancing Financial Innovation and Access in Nigeria (EFInA), *Key Findings: EFInA Access to Financial Services in Nigeria Survey* (2020), available at https://a2f.ng/wp-content/uploads/2021/06/A2F-2020-Final-Report.pdf, accessed on 14 January 2021.

National Identification Management Commission (NIMC), *A Strategic Roadmap for Developing Digital Identification in Nigeria: Approved Report* (2017), available at https://www.nimc.gov.

ng/docs/reports/strategicRoadmapDigitalID_Nigeria_May2018.pdf, accessed on 2 November 2019.

Nigeria National Bureau of Statistics, *Labour Force Statistics: Unemployment and Underemployment Report* vol 1 (Q4 2017-Q3 2018) (2018).

Nigeria National Bureau of Statistics, Nigerian Gross Domestic Product Report (Q2 2019) (2019).

Nigeria National Bureau of Statistics, *Vision and Mission*, available at https://nigerianstat.gov.ng/page/vision-mission, accessed on 2 August 2019.

SEC Nigeria, Public Notice on Investments in Cryptocurrencies and Other Virtual or Digital Currencies (2017), available at http://sec.gov.ng/public-notice-on-investments-in-cryptocurrencies-and-other-virtual-or-digital-currencies/, accessed on 20 November 2019.

Technical reports

Adeyoju, Ademola *Financial Technology and Artificial Intelligence: A Disruptive Union* (2019) 2, available at https://www.aelex.com/wp-content/uploads/2019/03/FINANCIAL-TECHNOLOGY-ARTIFICIAL-INTELLIGENCE_-A-DISRUPTIVE-UNION-_compressed-1.pdf, accessed on 3 December 2019.

Alexander, Kern *Financial Inclusion: The Role of Fintech and Digital Financial Services* (2017), available at https://unctad.org/meetings/en/Presentation/c1mem5_2017_115_S3_Alexander_2.pdf, accessed on 24 November 2019.

Anderson, C. Leigh Anderson, Pierre Biscaye, Sarah Coney et al *Review of National Identity Programs ITU: Focus Group Technical Report* (2016), available at https://www.itu.int/en/ITU-T/focusgroups/dfs/Documents/09_2016/Review%20of%20National%20Identity%20Programs.pdfm.

Bailey, Ronald, 'The other side of slavery: Black labor, cotton, and textile industrialization in Great Britain and the United States' (1994) 68 (2) *Agricultural History* at 35–50, available at https://www.jstor.org/stable/3744401, accessed on 26 July 2019.

Bankable Frontiers Associates, The Mzansi Bank Account Initiative in South Africa: Final Report (2009), available at http://www.finmark.org.za/wp-content/uploads/2016/02/Rep_MsanziBankAccInitiativeSA_2009.pdf, accessed on 26 July 2019.

Bourreau, Marc & Valletti, Tommaso, *Enabling Digital Financial Inclusion through Improvements in Competition and Interoperability: What Works and What Doesn't*? CGD Policy Paper 065 26, available at https://www.cgdev.org/sites/default/files/CGD-Policy-Paper-65-Bourreau-Valletti-Mobile-Banking.pdf, accessed on 17 July 2018.

Central Bank of Nigeria, 'CBN clarifies diaspora remittances, says official inflows is $2.6bn, $26bn' (2019) *Thisday* 13 October, available at https://www.thisdaylive.com/index.php/2019/10/13/cbn-clarifies-diaspora-remittances-says-official-inflows-is-2-6bn-not-26bn/, accessed on 5 December 2019.

Claessens, Stijn & Rojas-Suarez, Liliana, *Financial Regulations for Improving Financial Inclusion: A CGD Task Force Report*, available at https://www.cgdev.org/sites/default/files/CGD-financial-regulation-task-force-report-2016.pdf, accessed on 13 November 2018.

David-West, Olayinka *Digital Financial Services: State of the Market Report* (2016), available at http://sustainabledfs.lbs.edu.ng/FI-Resources/SoMR-Full_Report.pdf, accessed on 17 March 2017.

David-West, Olayinka, Ihenachor, Nkemdilim, Ajai, Olawale et al *Digital Financial Services: State of the Market Report* (2018), available at http://sustainabledfs.lbs.edu.ng/FI-Resources/SoMR_Full_Report_2018.pdf, accessed on 16 May 2019.

David-West, Olayinka, Ajai, Olawale, Salami, Adedoyin et al *Digital Financial Services: State of the Market Report* (2017), available at https://www.researchgate.net/publication/322315266_Digital_Financial_Services_in_Nigeria_State_of_the_Market_Report_2017, accessed on 13 August 2018.

Deloitte, *The New Physics of Financial Services: How Artificial Intelligence Is Transforming the Financial Ecosystem*, available at https://www2.deloitte.com/content/dam/Deloitte/uk/Documents/financial-services/deloitte-uk-world-economic-forum-artificial-intelligence-summary-report.pdf, accessed on 14 November 2019 5.

Deloitte, *Fintech in Nigeria and the Women who Lead* (2019), available at https://www2.deloitte.com/content/dam/Deloitte/ng/Documents/financial-services/ng-fintech-in-Nigeria-and-the-women-who-lead-29032019.pdf, accessed on 19 November 2019.

Deloitte, Regulatory Sandbox Making India a Global Fintech Hub (2017), available at https://www2.deloitte.com/content/dam/Deloitte/in/Documents/technology-media-telecommunications/in-tmt-fintech-regulatory-sandbox-web.pdf, accessed on 13 July 2019.

Demirgüç-Kunt, Asli & Klapper, Leora *Measuring Financial Inclusion Explaining Variation Across and Within Countries,* Policy Research Working Paper 7255 (2014), available at https://www.brookings.edu/wp-content/uploads/2016/07/2013a_klapper.pdf, accessed on 17 May 2019.

Henry-Nickie, Makada *How Artificial Intelligence Affects Financial Consumers: Brookings Institution Report* (2019), available at https://www.brookings.edu/research/how-artificial-intelligence-affects-financial-consumers/, accessed on 26 October 2019.

InterMedia, Kenya Wave 5 Report June–July 2017 (2018), available at http://finclusion.org/uploads/file/kenya-wave-5-report_final.pdf, accessed on 14 July 2019.

International Finance Corporation, *Can Blockchain Technology Address De-Risking in Emerging Markets?* (2017), World Bank Group Note 38, Washington DC, available at https://www.ifc.org/wps/wcm/connect/f0defcac-ebac-487e-912a-8d8a7a8b07ff/EMCompass+Note+38+Derisking+and+Blockchain+5-24+FINAL.pdf?MOD=AJPERES&CVID=lMWVNUO, accessed on 20 November 2019.

International Financial Corporation and MasterCard Foundation, *Data Analytics and Digital Financial Services*, available at https://www.ifc.org/wps/wcm/connect/369c10de-1703-4497-876f-9cdf0367a4d4/IFC+Data+Analytics+and+Digital+Financial+Services+Handbook.pdf?MOD=AJPERES&CVID=lRrkzEd, accessed on 12 November 2019.

Rojas-Suarez, Liliana & Pacheco, Lucía *An Index of Regulatory Practices for Financial Inclusion in Latin America: Enablers, Promoters, and Preventers,* CGD Working Paper Series 468, available at https://www.cgdev.org/sites/default/files/index-regulatory-practices-financial-inclusion-latin-america_0.pdf, accessed on 1 October 2019.

Shamika, Ravi *Accelerating Financial Inclusion in India* (2019), available at https://www.brookings.edu/research/568486/, accessed on 26 June 2019.

News media

Abioye, Oyetunji, 'Four banks earned N49bn from maintenance charges in 2017' *The Punch* 1 April 2018, available at https://punchng.com/four-banks-earned-n49bn-from-maintenance-, accessed on 28 July 2018.

Abioye, Oyetunji 'CBN suspends cashless policy in 30 states' *The Punch* 22 April 2017, available at https://punchng.com/cbn-suspends-cashless-policy-in-30-states/, accessed on 26 June 2019.

Adepetun, Adeyemi 'NCC, CBN sign MoU on mobile money, financial inclusion' 12 April 2018, *Guardian*, available at https://guardian.ng/business-services/ncc-cbn-sign-mou-on-mobile-money-financial-inclusion/, accessed on 27 February 2019.

Adepetun, Adeyemi 'Smartphone penetration hits 30% in Nigeria', *Guardian* 8 July 2016, available at https://guardian.ng/business-services/smartphone-penetration-hits-30-in-nigeria/, accessed on 26 February 2017.

Adepetun, Adeyemi 'What3words will boost Nigeria's addressing system', *Guardian* 16 August 2017, available at https://guardian.ng/technology/what3words-will-boost-nigerias-addressing-system/, accessed on 4 June 2019.

Akinkuotu, Eniola '84.2 million registered to vote in 2019, says INEC' *The Punch* 7 September 2018, available at https://punchng.com/84-2-million-registered-to-vote-in-2019-says-inec/, accessed on 25 August 2019.

Alo, Jebun Nesa 'Deposit through agent banking rises' 14 February 2019 *Daily Star,* available at https://www.thedailystar.net/business/banking/news/deposit-through-agent-banking-rises-122pc-1701760, accessed on 17 June 2019.

Baradaran, Mehrsa 'Facebook's cryptocurrency won't help the poor access banks: Here's what would' *Washington Post* October 29, 2019, available at https://www.washingtonpost.com/outlook/2019/10/29/facebooks-cryptocurrency-wont-help-poor-access-banks-heres-what-would/, accessed on 15 November 2019.

Central Bank of Nigeria, 'CBN clarifies diaspora remittances, says official inflows is $2.6bn, $26bn' *Thisday* 13 October 2019, available at https://www.thisdaylive.com/index.php/2019/10/13/cbn-clarifies-diaspora-remittances-says-official-inflows-is-2-6bn-not-26bn/, accessed on 5 December 2019.

CNN, *MPesa at 10,* available at http://edition.cnn.com/2017/02/21/africa/mpesa-10th-anniversary/index.html, accessed on 28 July 2019.

Cuaresma, Bianca 'More banks opt for 'branch-lite' strategy to expand reach in rural areas' 2 January 2019 *Business Mirror,* available at https://businessmirror.com.ph/2019/01/02/more-banks-opt-for-branch-lite-strategy-to-expand-reach-in-rural-areas/, accessed on 1 July 2019.

Dennis Erezi 'CBN slams ₦800 million fines on banks for flouting cryptocurrency order' Guardian 06 April 2022, available at https://guardian.ng/news/cbn-slams-%E2%82%A6800-million-fines-on-banks-for-flouting-cryptocurrency-order/, accessed on 8 April 2022.

Economist, 'The world's most valuable resource is no longer oil, but data' 6 May 2017, available at https://www.economist.com/leaders/2017/05/06/the-worlds-most-valuable-resource-is-no-longer-oil-but-data, accessed on 12 November 2019.

Fisher-French, Maya 'Mzansi accounts reach dead end' 17 Feb 2012 *Mail and Guardian,* available at https://mg.co.za/article/2012-02-17-mzansi-accounts-reach-dead-end, accessed on 10 July 2019.

Guardian, 'Firm to assist MSMEs' 19 June 2019, available at https://guardian.ng/business-services/firm-to-assist-msmes/, accessed on 13 August 2019.

Islam, Shariful 'The rapid growth of agent banking in Bangladesh Dhaka' *Tribune Sunday,* 9 June 2019, available at https://www.dhakatribune.com/business/2018/06/03/the-rapid-growth-of-agent-banking-in-bangladesh, accessed on 17 July 2019.

Khan, M Ilyas 'Pakistan's experience with identity management' *BBC News,* Islamabad, available at http://www.bbc.com/news/world-asia-18101385, accessed on 23 June 2019.

Komolafe, Babajide 'CBN, NIBSS unveil regulatory sandbox to empower fintechs' 26 March 2018 *Vanguard,* available at https://www.vanguardngr.com/2018/03/cbn-nibss-unveil-regulatory-sandbox-to-empower-fintechs/, accessed on 13 July 2018.

Mbele, Lerato 'Why M-Pesa failed in South Africa' *BBC Africa Business Report,* Johannesburg, 11 May 2016, available at http://www.bbc.com/news/world-africa-36260348/, accessed on 28 May 2018.

Merry, Alice 'Women worldwide struggle to access banking services: Bitcoin is only making that worse' October 29 2018, *Time*, available at https://time.com/5431809/blockchain-financial-inclusion-gender-gap/, accessed on 15 October 2019.

Monks, Kieron 'M-Pesa: Kenya's mobile money success story turns 10', *CNN*, 24 February 2017, available at https://edition.cnn.com/2017/02/21/africa/mpesa-10th-anniversary/index.html, accessed on 6 May 2018.

Nwokoji, Chima 'We chose bank-led mobile money to protect users from losses—CBN' *Nigerian Tribune* 5 June 2018, available at http://www.tribuneonlineng.com/chose-bank-led-mobile-money-protect-users-losses-cbn/, accessed on 10 June 2018.

Obulutsa, George 'M-Pesa helps drive up Kenyans' access to financial services' *Reuters* 03 April 2019, available at https://www.reuters.com/article/kenya-banking/m-pesa-helps-drive-up-kenyans-access-to-financial-services-study-idUSL8N21L2HK, accessed on April 2019.

Okonji, Emma 'NIMC registered 21.4 million Nigerians in five years' *Thisdaylive*, 13 September 2017, available at https://www.thisdaylive.com/index.php/2017/09/13/nimc-registered-21-4-million-nigerians-in-five-years/, accessed on 13 August 2019.

Olawoyin, Oladeinde 'How bank charges hinder financial inclusion in Nigeria' *Premium Times* 7 May 2019, available at https://www.premiumtimesng.com/business/financial-inclusion/328817-how-bank-charges-hinder-financial-inclusion-in-nigeria.html, accessed on August 31 2019.

Omarova, Saule & Graham Steele 'There's a Lot We Still Don't Know About Libra' *New York Times* November 4, 2019, available at https://www.nytimes.com/2019/11/04/opinion/facebook-libra-cryptocurrency.html, accessed on 14 December 2019.

Partington, Richard 'How the wheels came off Facebook's Libra project' *Guardian* 18 October 2019, available at https://www.theguardian.com/technology/2019/oct/18/how-the-wheels-came-off-facebook-libra-project, accessed on 4 December 2019.

Rainbow, 'CBN issues new guidelines for financial inclusion strategy' *Nigerian Voice*, 30 December 2013, available at https://www.thenigerianvoice.com/news/132831/1/cbn-issues-new-guidelines-for-financial-inclusion-.html, accessed on 27 March 2017.

Reuters, 'M-Pesa helps drive up Kenyans' access to financial services', available at https://www.reuters.com/article/kenya-banking/m-pesa-helps-drive-up-kenyans-access-to-financial-services-study-idUSL8N21L2HK, accessed on 16 June 2019.

Reuters, 'Nigeria's Nitel Privatisation ends in failure again', 15 June, 2011, available at https://uk.reuters.com/article/nigeria-nitel/update-1-nigerias-nitel-privatisation-ends-in-failure-again-idUKLDE75E27320110615, accessed on 30 May 2018

Vanguard, '30 million Nigerians get National Identity Number, *Vanguard Newspaper* 4 March 2018, available at https://www.vanguardngr.com/2018/03/30-million-nigerians-get-national-identity-number/, accessed on 4 September 2019.

General Internet sources

Akintaro, Samson *Goodbye NITEL … Hello! NTEL: New Network Operator Raises Broadband Hope* (2015), available at https://ittelecomdigest.com/goodbye-nitelhello-ntel/, accessed on 27 June 2018.

Anspach, Dana *What Is a Robo Advisor and How Do They Work?* (2019), available at https://www.thebalance.com/what-is-a-robo-advisor-and-how-do-they-work-4097134, accessed on 1 December 2019.

Alliance for Financial Inclusion, *AFI Official Members*, available at https://www.afi-global.org/sites/default/files/inline-files/AFI%20Official%20Members_8%20Jan%202019.pdf, accessed on 12 April 2019.

Alliance for Financial Inclusion, *Maya Declaration: Central Bank of Nigeria* 27 Nov 2011, available at https://www.youtube.com/watch?v=CX7sx-7ykxs&feature=youtu.be

Buy Bitcoin worldwide *Popular Exchanges to Buy Bitcoin in Nigeria* available at https://www.buybitcoinworldwide.com/nigeria/, accessed on 19 July 2020

Central Bank of Nigeria (CBN), *About CBN*, available at https://www.cbn.gov.ng/AboutCBN, accessed on 2 August 2019.

Central Bank of Nigeria (CBN), *Cash-less Nigeria*, available at https://www.cbn.gov.ng/cashless/, accessed on 19 May 2019.

Central Bank of Nigeria (CBN), *CPD FAQs*, available at https://www.cbn.gov.ng/Devfin/CPD_FAQs.pdf, accessed on 12 May 2019.

Central Bank of Nigeria, *Electronic Payments Incentives Scheme and Awareness Campaign Directive* BPSD/DIR/GEN/CIR/012 (2014) available at https://www.cbn.gov.ng/Out/2014/BPSD/CIRCULAR%20ON%20EPAYT%20INCENTIVES%20SCHEME.pdf

Centre for Financial Inclusion, *Mission and Vision*, available at https://www.centerforfinancialinclusion.org/about/mission, accessed on 30 April 2019.

Centre for Financial Inclusion, Definition of Financial Inclusion (2010), available at http://www.centerforfinancialinclusion.org/index2.php?option=com_content&view=article&id=579&Itemid=161, accessed on 22 March 2016.

Chiwete, *Welcome to the New FINT*, available at https://blog.fint.ng/2019/10/18/welcome-to-the-new-fint/, accessed on 10 November 2019.

Concurrences Glossary of Competition Terms, Dominant Position ([N.d.)], available at https://www.concurrences.com/en/glossary-of-competition-terms/Dominant-position, accessed on 5 May 2018.

De Koker, Louis and Jentzsch, Nicola 2011, *Financial Inclusion and Financial Integrity: Aligned Incentives?* in Shadow 2011: The Shadow Economy, Tax Evasion and Money Laundering: Proceedings of the 2011 Shadow Conference, University of Münster, Münster, Germany, pp. 1–28, available at https://dro.deakin.edu.au/view/DU:30041719, accessed on 30 January 2021.

Frankenfield, Jake 'Data analytics' *Investopaedia* 27 April 2019, available at https://www.investopedia.com/terms/d/data-analytics.asp, accessed on 12 November 2019.

Frankenfield, Jake 'What is a robo-advisor?' *Investopaedia* 1 October 2019, available at https://www.investopedia.com/terms/r/roboadvisor-roboadviser.asp, accessed on 27 November 2019.

Guaranty Trust Bank, *Instant Transfer FAQs,* available at https://www.gtbank.com/personal-banking/services/e-banking/instant-transfer-faqs, accessed on 11 September 2019.

Independent National Electoral Commission, *Permanent Voters Card*, available at http://www.inec.gov.ng/permanent-voters-card-pvc/, accessed on 15 August .2019.

Independent National Electoral Commission, *About INEC*, available at http://www.inec.gov.ng/home/about-inec/, accessed on 11 September 2019

Independent National Electoral Commission, *INEC Nigeria,* available at https://www.inecnigeria.org/, accessed on 16 May 2019.

Independent National Electoral Commission, *Total Registered Voters and PVC Collection*, available at http://www.inec.gov.ng/, accessed on 4 May 2019.

Magdas, Adriana *Cryptocurrencies and Financial Inclusion – Why I Am a Skeptic … For Now at Least* (2014), available at https://www.centerforfinancialinclusion.org/cryptocurrencies-and-financial-inclusion-why-i-am-a-skeptic-for-now-at-least, accessed on 15 September 2019.

Mcash, *About,* available at http://www.mcash.com.ng/, accessed on 5 May 2018.

Ministry of Information and Communications Technology and Security Guidance (Uganda), *National Security Information System*, available at https://ict.go.ug/projects-programmes/national-security-information-system/, accessed on 10 July 2019.

Michael Kapilkov *JPM Blockchain Creator Says the Project Was Going Nowhere, JP Morgan Wwanted Rid of It,* available at https://cointelegraph.com/news/quorum-s-creator-says-the-project-was-going-nowhere-jpmorgan-wanted-rid-of-it, accessed on 22 March 2022.

Mondato, Do Bank-Led Models Stall Progress? (2018), available at https://blog.mondato.com/do-bank-led-models-stall-progress/, accessed on 20 June 2018.

Mondato, *The Regulatory Sandbox* (2016), available at http://blog.mondato.com/the-regulatory-sandbox/, accessed on 7 July 2018.

NADRA, *National Identity Card*, available at https://www.nadra.gov.pk/identity/identity-cnic/, accessed on 9 July 2019.

National Identification Management Commission (NIMC), *About the NIN*, available at https://www.nimc.gov.ng/about-nin/, accessed on 17 October 2019.

National Identification Management Commission (NIMC), *Learn about the NIMC*, available at https://www.nimc.gov.ng/, accessed on 12 May 2018.

National Identification Management Commission, *Vision and Mission*, available at https://www.nimc.gov.ng/vision-mission, accessed on 2 August 2019.

National Identification Management Commission, *Why Your NIN is Important*, available at https://www.nimc.gov.ng/nin-importance, accessed on 22 August 2019.

National Identity Management Commission (NIMC), *Functions and Powers*, https://www.nimc.gov.ng/functionspowers/, accessed on 2 August 2019.

National Identity Management Commission (NIMC), *How to Enrol (Adults)*, available at https://www.nimc.gov.ng/how-to-enrol-adults/, accessed on 15 August 2019.

National Identity Management Commission (NIMC), *NIMC Enrols over 28m Nigerians and Legal Residents* (2019), available at https://www.nimc.gov.ng/nimc-enrols-over-28m-nigerians-and-legal-residents/, accessed on 25 August 2019.

National Identity Management Commission (NIMC), *NIMC EnrolmentCentres,* available at https://www.nimc.gov.ng/nimc-enrolment-centres/, accessed on 4 September 2019

National Pension Commission, *About Us',* available at https://www.pencom.gov.ng/about-us/, accessed on 2 August 2019.

Nigerian Deposit Insurance Corporation, *Mandate, Powers & Functions,* available at https://ndic.gov.ng/about-ndic-3/mandate-powers-functions, accessed on 2 August 2019.

Nigerian Interbank Settlement System (NIBSS), *About*, available at https://nibss-plc.com.ng/bvn/, accessed on 11 September 2019.

Nigeria Deposit Insurance Corporation (NDIC), *About NDIC*, available at https://ndic.gov.ng/about-ndic-3/, accessed on 2 August 2019.

Nigerian Communications Commission (NCC), *About the NCC*, available at https://www.ncc.gov.ng/about-ncc/who-we-are, accessed on 2 February 2019.

Nigerian Communications Commission (NCC), *Industry Statistics,* available at https://www.ncc.gov.ng/stakeholder/statistics-reports/industry-overview#view-graphs-tables-6, accessed on 5 December 2019.

Nigerian Postal NIPOST, *Financial Services*, available at http://www.nipost.gov.ng/Financial_Services, accessed on 2 August 2019.

Nigerian Postal Services, *Vision and Mission*, available at http://www.nipost.gov.ng/Vision_Mission, accessed on 2 August 2019.

Patrick Thompson JPMorgan Offloads Unprofitable Quorum Network 31 August 2020, available at https://coingeek.com/jpmorgan-offloads-unprofitable-quorom-network/#:~:text=JPMorgan%20sold%20Quorum%20because%20they,to%20adopt%20and%20implement%20Quorum, accessed on 22 March 2022.

Polaris Bank, *Our History*, available at https://www.polarisbanklimited.com/about-us/our-history/, accessed on 26 July 2019.

Quorum, *Evolve with Quorum: The Proven Blockchain Solution for Business*, available at https://www.goquorum.com/, accessed on 23 September 2019.

Securities and Exchange Commission, *About*, available at https://sec.gov.ng/about/, accessed on 2 August 2019.

Securities and Exchange Commission, *What We Do*, available at https://sec.gov.ng/about/what-we-do/, accessed on 2 August 2019.

SnooCODE, *About SnooCODE*, available at https://snoocode.com/about, accessed on 2 September 2019.

Techopedia, *Definition: What Does Mobile Network Operator (MNO) Mean?* available at https://www.techopedia.com/definition/27804/mobile-network-operator-mno, accessed on 12 May 2019.

Unique Identification Authority of India, *What Is Aadhaar*, available at https://uidai.gov.in/what-is-aadhaar.html, accessed on 9 July 2019.

United Bank of Africa, *Hi I Am Leo*, available at https://www.ubagroup.com/nigeria/personal-banking/digital-banking/chat-with-leo/, accessed on 2 December 2019.

United States of America Embassy in Nigeria, *Nigeria Fact Sheet*, available at https://photos.state.gov/libraries/nigeria/487468/pdfs/Nigeria%20overview%20Fact%20Sheet.pdf, accessed on 18 April 2018.

Universal Postal Union, *About Financial Services*, available at http://www.upu.int/en/activities/financial-services/about-financial-services.html, accessed on February 2019.

Van Zyl, Gareth 'Why Vodacom M-Pesa Has Flopped in SA (2016) fin24tech', available at https://www.fin24.com/Tech/Companies/why-vodacom-m-pesa-has-flopped-in-sa-20160509, accessed on 9 May 2021.

What3words Limited, *What is What3words?* available at https://what3words.com/about-us/, accessed on 12 September 2019.

World Bank, *Population Total* (2015), available at http://data.worldbank.org/indicator/SP.POP.TOTL, accessed on February 2017.

World Bank, *Rural Population: % of Total Population*, available at http://data.worldbank.org/indicator/SP.RUR.TOTL.ZS?locations=NG, accessed on 26 February 2017.

Index

Page numbers followed by "n" indicate a note on the corresponding page.

556 Local Government Areas (LGAs) 79
2014 Pension Reform Act 21

Abioye, Oyetunji 83n27, 85n114
Abraham, Facundo 138n171, 139nn175, 179, 183
Access Bank 101, 110
account opening complexity 80–82
Adeleke, Adekoge 107n19, 108n24
Aderinokun, Kunle 133n15
Adeyoju, Ademola 138n167
Aella Credit 127
Agarwal, Khushboo 64n76
Akinkuotu, Eniola 107n11
Alexander, Kern 140nn214, 216, 218
Alliance for Financial Inclusion (AFI) 40
Anderson, C Leigh 47nn85, 87
Anspach, Dana 139nn178, 185
anti-competition in DFS 56–59
anti-money laundering (AML) 3, 112, 121
application programming interface (API) 124–126; Equity Bank 125; MTN Uganda 125; MTN Uganda 125; Nedbank 125; Open APIs 125; Payment APIs 125; Private APIs 125
Artificial intelligence (AI) 121–123
automated teller machine (ATM) card 7
Aveni, Tyler 140nn213, 140n217
Ayua, I 34

Baderin, Mashood 33–34, 44n8, 45nn24, 27, 35
Bailey, Ronald 46n59
Baker, Tom 139n181
Bangladesh, financial inclusion in 42
Bank Verification Number (BVN) 81, 125
bank/non-bank institutions 4
Bankable Frontiers Associates 47n115
bank-centred regulatory model 51
banked 7
bank-led model 50–51
Banks and Other Financial Institutions Act (BOFIA) 18–19, 41
Bara, A 63n34
Baradaran, Mehrsa 135nn65, 67
Benson, Carol 25nn21, 24, 26
Bertino, E. 141n231
Bester, Hennie 63n38, 107n18
big data 120–122
Binance, cryptocurrency exchange 110
biometrics 129
Bitcoins 113–114, 116, 133n10
BitPesa, cryptocurrency exchange 110
blockchain 111–112
Boateng, Kwadwo 47n89
Bordo, Michael D 136nn86, 99, 137nn111, 114
Boulanger, Christian 39, 46n62
Bourreau, Marc 63n54
Branch, mobile financial services provider 110
Brazil, financial inclusion in 42
Breul, Philippe 137n139, 138nn142, 147, 159

Cairns, John 46n51
Carstens, Agustín 137n107
cash, importance 103–104
cash-in-cash-out (CICO) 55, 74
Central Bank Digital Currencies (CBDCs) 116–120; eNaira 16, 116, 119–120; launch 117; risks 117; token-based 118

Central Bank of Nigeria (CBN) 2, 18–20, 47nn79, 81, 83
Cheston, Susy 140n222
Chibuzor, Oluchi 139n202
Chima, Obinna 62n21
Claessens, Stijn 63n55, 64n59
Clark, Julia 141n259
Clotteau, Nils 25nn21, 24, 26
Code 110
Coeuré, Benoît 136nn84, 88
Competition and Tariff Commission (CTC) 59
ConsenSys 115
Consultative Group to Assist the Poor (CGAP) 2, 139n187
consumer perceptions, insights from 100–101
corporation-led model 50
Credit Reporting Act 2017 16, 18
Credpal 110
cryptocurrencies 113–116, 131

Dai 115
data analytics and big data 120–122
David-West, Olayinka 84n37
Davis, Kevin 44nn4, 9
de Koker, Louis 86n115, 134nn33, 53, 136n105, 139n199, 141n248
demand-side barriers 94–95
Del Duca, Louis F 46n67
Demirgüç-Kunt, Asli 24nn1, 2, 25n13, 26nn49, 51, 47n96
Diem cryptocurrency 114–115, 131
digital financial services (DFS) 2, 4, 49–60; competitive advantages for 54–56; consumer perception of 99–101; dominance and anti-competition in, determining 56–59; mobile network operators (MNOs), perceptions about 99–100; postal service, perceptions about 100; regulatory sandboxes and prospective use cases 59–60; *see also* financial sector regulator
digital identification 128–130; biometrics 129; blockchain-backed ID 129; fingerprinting 130; mobile authentication 129
Dimitrova-Grajzl, Valentina 37, 39, 46n64
Diofasi, Anna 142n264
Direct Pay Online 110
distributed ledger technology (DLT) 111–113, 119
Dogecoin 116
Dzirutwe, MacDonald 133n5

eBay 114
Econet's mobile money service (EcoCash) 59
eNaira 16, 116, 119–120
Enhancing Financial Innovation and Access in Nigeria (EFInA) 10, 22, 24n6, 63n19
Enyinnaya, Chris 83nn24, 30
Equity Bank 125
Estenssoro, Amalia 136nn83, 87, 95
Ethereum blockchain technology 115
Europay, MasterCard, and Visa (EMV) chip 13

Federal Capital Territory (FCT) 77
Federal Competition and Consumer Protection Act 2019 (FCCP) Act 56
finance access, barriers to 94–97
Financial Action Task Force (FATF) 3, 121
financial capability 6–7
financial exclusion in Nigeria: age range of 10; by gender 10; by level of education 10–11; rural/urban exclusion 10
financial health 5–6
financial inclusion 2–4, 31–44, 102–105, 109–132; bank/non-bank institutions 4; banked 7; cash, importance 103–104; Central Bank Digital Currencies (CBDCs) 116–120; concepts in, definition 2–7; conventional banks difficulties 102–103; cryptocurrencies 113–116; data analytics and big data 120–122; digital financial services (DFS) 2, 4; digital identification 128–130; dimensions of 7–8; distributed ledger technology 111–113; emerging technology trends 111–130; financial health 5–6; financial literacy and capability 6–7; financial stress 6; financially excluded 8; formal other 7; geographical representation by geo-political zones 11; importance 8–9; inclusive finance 5; informal only 7; mobile network operator (MNO) 4–5; Nigeria's journey to achieving 9–11; religious bias and 15; stakeholder and industry profile 11; tailored regulatory policies 104–105; *see also* law and development context of financial inclusion

financial inclusion in Nigeria, barriers to 67–82; account opening complexity 80–82; agent banking/network 74–77; ATM charges 69–70; bank verification number (BVN) 81; cash preference 77–78; cost of financial services 68–70; distance 72–77; geographical spread of financial access points 73–74; identification documentation 78–80; illiteracy 70–72; irregular income 67–68; Know-Your-Customer (KYC) compliance 80–81; permanent voter card (PVC) 79–80; proof of address 81; unemployment 67–68
financial literacy 6–7
financial sector regulator 49–53; approval-in-principle 52; bank-centred regulatory model 51; Grameen Bank 52; market competition and 53–54; *see also* digital financial services (DFS) regulation
Financial Service Innovators Association of Nigeria (FSI) 60
financial service technologies, legal issues raised by 131–132
financial services in Nigeria 66–82; *see also* financial inclusion in Nigeria, barriers to
financial stress 6
financially excluded 8
First Bank 101
formal other 7
Framework and Guidelines for Mobile Money 2015 18
Frankenfield, Jake 134n46, 137n138, 138nn170, 174, 139n182
Freehills, Herbert Smith 64n77

Gallo, Alberto 136n98
Garoupa, Nuno 37–38, 46nn46, 56
Gelb, Alan 141nn243, 259, 142n264
general multipurpose card (GMPC) 78
Ghana, financial inclusion in 41–42
Gifford, Karen 138n150
Gili, Ricard Murillo 136n106
Giné, Xavier 141nn258, 260, 142n268
Global Policy Forum (GPF) 11
Global System for Mobile Communications (GSM) in Nigeria 57
Grajzl, Peter 37, 39, 46n64
Grameen Bank financial inclusion model 52
Guaranty Trust Bank 101
Guidelines for Licensing and Regulation of Payment Service Bank 2020 18
Guidelines on Mobile Money Services 50

Halpin, Dan 134n53
Hansen, Espen Marinius 136nn93, 96
Henry-Nickie, Makada 133n19, 138n163

identification (ID) 128–130
identification documentation 78–80
inclusive finance 5
Independent National Electoral Commission (INEC) 15
India, financial inclusion in 41
indigenous savings systems 97–99
informal only 7
International Financial Corporation (IFC) 1
International Telecommunications Union (ITU) 2–3
Internet of Things (IoT) 121
Investments and Securities Act 29 of 2007 22

Jenik, Ivo 64nn63, 69, 75, 80
Jentzsch, Nicola 137n135, 138nn144, 149, 152
Jörgensen, Fredrik 39, 44n12, 46n68
JP Morgan Bank 115
Jubraj, Roy 138n162
Juden, Matt 133nn23, 27, 134n43

Kagan, Julia 25n31
Kenya, financial inclusion in 43
KiaKia 127
Kleinbaum, Dan 139nn190, 194, 140n206
Know-Your-Customer (KYC) compliance, complexity 80–81
Koksal, Ilker 134n36
Komolafe, Babajide 62n18, 64n78
Kynge, James 136n85

Landerreche, Esteban 134n41
Lauer, Kate 64n63
law and development context of financial inclusion: intersections 33–35; moments 31–33; theory in 35–36; *see also* legal transplants
Lee, Yong-Sik 33, 34, 40, 45nn20, 23, 25, 28, 31, 40, 46n70
legal landscape for financial inclusion in Nigeria 16–18
legal transplants 36–44; background to 36–37; based on an imperialist predisposition 38; cultural affinity in 38–39; motivating factors for 37–40
Legrand, Pierre 37, 46n47
Levasseur, Alain A 46n67

Levin, Andrew T 136nn86, 99, 137nn111, 114
Litecoin 116
Lizarazo-Rodriguez, Liliana 44n1, 45n17
Lorini, Roberto 136n89, 137n113
Loufield, Ethan 134nn34, 44, 138nn141, 145, 157
Louis, Lydie 61n17

Macmillan, Rory 48n113, 62nn24, 28, 63n37, 64nn58, 60
Magdas, Adriana 134n54, 136n80
market competition 53–54
Mas, Ignacio 63n33
Mastercard 114
Maurushat, Alana 134n53
Maya Declaration 11–13
Mazer, Rafe 63n56
McLean, Sue 64nn73–74, 82
Merry, Alice 134n42
Mexico, financial inclusion in 42
Miriri, Duncan 62n29
mobile network operators (MNOs) 4–5, 11, 50–51, 99–100
modernisation theory 32
Monaco, Marco 136n89, 137n113
Monero 116
Mousourakis, George 36–38, 46nn45, 49, 52, 55, 57, 60, 61, 66
MTN Uganda 125
Muhammad, Yunus 52
Mukherjee, Anit 141n243

NairaEx, cryptocurrency exchange 110
Nakamoto, Satoshi 113
National Bureau of Statistics (NBS) 22
National Financial Inclusion Strategy (NFIS) 3, 11, 13–16, 36, 40–41
National Financial Literacy Framework (NFLF) 12
National Identification Management Commission (NIMC) 11, 22–23, 78–79, 96, 130, 140n227
National Identity Number (NIN) 96
National Insurance Commission (NAICOM) 20
National Pension Commission (PENCOM) 21–22
National Youth Service Corps (NYSC) 15
Nedbank 125
Nelson, Bill 136n91
NIBSS Electronic Funds Transfer (NEFT) 13
NIBSS Instant Payment (NIP) 125
Nigeria 59–60; commitment to the Maya Declaration 11–12; regulatory sandboxes and prospective use cases in 59–60
Nigeria, financial inclusion in 8–9; access strands 10; Central Bank of Nigeria (CBN) 19–20; demographic profile of the excluded in the pre-2011 era 10; importance 8–9; institutional landscape for 18–23; journey to achieving 9–11; National Bureau of Statistics (NBS) 22; National Identification Management Commission (NIMC) 22–23; National Insurance Commission (NAICOM) 20; National Pension Commission (PENCOM) 21–22; Nigeria Deposit Insurance Corporation (NDIC) 21; Nigerian Communications Commission (NCC) 20; Nigerian Postal Service (NIPOST) 23; performance 23–24; Securities and Exchange Commission (SEC) 22
Nigeria Deposit Insurance Corporation (NDIC) 16, 21, 93
Nigeria Interbank Settlement System (NIBSS) 60
Nigeria Postal Service (NIPOST) 11, 23
Nigeria Telecommunications Limited (NITEL) 57
Nigeria Uniform Bank Account Number (NUBAN) 13, 125
Nigerian Communications Commission (NCC) 20
Niglia, Leone 40, 46n74
NITDA Data Protection Act 2019 130
non-bank-led model 50–51
non-proof-of-work chains 112
not-for-profit organisations 2

Obulutsa, George 26n53, 45n43
Ogus, Anthony 37–38, 46nn46, 56
Ohnesorge, John 45nn26, 34
O'Keefe, Daniel 139n176
Okonji, Emma 86n126
Olawoyin, Oladeinde 83n31
Omarova, Saule 135n62
Onecoin 116
OneFi 110
Open APIs 125
Open Technology Foundation (OTF) 125
Oradian company 110, 113
Ordor, Ada 32–34, 45nn15, 18, 22, 38
Ostrovsky, Sima 63n43
over-the-counter (OTC) services 55

Pacheco, Lucía 140n219
Pakistan, financial inclusion in 41
Partington, Richard 135n60
Payment APIs 125
PayPal 114
PayWithCapture 110
Peerenboom, Randall 46n50
peer-to-peer (P2P) lending 111, 126–127, 131
Penca, Jemeja 40, 46n72
permanent voter card (PVC) 79–80
Philippines, financial integrity in 41–42
PiggyVest 110
Pisa, Michael 133nn23, 27, 134nn43, 55–57, 135n66
Podder, Suman 139n199
postal service, perceptions about 100
Private APIs 125
proof of address complexity 81
public–private partnership 130
Puglisi, Alfio A. 134n33

Quick Response (QR) 16
quorum cryptocurrency 113–115, 131

Ramachandran, Vijaya 133n25, 134n38, 137nn132, 137, 141nn252, 254
Reach fintech 110
Regulation of Agent Banking and Agent Banking Relationships 2013 75
regulatory sandboxes 59–60
Rhine, Elisabeth 26n34
Ripples 116
robo-advisors 123–124, 131
Rojas-Suarez, Liliana 140n219
Rudman, Desmond 63nn40, 43
rural digital financial exclusion, community case study 88–107; *see also* Ubulu-Uku, rural digital financial exclusion case study
rural/urban exclusion 10

Safaricom 61n1
Salmeron, Adrià Morron 136n106
Santos, Alvaro 32, 44n2, 45n30
Secured Transactions in Movable Assets Act 2017 16, 18
Securities and Exchange Commission (SEC) 22
Seth, Shobhit 136n94
Shared Agent Network Expansion Facility (SANEF) 76
significant market power (SMP) 56
Silvergate Capital Corporation 115
Small and Medium Enterprise Development Agency of Nigeria (SMEDAN) 11
small but significant and non-transitory increase in price (SSNIP) 56
Social Lender 127
Specta social lender 110
stable currency 131
States Accelerated Broadband Initiative (SABI) 20
Steele, Graham 135n62
Stella company 110, 113
Stevens, Marc 134n41
Sturgeon, John A. 26n41
Suárez, Sandra 62n32
Sultan, Karim 133nn21, 26, 28, 134n39
supply-side barriers 95–96
SureCredit 127

Tamanaha, Brian 32, 44n7, 45nn13, 16, 33
Techopedia 25n28
Tether 115
Third World Approaches to International Law (TWAIL) 33
Thun, Jonathan 136nn93, 96
token-based CBDC 118
Torpman, Jan 39, 44n12, 46nn63, 68
Transactions Switching Guidelines 18
Trebilcock, Michael 44n4
Trubek, David 32–33, 44nn2, 5, 10, 45nn14, 19, 30, 42
Tsai, Chang-Hsien 140n210

Ubulu-Uku, rural digital financial exclusion case study 88–107; accessing finance, barriers to 94–97; banks use 97; cash, importance 103–104; consumer perception of DFS 99–101; conventional bank difficulties 102–103; coping strategies 97–99; demand-side barriers 94–95; face-to-face interviews 90; financial inclusion initiatives 91–92; financial inclusion themes 91–102; financial inclusion, lessons for 102–105; financial services adoption and usage patterns 92–94; in-depth interviews (IdIs) 90; indigenous savings systems use 97–99; local savings clubs 98; outline of study 88–89; participants, identifying and selecting 89–90; point of sale (POS) machines 93; regulatory barriers 96–97; supply-side barriers 95–96; tailored regulatory policies 104–105; user recommendations 101–102
Uganda, financial inclusion in 41
United Bank of Africa (UBA) 101

United States Agency for International Development (USAID) 140nn228, 230
Universal Finance Access (UFA) 1
Universal Postal Union (UPU) 42
Unstructured Supplementary Service Data (USSD) 15–16, 18
USD Coin 115

Valletti, Tommaso 63n54
van Zyl, Gareth 26n54, 45n44
Visa 114

Watson, Alan 36–37, 46n53
White, Olivia 141n244
Wire Nigeria Project (WIN) 20
Woodsome, Jim 133n25, 134n38, 137nn132, 137, 141nn252, 254
World Bank Group 47n114

Yu, Sun 136n85
Yusuf, Damola 139n198

Zelazny, Frances 141n256
Zenith Bank 110
Zhou, Mimi 64n81

FSC
www.fsc.org
MIX
Papier | Fördert gute Waldnutzung
FSC® C083411

Kolibri 360 GmbH
Ferdinand-Jühlke-Straße 7
99095 Erfurt, Deutschland
produktsicherheit@kolibri360.de